Looking for History on Highway 14

14
WEST
BOUND

LOOKING for HISTORY on HIGHWAY 14

JOHN E. MILLER

Iowa State University Press / Ames

JOHN E. MILLER, who lives two blocks from Highway 14, is professor of history at South Dakota State University.

Frontispiece: Highway 14 near Fort Pierre sometime after World War II. (Courtesy of South Dakota State Historical Society)

Map of the route of Highway 14 in South Dakota by Orville Gab.

♾ Printed on acid-free paper in the United States of America

First edition, 1993

Library of Congress
Cataloging-in-Publication Data

Miller, John E.
Looking for history on Highway 14 / John E. Miller.—1st ed.
p. cm.
Includes bibliographical references and index.
ISBN 0-8138-1246-1 (acid-free paper)
1. South Dakota—History, Local. 2. United States Highway 14. 3. Automobile travel—South Dakota. 4. South Dakota—Description and travel. I. Title.
F651.M47 1993
978.3—dc20 92-30506

CONTENTS

INTRODUCTION

I went looking for history on Federal Highway 14 and, not surprisingly, found some. Not surprisingly, I say, because people have a way of finding what they are looking for. On the other hand, much of what I discovered was not, and could not have been, anticipated. This was a trip of discovery—an enjoyable and educational journey down a road I had taken many times before without seriously asking what it was that I was seeing along the way.

It is necessary to emphasize *some* in the introductory sentence, for this book makes no pretense of providing the definitive history of the towns on Highway 14 and, in fact, suggests that no such history can be written. The people we encounter and the stories we hear while traveling down the highway are reminders of just how much we are all influenced in our perceptions and thoughts by our backgrounds and situations, by our hopes and dreams and memories. Ask ten different people to relate what happened a year, ten years, or fifty years ago, and you will probably get ten differing versions of it.

Yet, while details and interpretations may differ, these stories collectively form an account that bears a resemblance to the truth. Living in the late twentieth century, we confront philosophies that deny the possibility of truth, psychologies that reduce knowledge to dreams and fantasies, literary theories that replace human experience with language games, and historical approaches that spout skepticism and relativism. Yet despite the difficulty of fully or accurately knowing what happened in the past, we instinctively operate on the assumption that "something happened." It is toward describing how we remember that something—through physical reminders, written records, photographic and visual evidence, stories that get told and retold, and enduring dreams and myths—that this study is directed.

Truths await our discovery of them, but these are always

contested truths. Memories falter, stories vary and sometimes lie, while reconstructions of the past fall short of the mark. The original evidence is often dim and sometimes lacking altogether. Searching out the truth is imperative, but discovering the truth is often impossible. What we think about the past influences what we do today and hope for tomorrow. The more we know about where we have come from, the better we can understand our present condition and fashion our future directions.

The business route through Brookings on Highway 14 runs two blocks north of where I live. I attended high school for a while in Arlington Heights, Illinois, just two blocks from the highway; worked at a canning factory for a summer in Sleepy Eye, Minnesota, right on the highway; and went to graduate school at Madison, Wisconsin, another town on the route. But all that is mere coincidence. Having grown up and lived in half a dozen small towns in the Midwest, I wanted to do some small town history. Choosing a string of towns along a highway seemed to be a sensible way to proceed.

One could easily demonstrate that, as a collection, the towns on Highway 14 constitute the most interesting group of towns in the state. Along that stretch of highway lie the state's land grant university, the state fair site, and the state capital. One of the towns on the route is De Smet—the "little town on the prairie" made famous by five of Laura Ingalls Wilder's novels. Eight miles west of it is Manchester, near the homestead where South Dakota's most celebrated artist—Harvey Dunn—grew up. Wall Drug, dominating the town where Highway 14 links up with Interstate 90, is one of America's well-known tourist attractions. Beyond it to the west, Mount Rushmore, which is not on the highway but close to it, was carved with the images of four famous presidents in large part because of the desire to boost tourist traffic along the route during the 1920s. The chapters progress from east to west partly because of my own vantage point at the eastern end of the route, mostly because that historically has been the direction of traffic and migration in the area. One could read the chapters backwards, from west to east, with little being lost, although the first chapter on Elkton—the easternmost town on the highway in South Dakota—provides some useful background on the building and development of the highway itself. (Note: I should say Elkton is *near* the highway, because when the road was resurfaced in the mid-1930s, it was also rerouted two miles north of town.)

The stories told here are confined to South Dakota because that is what I am most familiar with and because it seemed useful to focus upon a set of more or less homogeneous towns and to portray some of the interconnections among them. One could certainly go east and west—to the start of Highway 14 in Chicago and to its terminus in Yellowstone National Park—and do something like what I have done in the chapters included here. The people and the stories would be different, but the general point would be the same: that history reveals itself to the observer in a variety of different and interesting ways and that we can sensitize ourselves to this history by staying alert and by training ourselves to look and listen for the historical signs that are present everywhere.

We live in space and time, and our journeys through these dimensions give us all we know of life. Our roots in place and time, increasingly attenuated in modern (or, better, postmodern), industrialized, urban, media-saturated Western society define much of our character. A trip down Highway 14 in South Dakota can be a way of reminding ourselves just how much has been lost as these roots in place and time have diminished in the face of constant pressure from an increasingly mobile, rootless, historyless society.

Looking for history, we also look for ourselves. Discovering the stories of particular people who lived in particular places and times, we come upon mirrors in which we can reflect upon our own particular experiences in place and time. A little probing soon reveals that the stories that could be told are endless, the meanings that can be extracted are innumerable.

We live in an impatient society—one that demands instant judgments, that lacks the willingness to stop and linger if excitement and titillation are not quickly forthcoming. A journey down Highway 14 forces us to slow down, stop for a cup of coffee, and take a moment to listen and reflect. What do these people, these barns and buildings, these streets and roads, these old photographs and records, these bridges, water pumps, and junkyards tell us?

The stories I have related in this volume are the ones I ran into during the past five years or so I have spent in traveling the highway. They are just a few of the many that could be told. Told by different people, and even by the same ones at different times, the stories take on slightly different twists. But for each person they have special meanings attached to them. They provide identity, they provide attachments, and they provide significance. The people who live and have lived along the highway are no different from you or me in what they bring into this world, but each is a unique person with unique value and importance.

Traveling along a route of transportation in search of enlightenment and edification is not a new idea. Nineteenth-century European visitors to the United States frequently wrote about their experiences here, searching for themes and lodestones that would explain, for their own satisfaction and their readers', the true meaning or significance of America. Some of these works—for example, those of Frances Trollope, Harriet Martineau, Charles Dickens, Robert Louis Stevenson, and Bjørnstjerne Bjørnson—are more or less insightful and were often highly controversial. Others—particularly those of Alexis de Tocqueville and James Bryce—have taken on the status of classic commentaries on American life.[1]

During the twentieth century, Americans themselves took to the road in increasing numbers on voyages of discovery and self-discovery. In the process of looking for America, many hoped to find themselves. In carrying out their investigations, some authors were more historically oriented than others. A few put historical context at the center of their portraits; for most it was peripheral. During the 1970s, *New York Times* reporter Harrison E. Salisbury in *Travels around America,* for example, traced his own family's path west across the country from Chepachet, Rhode Island, to Minneapolis, Minnesota, and proceeded from there to talk to people who had been involved in or who could comment on the history that had been made after World War II. Back in 1947, John Gunther in *Inside U.S.A.*, an amazingly broad collective portrait of the American people, rooted his observations in the historical context of the states that he visited. Consciously aiming to provide a modern-day sequel to Gunther's volume, Neal R. Peirce and Jerry Hagstrom imitated his historical bent when they wrote *The Book of America: Inside Fifty States Today.*[2]

In efforts to update Tocqueville, Richard Reeves and former senator Eugene J. McCarthy used the Frenchman's observations and interpretations as a baseline from which to make comparisons with modern society. Other recent investigators also drew heavily upon history in their descriptions and analyses, for example, Berton Roueché in *Special Places: In Search of Small Town America* and Geoffrey O'Gara in *A Long Road Home: Journeys through America's Present in Search of America's Past.* While working on his book *Great Plains,* Ian Frazier discovered a powerful sense of history in the region, noting that "for many places on the Great Plains, the past is much more colorful and exciting and populous than the present. Historical markers are everywhere."[3]

More typical, however, are those for whom history is merely incidental and in some cases totally lacking. Bill Moyers's *Listening to America: A Traveler Rediscovers His Country* was based primarily upon interviews that he tape-recorded on his journey around the country. Journalistic predecessors and contemporaries of his such as Ernie Pyle and Charles Kuralt likewise relied primarily upon what people told them. The same can be said for novelists such as Erskine Caldwell and John Steinbeck, who traveled the country in search of its essential characteristics.[4]

Living and traveling in large cities led the Nobel Prize–winning Steinbeck to realize that for too long he had been cut off from ordinary people and activities. "Thus I discovered that I did not know my own country," he observed at the beginning of *Travels with Charley: In Search of America.* "So it was that I determined to look again, to try to discover this monster land." Steinbeck's keen ear and observant eye stood him in good stead as he roved about in his pickup camper. His fear that being famous would prevent people from opening up to him quickly evaporated; not one person on his ten-thousand-mile journey recognized him! Steinbeck's stories and observations are engaging and informative, but his conversations seldom were very drawn out or penetrated very deeply. An observation he made about one of his encounters reflected his reticence: "There's a gentility on the road. A direct or personal question is out of bounds."[5]

A problem with travel accounts by commentators who dart from place to place without stopping for long in any of them is that they have to depend almost entirely upon the observational and narrative powers of the author and upon chance encounters with informants who can provide particularly revealing information and anecdotes. In addition, as anyone who has traveled much knows, staying alert, paying attention, and remaining interested over long periods of time are hard to do. It takes curiosity, determination, energy, and stamina—qualities that tend to diminish after the thousandth or five thousandth mile registers on the odometer. Furthermore, even when the traveler possesses all of these to a high degree, the opportunity to probe very deeply in a place where one spends only a few minutes or hours or, at most, a day or two is somewhat limited. Roueché's practice of staying for a week or even several in the seven communities he visited provided him opportunities to get to know people better and to follow up on leads. Quick in-and-outers like Bill Bryson are forced to rely on surface impressions and lots of imagination to tell their stories. Bryson seldom stopped to talk to people, or even get out of his car for that matter, and was generally content to criticize, poke fun at, and sometimes sympathize with the people he encountered, which led him one Friday evening in his home state of Iowa to observe, "I felt guilty for mocking them. They were good people."[6]

The traveler will do better to avoid the superhighways and instead take what William Least Heat Moon called the "blue highways"—two-lane routes marked in blue on his road maps that connect the small towns and cities of America, the mountain valleys and country crossroads. This is not to say that large roads are unimportant or that they shouldn't be studied. Angus Kress Gillespie and Michael Aaron Rockland's *Looking for America on the New Jersey Turnpike* provides an example of how much can be learned by studying such a route. They succeeded because they took a historical approach and because they took time to stop to see what went on in the rest areas and what life was like for people living beyond the chain-link fences and sound barriers. Unfortunately, driving the interstate highways and other large, heavily traveled roads today makes it difficult to take things slowly and to stop and look around. Steinbeck consciously drove slowly on his trip so he could take more in, and he did his best to bypass cities. Salisbury lamented, "Not many of us *see* the American continent. We course it on concrete magesterials, directional lights flashing as we pull a steady 75–80 miles an hour ('Not a single stoplight all the way!') from coast to coast." Kuralt likewise marveled, "Thanks to the Interstate Highway System, it is now possible to travel across the country from coast to coast without seeing anything. From the Interstate, America is all steel guardrails and plastic signs, and every place looks and feels like every other place."[7]

Kuralt's alternative: "We stick to the back roads." While on them, the way to learn something is to talk to people and to stay attentive to what they say and what you see. That was also the advice of President Franklin Roosevelt in 1939 to a young man hoping to learn something about the country by driving across it: "Take a second-hand car, put on a flannel shirt, drive out to the Coast by the northern route and come back by the southern route. . . . Don't talk to your banking friends or your chamber of commerce friends, but specialize on the gasoline station men, the small restaurant keeper, and farmers you meet by the wayside, and your fellow automobile travelers."[8]

Once you talk to people like this, you realize how much you can learn from them, and you also appreciate a little bit of what they have been through and accomplished. The second lesson to be learned from such adventures, therefore, is the wealth of information to be had from "ordinary folks." Simply watching people through the windows of a moving car is an invitation to stereotype them, downgrade them, laugh at them, and worse. Getting to know them is to discover their worth and to observe their interesting qualities. Thus, Pyle in the 1930s: "The job of being a roving reporter teaches you one thing: he who laughs too long and too loud at other people is liable to get sand in his mouth. The more you travel around and see all sorts of people the less inclined you are to stand up on a dais and look down at anybody, or laugh at him. Because he may be looking up, laughing at you." Likewise, a traveling actor talking to Steinbeck in the 1950s: "You know when show people come into what they call the sticks, they have a contempt for the yokels. It took me a little time, but when I learned that there aren't any yokels I began to get on fine. I learned respect for my audience."[9]

Lesson number three is to recognize the complexity of human character and history. No person is simply one thing. Few generalizations hold. "I thought how every safe generality I gathered in my travels was canceled by another," Steinbeck mused. Upon contemplating predecessors of his such as Steinbeck, Tocqueville, and Mark Twain, Kuralt observed, "Each of them caught a little bit of the truth about America and wrote it down. Even the best of them never got it all into one book, because the country is too rich and full of contradictions." Moyers refused to paint a simple portrait of America but rather catalogued its many contradictions: "troubled, spirited, inspired, frightened, complacent, industrious, selfish, magnanimous, confused, spiteful, bewitching." All Salisbury could do, he wrote, was to "see my America with my own eyes. Put it down in my own words. It will not be everyone's America. It cannot even be all of my own because the images twist and turn, dissolve and resolve again in changing form. There are a thousand strands in the American tapestry. The warp and woof is beyond the art of a weaver like myself."[10]

Complexity, contradiction, change. All of these mean that our vision emerges as highly personal, imprecise, and incomplete. The fourth lesson worth emphasizing is that not only are our own views in flux but the reality that we are trying to fix for ourselves and our readers is constantly changing. "The mood of America," wrote Kuralt, "is infinitely complex and always changing and highly dependent on locale and circumstance."[11] The people and places that I visited on Highway 14 reflect this basic reality. By the time I visited these communities while on sabbatical leave from South Dakota State University during the fall of 1985, I had already taken an interest in them for several years, for instance teaming up with a colleague in the speech department in 1982 to put together a couple of half-hour radio programs on De Smet and Lake Preston. At that time we noticed the kinds of changes—empty storefronts, new houses and building projects, road improvements, park developments—that were going on in the communities. As I returned in 1988 and 1989, change continued to unfold. Several of the people I talked to had since died. Economic pressures on these small towns continued to intensify. All that we can be sure of about the future is that change will continue to occur. While a casual visitor might assume that these towns are frozen in time, the truth is that they have been in the throes of change from the very beginning.

The method employed here draws upon my own experience and background. Having been a small town resident for most of my life, my affection for small town people and the small town way of life may show through here. I hope, however, that my training as a historian as well as my desire to be fair and objective have served as a balance wheel and will make this study of interest to everyone who is curious about small town America. America is like life, E. M. Forster once said, because "you can usually find in it what you look for."[12] If I found some of the things I was looking for, I also discovered many unanticipated things.

Most influential on this study has been my historical training. Recently, books have proliferated on small town history and on highway history. Most of the highway books deal with well-known ones like the Lincoln Highway, Highway 40, Route 66, the Los Angeles Freeway, and the New Jersey Turnpike. The connection between history and highways is not a new subject; during the 1930s the Federal Writers' Project, operating under the Works Progress Administration, put special emphasis on highway routes and the history associated with them.[13]

Historical geography provided a second source of ideas for how to conduct research for this book. Historical geographers have naturally been attracted to roads and waterways as subjects. Their insistence that the vernacular landscape—the ordinary structures, places, and sites that surround us—is worthy of study offers a refreshing perspective. John Brinckerhoff Jackson reminded us that there is beauty in the landscape and that it derives from the human presence there, not just because it reflects some ideal standard of beauty. Paying close attention to townscapes and countryscapes opens up new avenues of historical understanding for us. It helps us discover meaning where none may have been apparent. D. W. Meinig pointed out that "every landscape is a code, and its study may be undertaken as a deciphering of meaning, of the cultural and social significance of ordinary but diagnostic features, as shown in numerous revealing essays by J. B. Jackson."[14]

Historians are increasingly using oral history to enrich their understanding of the past. Armed with tape recorders, they can fill in many lacunae otherwise condemned to obscurity. An oral history–journalistic approach thus was also useful for gathering information about my subject. I interviewed more than a hundred people who lived on or near the highway. At times I felt a sense of identity with Kuralt. (And several people even said that I reminded them of him!) While discovering patterns and regularities of the type that historians look for, Kuralt's observation rings true: "The small towns are full of surprises."[15] Blending history and journalism proved to be a natural sort of thing to do, fitting perfectly the purposes of this investigation.

Not being pressed with a deadline offered an advantage that most journalists don't have the luxury of. I could stay in a town for a few days, return to it several times, keep in touch with people I had met there, and go back and ask questions after further historical research. My thoughts during all of this echoed those of Steinbeck when he observed during his drive across America, "On the long journey doubts were often my companions. I've always admired those reporters who can descend on an area, talk to key people, ask key questions, take samplings of opinions, and then set down an orderly report very like a road map. I envy this technique and at the same time do not trust it as a mirror of reality. I feel that there are too many realities."[16]

Literary critics are quick to point out the many-sided nature of the realities we conjure up. I do not happen to agree with those who deny a foundation existing beneath the signs and symbols we use to depict the "real world," but I think we can learn something from their emphasis on the relational quality of our knowledge of past and present and from their insistence on the importance of language in shaping our perceptions and ideas. Jonathan Culler, for example, in an article on the semiotics of tourism, noted how people frequently surround objects with markers or signs that frame them as sights for tourists. Thus, rather than trusting people to make their own observations and interpretations, we tell them what to see and what it means. "The existence of reproductions is what makes something an original, authentic, the real thing—the original of which the souvenirs, postcards, statues etc. are reproductions—and by surrounding ourselves with reproductions we represent to ourselves . . . the possibility of authentic experiences in other times and in other places."[17]

A fifth influence on my investigation was the American Studies movement. Its concern with cultural meanings and interpretation leads one to stay alert to the significance of seemingly insignificant things. Although I am not convinced that they found America, I like the imaginative approach and broad sweep of the authors of *Looking for America on the New Jersey Turnpike;* they teach in the American Studies program at Rutgers University.[18] The slice of America that is crossed by Highway 14 through South Dakota is only a small and obscure part of the country but, in my opinion, important nevertheless. While the title of this book is *Looking for History on Highway 14,* it might also be called *Looking for Meaning on Highway 14,* since always, in looking at the past and for its traces, we are trying to discover the meaning that it ultimately has for us.[19]

Material culture studies have proliferated of late and provided a sixth perspective for me. Like the other approaches already mentioned, the investigation of architecture, roadways, automobiles, artifacts, and other aspects of material culture requires an interdisciplinary approach. By reconstructing the material environment that people lived in, we can better understand the ways they believed, felt, and acted.[20]

Finally, illustrations are an integral part of this study. Pictures themselves are seldom clear or unambiguous, and the meanings we derive from them or impose upon them require placing them in context and obtaining supplemental information about them. The value of photographs, art, and other visual forms is evident in the works of artists, such as George Catlin and Karl Bodmer, who came up the Missouri River during the nineteenth century; of photographers for the Farm Security Administration who documented the devastation wreaked by drought and depression during the 1930s; and of countless snapshots preserved in family albums and dresser drawers documenting ordinary daily life in the small towns. Such visual evidence provides a wonderful supplement to the documentary record and personal memories that can be recorded on tape.[21]

Originally my purpose in visiting the towns on Highway 14 was to respond to my own curiosity about the towns and their inhabitants. My purpose in this book is to illustrate some of the many ways there are to learn about the past. It is to disabuse those who might think that all of these towns are identical. It is to stimulate the imagination of those passersby who think they may be boring. It is to encourage people who travel by at fifty-five miles an hour to think about stopping for an hour or two, or for a day or a week, and perhaps even to come back and visit. It is to show how by approaching history from a variety of perspectives one can enliven and enrich one's view of the past and look at it through different eyes.

The fifteen towns featured here were the ones I found the most interesting stories in. Someone else might have uncovered entirely different stories. Mount Rushmore was included because it is the goal of so many tourists who travel the highway and because of its close association with the efforts to publicize and improve the highway during the 1920s. All of these towns once were, and most of them originated as, railroad towns located on the Dakota Central branch of the Chicago and North Western Railway, which laid its track east of the Missouri River in 1879–80 and west of the river in 1906–7.

Some of the towns along the track grew and prospered, some of them held their own, and others withered and declined. My purpose here is not to recount the histories of those towns, although much of their history does come through in the stories that are told. That history, in fact, should be written down, because it is interesting in itself and because the present is a transitional period in which the fate of these small towns lies in the balance. In another twenty or thirty years, more of these towns will succumb to the inexorable pressures of economic and social change. Already the face of the countryside has altered dramatically, and what the future will bring remains cloudy. Suffice it to say, there is much worth preserving here, but whether it will be or not is in the hands of the people who live here and the outside forces—political, economic, and social—that determine the fate of rural and small town America.

LOOKING FOR

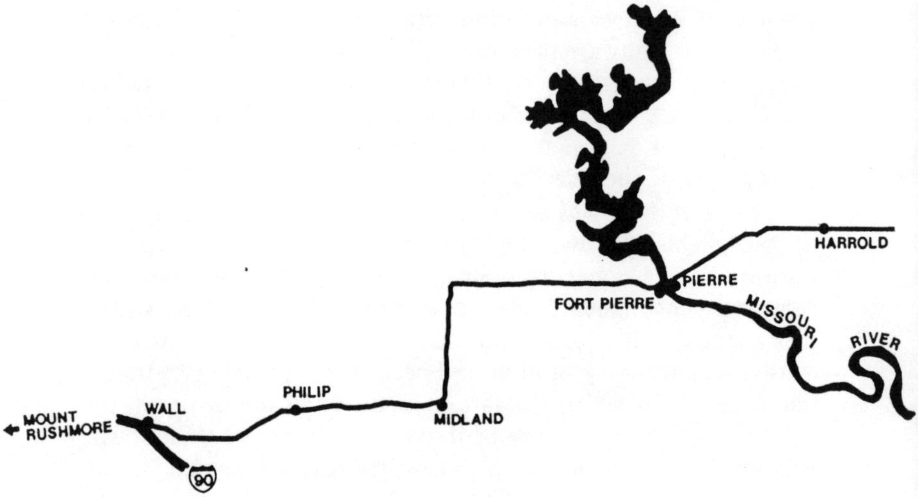
HARROLD
PIERRE
FORT PIERRE
MISSOURI
RIVER
PHILIP
WALL
MIDLAND
MOUNT RUSHMORE
90

HISTORY ON HIGHWAY 14

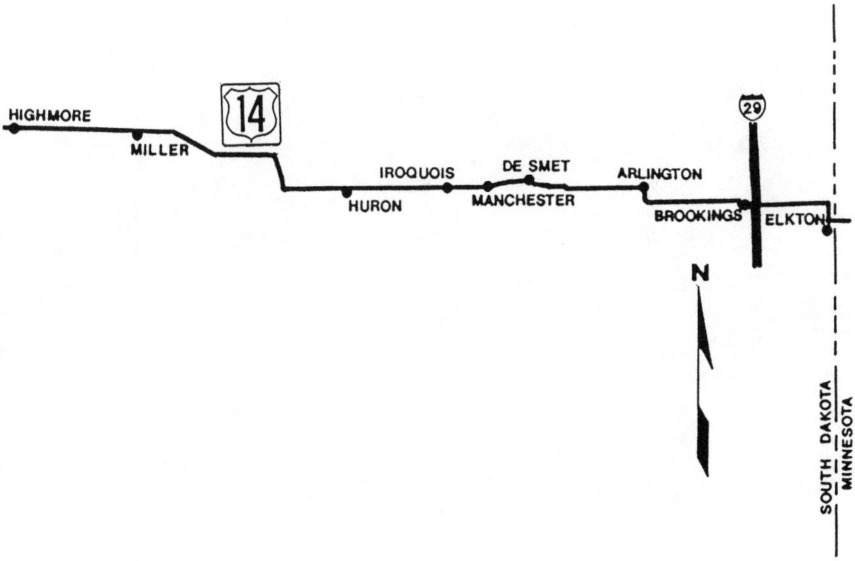

ELKTON

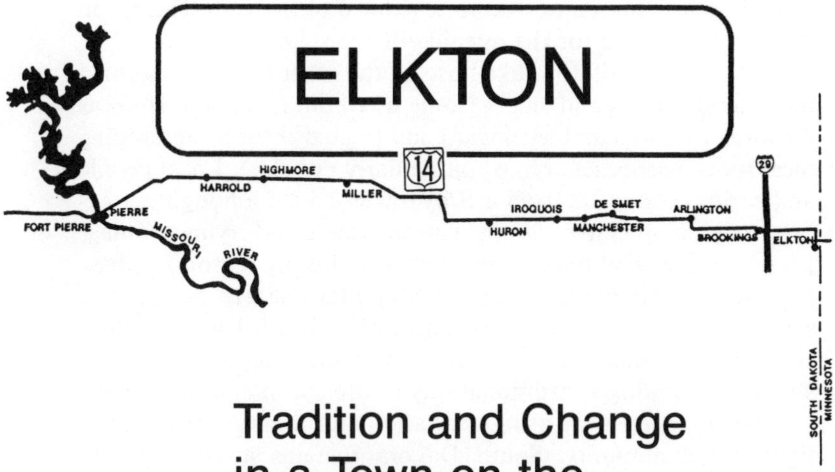

Tradition and Change in a Town on the Black and Yellow Trail

Monday morning, May 29, 1989, Elkton, South Dakota. I had planned to get over there by 7:30 in order to look around a while and see what was happening before the Centennial Wagon Train broke camp on the edge of town at 8:00. But plans seem to have a way of going awry, and it was almost 7:30 by the time I pulled out of Brookings heading east on Highway 14. The blacktop roadway was smooth, and encountering hardly any traffic on it, I easily covered the twenty miles and pulled into a parking space in time to see the horses and wagons parade past a rather thin crowd of spectators who had come out to watch them.

The Centennial Wagon Train was one of the major events devised by planners for South Dakota's 1989 centennial celebration. Elkton was the eighteenth stopover for the eastern division of the route (a separate group was simultaneously crisscrossing the region west of the Missouri River). Newspaper reporters and television Minicam units chronicled the picturesque procession as it meandered in a generally northward direction from its starting point on May 10 in Elk Point, in the southeastern tip of the state. *Time* even ran a story on it.[1] Most of the drivers had installed rubber tires on their wagons for smoother traveling, but some of the classic old Conestogas rumbled over the blacktop on creaky old wooden ones. Traveling at a rate of three or four miles per hour along state and county highways, the hundred or so wagons in the group (the size fluctuated as wagons broke down and had to be fixed and as others joined the train for brief stretches as it neared their communities) were scheduled to arrive in Huron on August 29, in time for the opening of the state fair.

The folks at Elkton, like hosts in the other towns, welcomed the wagon drivers and riders (some of whom had come from as far away as Texas and Michigan) and treated them to an evening meal (pork barbecues seemed particularly popular). Local people and curious observers from nearby towns drifted among the wagons, striking up conversations with the riders and trying to imagine how things had once been. That was also my reason for driving over on this humid, overcast May morning—to recapture a sense of history and to envision an earlier South Dakota before railroads, automobiles, telephones, and radio ushered in new lifestyles, obliterating a traditional way of life that had moved to the rhythms of horse-drawn transportation and found nurturance in tight-knit community. South Dakota remains a young state. There are many people, however, who can recall an automobileless society and more who remember when people farmed with horses and still rode in horse-drawn buggies even after the arrival of the automobile.

As the wagon train slowly wound its way north up Elk Street, the main street in town, I clicked off a few pictures. Some of the riders looked picturesque and weather-beaten; most were just ordinary looking, because they were just ordinary people taking time out of their lives to experience something that they would long remember. North of the business district, the caravan swung left and moved onto County Highway 13. Ten miles west of Elkton they angled right, drove through the town of Aurora, and a mile and a half north of town cut back west onto Highway 14. By late afternoon they had covered the last five miles of open road for the day and were coming into Brookings, where the third crowd of the day was waiting to greet them. After a day of rest the train pulled out again on May 31, heading west along Highway 14 toward Volga, Arlington, Lake Preston, and De Smet, where the route left the highway and veered north again toward Willow Lake, Clark, Watertown, and other communities in the northeastern part of the state.

Karroll Kyburz, a retiree who had come to watch the parade, invited me over to the Elkton Drive-In, located a block off Main Street, for a cup of coffee. He gave me the names of several people to talk to about local history and introduced me to John Even, who was eating breakfast there with his daughter and son-in-law. Even, who was eighty-five, told me about the time in 1912 when his father brought home his first car—a Model T Ford. Afterward, Karroll and I walked over to the city auditorium to attend the 9:45 Memorial Day observances, which for the past several years have been switched over from May 30 to the last Monday in May, allowing people to enjoy a three-day weekend. The speaker of the day was Ralph Perkins, a World War II veteran and Legionnaire from Gary, South Dakota, located thirty miles north of Elkton. His son Merle, an Elkton Legionnaire who served as master of ceremonies, appeared to be the youngest veteran involved in the exercises. Before launching into an address mixing personal reminiscences from his wartime service with ringing affirmations of patriotism and freedom, the elder Perkins noted disapprovingly that the day for honoring America's heroic veterans had been converted into more of a convenience for vacationers than a patriotic day of remembrance.[2]

Several hundred people occupied the folding chairs that had been set up on the gymnasium floor, while others sat in the bleachers along the sides. A number of families were in attendance, but the audience was heavily weighted toward older people on the one hand and high school students on the other, the latter

The South Dakota Centennial Wagon Train moving north on Elk Street.

there to play in the band. A color guard led the procession of honored guests up onto the stage. Father McPhillips, the Catholic priest, gave the invocation, after which the assembly rendered rather tentatively "The Star-Spangled Banner," followed by the Pledge of Allegiance and a special tribute to the South Dakota flag. Besides the address of the day, short essays on patriotism and Americanism were read by high school students, a musical selection was rendered by the high school chorus (most of whom were also band members), and citizenship awards were presented to several outstanding students. Following the benediction, the crowd reassembled on the lawn outside near several dozen wooden crosses that had been inscribed with the names of servicemen who had sacrificed their lives to protect the freedom and liberty of their families and friends. Elementary schoolchildren carefully installed small American flags in holes drilled in the tops of the crosses while names of the heroes they honored were solemnly read.

Compared to similar ceremonies in other towns, Elkton's Memorial Day exercises are more elaborate and better attended. By carrying on these traditions, the older generation impresses upon children and grandchildren the importance of the sacrifices made by those who have gone before them. In so doing they reinforce values and symbols that are central to both local and national cultures. A military tank is on the lawn in front of the auditorium, and a memorial signboard lists the names of all the servicemen and women from the Elkton area who served in World War I, World War II, and the Korean and Vietnam Wars (those from the last two are listed together for some reason). Stars mark the names of those who died in the service. In ways such as this historical memory is preserved in towns like Elkton, and generational boundaries are bridged. Local residents thus remember and honor those neighbors, friends, and loved ones whose lives were cut short. All can feel thereby their connectedness to a larger whole—a community that consists of more than the sum of its individual parts.

Memorial Day isn't quite what it used to be, however. All over South Dakota, during the early years of settlement and into the twentieth century, Memorial Day—or "Decoration Day," as it was more commonly called—ranked with Christmas and the Fourth of July as big events on the community calendar. During the late 1800s most small towns contained active units of the Grand Army of the Republic. GAR veterans attended summer encampments with their wives and reminisced about their Civil War experiences, took a leading role in Republican politics, and proudly marched in ceremonies every May 30, while stores closed for an hour or two. Almost everybody in town came out to commemorate the significance of the day. If there was an opera house in town, and there usually was, the parade of war veterans, band members, women's auxiliaries, local officials, schoolchildren, and lodge members would wind up there after marching down Main Street and several side streets and settle down for the ceremony, which closely resembled the program of the day at Elkton in 1989. One of the biggest differences between then and now was the length of the oration, for folks back then were accustomed to listening to long speeches. From the opera house, many spectators would join a procession to the cemetery, where schoolchildren placed wreaths on the graves of departed soldiers.[3]

By the 1920s, declining interest in Memorial Day services and Fourth of July celebrations began to elicit comment and concern.[4] The declining significance of Memorial Day coincided with the rise of the automobile, which greatly increased people's mobility. During the 1920s, according to historian James Flink, "automobility became the backbone of a new consumer-goods-oriented society that has persisted to the present." Activities that earlier required considerable planning could now be undertaken on the spur of the moment. Trips that had taken an hour or more were now made in minutes. Farmers needing parts for their combines or a loaf of bread for lunch could hop in the car or pickup and be to town and back in less time than it had once taken to get ready to go. In the process of conquering space and time, automobiles brought tremendous changes in people's lives. On the one hand, heightened mobility eased the burdens of daily living, enhanced people's enjoyment of leisure time, and provided them with options that had been unimagined during horse-and-buggy days. On the other hand, in the process of reducing the constraints of space and time, the automobile was the single most important factor in attenuating ties of community that had earlier held sway. By shortening distances and compressing time, it tended to corrode and undermine the types of rituals and ceremonies—Memorial Day, the Fourth of July, Sunday churchgoing, and Saturday night shopping in town—that seemed to slow the clock for a moment and unite people within a particular locality in a sense of shared purpose and belief. Thus, increased mobility was a beneficial as well as a corrosive force as it transformed people's lives in towns like Elkton.[5]

The first automobiles to appear in South Dakota were luxury items, only for people affluent enough to afford the price tags they sported. Elkton's first automobile was a Case purchased by

Joe Noeth around 1905.[6] Roads in the country, like streets in town, consisted only of dirt; they raised clouds of dust in the summer and mired the unwary in mud in the winter and during rainy weather. Until landowners began to object to the practice, people had often cut diagonally across the prairie with their horse-drawn wagons and buggies, but after the arrival of the automobile, roads were mainly on the section lines, which crisscrossed the landscape at one-mile intervals in an endlessly repeating pattern.[7] Before cars arrived on the scene, nobody worried much about giving people directions, because, except for an occasional immigrant wagon or excursionist, few people ever drove more than several miles away from home. When they did, it was a simple matter to stop and ask for directions along the way from farmers or townspeople. Long-distance automobile traffic brought road signs, maps, facilities catering to drivers, and increasing demands for building better roads.[8]

The early settlers in Brookings County had made their way across the seemingly endless, grass-covered prairies by plowing furrows that they could follow to get from place to place. In 1875 a group of farmers extended one from the county seat at Medary, located on the Big Sioux River in the southern part of the county, in a generally northeasterly direction past the settlement at Lake Hendricks and on to Canby, Minnesota, the end of the line for the railroad at that time. People could walk or drive a wagon as far as fifty or sixty miles to get to Canby to pick up supplies. Such furrows were a common sight during the early days. As settlement picked up during the late 1870s in anticipation of the coming of the railroad, stagecoach lines began, linking the tiny inland settlements at Medary, Oakwood, and Fountain with other towns in the area such as Flandreau and Canby, Minnesota.[9]

Even earlier, the first roads in the area had been Indian trails, whose paths in pursuit of the buffalo could easily be discerned by the early white settlers. Several government roads also were laid out in Dakota Territory. The most famous was the Nobles Trail, which entered Brookings County from Minnesota near the "Hole-in-the-Wall," a gap in the hills that the Indians frequently used and which later would be used for the route of the Chicago and North Western Railway in 1879. Building the trail in 1857 simply amounted to constructing earthen mounds at regular intervals to mark it and laying rock fords in rivers and streams to make them passable for teams and wagons. The trail angled through Brookings County in a southwesterly direction, passing by the future site of Elkton and crossing the Big Sioux River near the point where Medary was located in the same year that the road was built.[10] In a sea of tallgrass prairie growing waist to shoulder-high, such trails and roads made scant impression. Today it is not always easy to determine exactly where they were located, but people at the time welcomed them just as we do our interstates today.

The coming of the automobile revolutionized transportation for towns like Elkton. As early as 1905, future governor Peter Norbeck completed the first automobile trip from the Missouri River to the Black Hills, although roads all over South Dakota remained terrible and in many places virtually nonexistent.[11] By the second decade, the state began taking part in a national movement to build better roads, and the idea of constructing coast-to-coast highways and other extended routes rapidly gained popularity. The Lincoln Highway, which started in New York City, following the route of the old National Road and then continuing west to San Francisco, established a model for others to imitate. Its promoters were Henry Joy, president of the Packard Motor Car Company, and Carl Graham Fischer, owner of Prest-O-Lite, a carbide gas auto headlight company, and founder of the Indianapolis Motor Speedway. Beginning in 1912, they organized an association to raise funds, locate a route, publicize it, encourage local boosters, and generate support for the better roads movement. The first improvements along the route were made by local sponsors who recognized the commercial advantages of being located along it. Emphasis quickly shifted to soliciting governmental aid for building and maintaining the highway.[12]

Other highway and trail associations were emerging about the same time. These organizations printed maps, marked the trails, advertised them, and sought funds to improve them. By the mid-1920s, the United States had an estimated 250 marked trails. In South Dakota these included the Custer Battlefield Trail, which ran west from Sioux Falls through Mitchell and Chamberlain and past the Black Hills; the King of Trails, which ran from Winnipeg to the Gulf Coast, passing through Brookings; and the Yellowstone Trail across the northern part of the state through Milbank, Aberdeen, and Mobridge, with termini in Boston and Puget Sound. The latter's father and chief promoter was J. W. Parmley of Ipswich, sometime state legislator and full-time road enthusiast and the outstanding spokesman for better roads in the state.[13]

In 1912, the year Fischer started promoting the Lincoln Highway and Parmley organized the Yellowstone Trail Association, another group began boosting a parallel route to Yellowstone National Park running through the middle of the state.

Since this highway began in Chicago and terminated at Yellowstone, its promoters called it the "Chicago to Black Hills and Yellowstone Park Highway" (or "Trail"). It soon became popularly known as the "Black and Yellow Trail." During 1912 and 1913, pathfinders traversed the route of the proposed highway, fixing its location and soliciting support from local businesses. A rudimentary organization emerged that solicited funds, pushed the idea of tourism, and called for governmental subsidies for road building. A two-day conference of state road enthusiasts that met in Deadwood in April 1913 projected an extension that would continue all the way to Portland and Seattle.[14]

To mark the highway, local boosters painted black and yellow stripes on telephone poles and fence posts and on anything else that was handy, including boulders, bridge abutments, and even water towers. Only brave and hardy travelers, however, ventured very far on these dirt trails until after World War I. In 1913 the State Highway Commission was established by the legislature (it was reorganized in 1919), and larger legislative appropriations gradually became available for building and improving roads.[15] After the war, as car ownership expanded and travel increased, trail boosters stepped up their activities. Governor Norbeck addressed the annual meeting of trail boosters in Pierre in June 1920, speaking on the subject of road construction in South Dakota. Two months later, at the national headquarters of the association in Huron, the board of directors perfected a plan to develop and advertise the highway. The secretary of the association, O. M. Phelps of Huron, announced an expanded publicity campaign and the intention to completely remark the trail from Chicago to Yellowstone and indicated that the organization would encourage towns to establish free campgrounds for traveling tourists.[16]

By 1923, seventy-three tourist camps had been established in the 120 or so towns that lay along the 1,605 miles of the trail, and other towns were considering putting in their own. A full-time general manager, H. L. Kyes of Huron, was hired, and the budget of the organization, which had been less than $3,000 three years earlier, was increased to $20,000. A newsletter for members and backers called the *Straight Away* also made its appearance that year. Published sporadically thereafter, it advertised the trail and reported on activities of the organization, seeking to whip up enthusiasm among businessmen and women and other potential contributors. The organization adopted a pledge and a code of ethics. It played up the Black and Yellow Trail as "The Shortest and Most Scenic Route to Yellowstone National Park."[17]

Growing interest in the Black and Yellow Trail Association coincided with the graveling of the route and its designation as State Highway 30 in 1923. By the end of the year, its publicists were advertising that the entire route from Chicago to Pierre was either hard-surfaced or graveled and that links west of the Missouri River would soon be improved, too. In 1924, an expanded system of committees was set up to help plan and carry out the work of the organization, relieving the general manager of some of the responsibility. At the annual meeting in Huron in January of that year, businessman Charles Leavitt Hyde of Pierre spoke enthusiastically about opportunities for developing the West River region of South Dakota (the area west of the Missouri River) and asserted that the Black and Yellow Trail could play a major role in the project. State historian Doane Robinson, a good friend of Hyde's in Pierre, took as his topic "The Value of

PLEDGE

As a part Owner, having a proprietary interest in the "Black and Yellow Trail" I know that it offers wonderful scenery and increasing opportunity to the traveler. I believe that the slogan "he profits most who serves best" is just as applicable to trail associations as it is to the individual, and that I should ever be careful to see that one hundred cents worth of service is given for every dollar received. I realize that as part owner in a public highway I will be called upon to serve many people coming to my locality for the first time and I will earnestly endeavor to make them feel that they are not among strangers rather, that they are accumulating new friends. I further pledge my cooperation with highway officials and maintenence men that the "Black and Yellow" may eventually be known as

"The Scenic and Safe Route"

The pledge of the Black and Yellow Trail Association, adopted in 1923. (Courtesy of South Dakota State Archives, Pierre)

Historical and Scenic Markers to a Trail Association." He proposed carving statues of historical figures in rock formations in the Black Hills as a good method of attracting more tourists to the state. Previously, Robinson had accepted the chairmanship of a special marking committee to advertise historic points along the route of the Black and Yellow Trail.[18]

By the late 1920s, the improvement of roads like the Black and Yellow Trail was drawing increasing public interest. Robinson's brainchild eventuated in Mount Rushmore, which became a major attraction for travelers on the Black and Yellow and other trails through South Dakota. In 1926, as federal involvement in road building picked up, State Highway 30 was redesignated Federal Highway 14.[19] By the early 1930s, as tourist dollars came to be seen as one way to make up for the devastating financial losses wrought by the Great Depression, the call for better highways rang out even more stridently in South Dakota and surrounding states. The battle cry became "dustless highways," and by the end of the decade graveled roadbeds were rapidly being replaced by hard-surfaced ones.

The morning I talked to him over breakfast at the Elkton Drive-In, John Even told me what it had been like to live in the area when the Black and Yellow Trail first came through. He was eight years old at the time. Now he's a retired farmer. Before moving onto a farm seven miles north of Elkton in 1914, his family had lived near Ward, a smaller community six miles south and one mile east of town. Even remembered that he had been about six or seven years old when he had a chance to ride in one of the first cars to appear in the area. After learning about it, his father warned him that he'd get a licking if he tried to do it again, because automobiles were dangerous. Not long after that, in 1912, his dad bought a Model T that sometimes had its top removed so they could use it for farm work.

Even recalled that during the years when he was growing up on their farm north of Elkton, all of the roads were still dirt. Once, he said, a fellow speeded by their place going about sixty miles an hour, raising a cloud of dust that darkened the sky "for miles." The country school that Even attended was only about a mile away from home. To get there, he usually cut across a field. Neighbors generally got together more in those days than they do now. They'd drive over in their horse and buggy and put the horses in the barn. After a time, Even's father bought a Dodge touring car. In the wintertime, they could let the curtains down over the side to keep out the cold. Cars altered people's lives in many ways, but the changes did not come overnight. The Even family did not drive to Elkton very often; they would make the twenty-five miles over to Brookings maybe only a couple of times a year. Having an automobile, they could drive to the county fair instead of taking the train. Until better roads were built and automobile performance improved, however, driving was still something of an adventure.

While in Elkton, I also was able to talk to Dick and Mary Seivert in their two-story bungalow on Elk Street, a couple of blocks south of the business district. Mary recalled that when she was a little girl, her family's farm house, six miles west of Elkton, was next to the Black and Yellow Trail. She remembered telephone poles being painted with black and yellow stripes to mark the route of the highway. At first, the family's transportation was a surrey, but about the time she was seven, her father bought a new Model T. She told me that in those days nobody bought a used Model T. Rather, people generally drove them until they wore out and then parked them behind their barns. She recalled some families with several old cars no longer driven. Her mother never did learn to drive, but Mary started driving a Model A Ford when she was in her teens.

In 1920, when she was nine, the family moved into Elkton, and her father, Pat Culhane, started a garage on a corner a block and a half north and across the street from the family's home, the same house the Seiverts live in now. The garage was a big building, fifty feet wide and constructed of cement blocks, giving it an appearance typical of the time. Today the Ottertail Power Company's office occupies the lot. Pat Culhane's Garage sold Standard Oil products and did repair work. During the 1920s and 1930s, there were seven or eight places where you could buy gas in town. Nobody had much money in those days, and credit could run for years. Before Culhane died in 1936, he showed Mary his books, with thousands of dollars that people owed him, and told her to write off their debts when any of them died.

Until better cooling systems and permanent antifreeze arrived during the mid-1920s, people generally did not even try to drive their cars in cold weather. Whenever they went anywhere, they had to drain their radiators when they stopped and refill them before starting out again. Snowdrifts and muddy roads presented other hazards. Many Elkton car owners stored their automobiles over the winter in Pat Culhane's Garage. He charged them $3 a month. When Mary was fourteen, a fire broke out in a nearby building, and fearing that it might cross over to his garage, Culhane called the school so Mary could come help him drive all of the cars out just in case.

Mary's husband Dick worked on the construction of the new Highway 14 when it was rerouted north of town in 1935 and 1936. When the original road locators came through in 1912 and 1913, they had marked the route down the section lines, going right through the towns along the way and often right down the middle of Main Street. The result was a series of right angles that drivers had to negotiate as they made their way west across the state. In dirt road days, when few people were in a hurry to get anywhere, that posed no problems. But the graveling of the highway during the early 1920s and the arrival of higher performance cars and trucks put more and more of a premium on speed. By the mid-1930s, pressure had increased to improve and hard-surface major arteries like Highway 14. As the number of tourists steadily increased, business-minded people could see the makings of a new industry, and the cry for dust-free highways became more insistent.[20]

State highway officials in Pierre, responding to these pressures, decided to hard-surface Highway 14 and other major routes. In the process, they also determined to straighten out the kinks along the routes, thereby allowing faster vehicular speeds and also reducing the total mileage of the routes. In accomplishing this, they bypassed several towns along the highway, including Elkton and its neighbor to the west, Aurora. The new route, coming west from Lake Benton, Minnesota, crossed the state line two miles north of the old route, and when it got as far west as Elkton, turned north three miles and then cut directly west toward Brookings.[21]

In May 1935, a large delegation of Elkton residents descended on a public hearing in Brookings called by the state highway commission to hear objections to and discuss the proposed changes in the route north of Elkton. They noted the benefits that Elkton had derived from having the highway and argued that it was unfair to move it away from them now. Lake Benton, Minnesota, had four good roads leading into town, it was observed. Elkton, as the second largest town in Brookings County, deserved some consideration, they asserted. One member of the delegation noted that rerouting Highway 14 would virtually cut Elkton off in the winter since federal roads were the only ones kept free of snow. But their arguments were to no avail.

A Brookings resident made the point that obtaining federal funds to hard-surface the roadway required that they follow the highway commission's plan. Another person from Brookings contended that the welfare of the state as a whole should take precedence over the interests of particular places and that it was desirable to promote speed by straightening out the route and bypassing some towns, if necessary. A third Brookingsite observed that it was too late to change plans anyway, since both the South Dakota and the Minnesota highway commissions had already made the determination that the route should be changed. It was easy enough for people in Brookings, where the highway ran through the middle of town, to advise their Elkton counterparts not to be too upset by what was happening![22]

Dick Seivert was one of the men hired to build the new highway. In 1936, when the roadbed was graded, he drove one of six cabless trucks used to haul dirt, working the 6:00 A.M. to noon shift. A second crew took over at noon and worked till 6:00 in the evening. Altogether, there were about seventy-five men on the job. Besides building up the grade for the roadbed, they did cul-

Pat Culhane (behind counter) in his garage in Elkton.
(Courtesy of Mary Seivert)

vert work and built bridges. For his labor, Dick earned $12 a week ($2 a day for six days). He also worked for a while the following year, when the blacktop was laid. Gravel was mixed with oil and laid in windrows and then bladed to smooth it out. They didn't have any heavy rollers to pack the surface down, but for the time, the technology was modern and efficient.

Thus, in less than a quarter of a century the highway had come and gone at Elkton. In the early days of automobile travel, the new horseless carriages seemed to hold out great promise for small town residents as well as for their rural neighbors. For farm families, the benefits were obvious: their isolation would be reduced, they could get to town more easily to market their crops and produce and to shop and do their other business, they could partake of town culture, and they could ramble around the countryside on pleasure jaunts. The automobile, more than anything else, dissolved the old distinctions between country and town living. Townspeople, too, avidly toted up the benefits of automobile travel. They would have more business from rural residents and travelers, they could provide services for the vehicles themselves, they could get away to visit strange and exotic places, and they could march along with technological progress.[23]

South Dakotans, like other rural plains residents, were quick to purchase automobiles during the 1910s and 1920s. Reports during the 1920s ranked the state among the leaders in per capita car ownership. Motor vehicle registrations (passenger cars constituted over 90 percent of the total) in the state increased from 14,457 in 1913 to 120,395 in 1920, 168,230 in 1926, and 191,374 in 1928. In the latter year, with 272 motor vehicles registered per 1,000 population, South Dakota ranked behind only California (395), Nevada (356), Iowa (302), Kansas (291), Nebraska (278), and Oregon (275). It was tied with Michigan and slightly ahead of North Dakota (271). The national average was 204 per 1,000 population.[24]

When the Black and Yellow Trail was established, towns along the route perceived only the benefits they would derive from it. What people largely failed to anticipate was that what the automobile could give, it could also take away. Already by the 1920s, the impact of the auto was becoming apparent. Greater mobility enticed people into the larger towns with a greater variety of goods and services. Smaller towns like Elkton and Aurora increasingly would be passed by. Towns off the route of the highway, such as White, Bushnell, and Bruce in Brookings County, were at an even greater disadvantage. Already by the 1930 census most of them were beginning to show declines.

The economic consequences of the highway were significant, but the social implications were no less so. The rise of the automobile coincided with the beginning of the breakdown of the tightly knit sense of community that characterized both the small towns and the rural neighborhoods surrounding them.[25] Although increased mobility was by no means the only factor in this process, it was probably the most important one. The transition did not occur overnight. It included the consolidation of school districts and the abandonment of rural schools, the move of country churches into town, the closing down of many small town stores and businesses because of the rising competition of the bigger towns, and the centralization of medical services in clinics and hospitals in larger towns. The process also entailed the gradual disintegration of those informal social institutions and interactions that had been so pervasive and so taken for granted during the early decades, such as town baseball teams, tea parties, church picnics, livery stable conversations, and Saturday night.

One of the main things to be affected by the rise of the automobile culture was the social ritual and tradition that bound the community together, including Memorial Day, the Fourth of July, and other such days of remembrance and celebration. When horse and buggy was the common mode of transportation and farm families seldom got to a town, such days were expectantly looked forward to. People milked the experience for everything they could. When automobiles allowed them to go wherever and whenever they wanted to, to drive to Sioux Falls or even to Minneapolis, when radio, movies, television, and other diversions provided unlimited entertainment, and when the accelerated pace of everyday life often made neighbors into strangers and a sense of community attenuated at best, the commemoration of Memorial Day became an obligation devolving upon a smaller and smaller part of the population and something of a duty rather than a privilege.

What do people look forward to on Memorial Day now? Going to the lake in their automobiles, going shopping, watching a ball game on television, and, of course, watching the Indianapolis 500 auto race. If they are part of a declining group of patriotic citizens still aware of the significance of the day—or a high school student playing in the band or receiving a citizenship award—they will fit in the Memorial Day service as part of the day's schedule. Thus, in the change and continuity which characterize a small town that used to be on Highway 14 in eastern South Dakota, one can observe some of the history that can be found, if one wants to look for it.

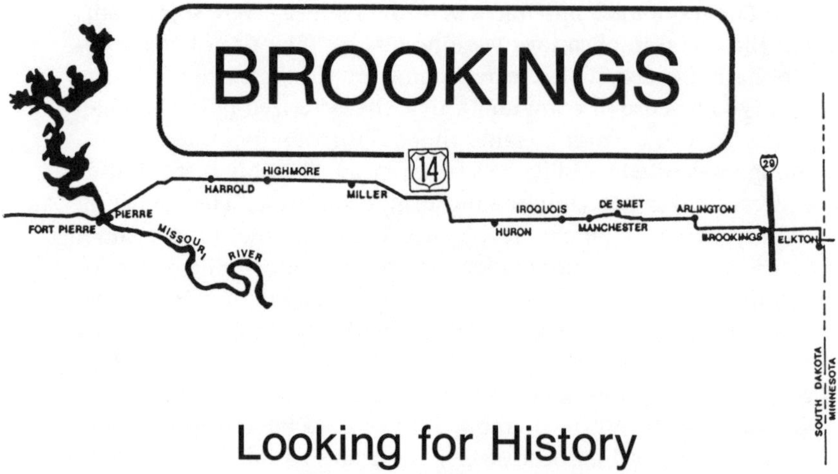

Looking for History in Small Town America

Where shall one search for history in a small town? If you happen to be in Brookings, South Dakota, there are many places to look. Larger than any other Highway 14 town in South Dakota east of Rapid City, Brookings also contains more historical resources than most of them. Shelves at the South Dakota State University library are lined with South Dakota books. The Brookings Public Library contains a special state and local history collection, including a variety of books, atlases, directories, pamphlets, personal reminiscences, scrapbooks, and newspaper clippings.

Strangely enough, significantly enough, until South Dakota celebrated its centennial in 1989, the only history of Brookings County available was a master's thesis done by Gustav O. Sandro at the University of South Dakota in 1936.[1] Partly because there were so many people capable of working on a new county history, they all seemed content to let somebody else take the initiative. In many other counties the history buffs realized that if they didn't start the ball rolling, nobody would. So during the last couple of decades, while counties all over the state were publishing their histories, Brookings County lagged behind, waiting until the state centennial arrived to get going on their project.[2]

Many people seem to prefer visiting historical museums or watching historical movies to reading history books. The Brookings County Historical Museum at Volga (eight miles west of Brookings on Highway 14) contains a typical array of artifacts, pictures, and printed materials. The State Agricultural Heritage

Museum on the South Dakota State University campus houses permanent displays of farm equipment and tools and rotating exhibits on other subjects. Down the street a couple of blocks is the South Dakota Art Museum, with its large collection of Harvey Dunn paintings portraying the prairie homestead experience during the late nineteenth century. The university itself promotes historical research and dissemination of information through its courses, library holdings, archives, and photo collection. *Writing Local History,* by the late Donald Dean Parker, a longtime member of the history department, was for several decades the standard handbook on local history research in the United States.[3] During his years on the faculty, Parker churned out scores of newspaper articles, books, and pamphlets on the history of the state and its counties and towns. Among the items in his voluminous files, which after retiring he deposited at the Center for Western Studies in Sioux Falls, is a three-hundred-page unfinished manuscript on the history of Brookings County.[4] While regularly carrying a four- to five-course teaching load, Parker managed to be a remarkably productive scholar.

At the county courthouse, more historical information can be discovered by those willing to ferret it out: property transactions in deed books, field notes recorded by the original land surveyors, property tax records, voting returns, vital statistics, criminal cases, and other materials. Scrapbooks and photo albums, letters and diaries, and personal recollections written down for grandchildren continue to gather dust in people's attics and basements and unfortunately often get thrown away when they move or die. Several years ago, a city librarian showed me some of her great-aunt's diaries—meticulously kept accounts of one woman's day-by-day life for more than thirty years from the 1930s to the 1960s. It constitutes a treasure trove of historical information about everyday life in Brookings, and some day will find its way into an archive. Too many similar records will wind up in the trash.

For fifteen years John Beatty, who followed his father into the jewelry business in Brookings and who is now retired, has run a Friday local history column called "Pokings" in the Brookings *Register.* Recently he added a second weekly column called "Sharings," which reprints excerpts from letters, diaries, interviews, and other items that people send in to him.[5] Beatty is a member of the clan of self-appointed local historians who can be found in almost every town—keepers of the past who preserve the historical memory of a community at a time when the noise level of the mass media tends to overwhelm local happenings and activities.

He is not alone, however. When people want to know something about some historical event or about somebody who lived in town, they soon find their way to George and Evelyn Norby.

Back in 1965 when workers who were tearing down the old Brookings *Register* office came across runs of old yellowing newspapers, they asked George, who worked for a local printing firm, if he wanted them. As a child, George had never really been interested in history. He never even finished high school. But now he and his wife Evelyn spent many fascinating hours poring over the ads and paragraph items in the old newspapers. She was especially interested in genealogy and what she could learn about her family, which had lived in the Sinai area, fifteen miles southwest of Brookings. After George retired in 1986, he had more time to read the papers, and the local Historical Preservation Commission asked him to help find information for a walking tour the committee was working on. Then the state centennial came along, and George and Evelyn were asked to share their findings. They put together a display of pictures and copies of newspaper articles depicting the history and growth of the community. Eventually they filled about two hundred cardboard sheets covered with plastic to protect the pictures. Some of the sheets have as many as twenty pictures on them. They spent many hours during the centennial year of 1989 talking to people who came to look at their display in the malls and at other places in town.[6]

Naturally enough, the Norbys wound up on the historical subcommittee involved in planning Brookings's celebration of the state centennial in 1989. Each month was assigned a special theme—celebrating the arts, transportation, harvest and hunting, and so forth. Pioneer past and heritage was the focus in January. Activities included an evening of dance (with dancers from the nearby Flandreau Indian School, Norwegian folk dancers, square dancers, jitterbuggers, and others), an ethnic food fest, and the printing of a historical calendar, with events from Brookings's history for every day of the year. To gather information for the calendar, George and Evelyn spent weeks poring through back issues of their own copies of the Brookings *Register* and the Brookings County *Press*.

The historical facts used in the calendar revolved around people ("L. A. Lemert new J.C. Penney mgr," February 5, 1925), places ("Newport Restaurant featuring Southern Cooking," July 21, 1910), firsts ("Downy Flake Doughnut Shop opens," September 24, 1931), and offbeat items ("Zoology & Pharmacy depts SDSC skin elephant," May 18, 1916). Most had a local focus, although some mentioned famous personalities passing through town or something in the national culture that bore upon local activities, for example, "John Philip Sousa and band performing at college," October 3, 1928, and "Fad Theatre showing Love with Greta Garbo," February 28, 1928.[7] While historical calendars like this illustrate the embeddedness of local happenings within wider national and international contexts, the predominant impression they give is one of people who take their days one at a time, attending to business, neighbors, and family, and not overly concerned about distant events and forces.

What imparts historical significance to these disconnected facts—these local items of historical trivia—is the background knowledge people carry that links together those isolated names,

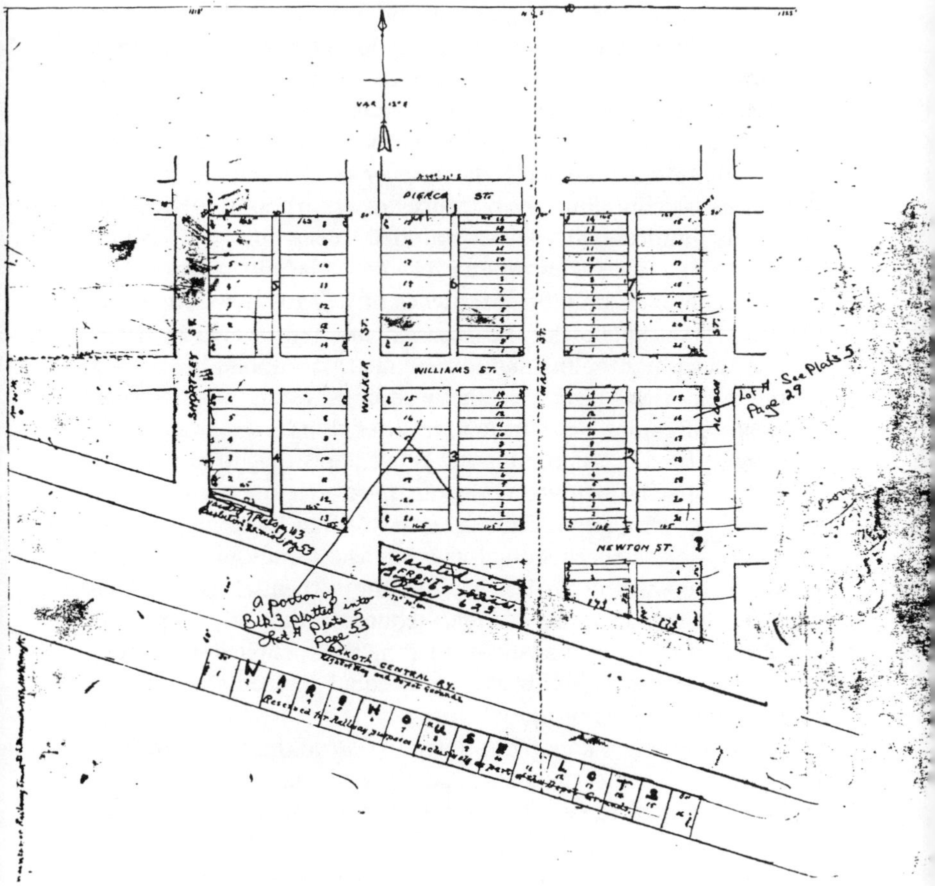

Original plat of Brookings done by Arthur Jacobi in 1879.
(Courtesy of Brookings County Register of Deeds)

dates, and facts. Knowing the context helps establish meaning. The stories that get told and retold, the people who tell the stories and act them out, the places where the action occurs—these constitute the setting for the names, dates, and facts recorded in the boxes on the calendar. Facts embedded in their historical context are meaningful; ripped out of that context they become factoids that are interesting only to trivia buffs. History, Carl L. Becker and many others have pointed out, is an extension of personal memory. "Knowledge or history," he noted, is "an enrichment of our minds with the multiplied images of events, places, peoples, ideas, emotions outside our personal experience, an enrichment of our experience by bringing into our minds memories of the experience of the community, the nation, the race."[8]

The 1881 bird's-eye drawing of Brookings featured on the cover of the calendar illustrates the tendency of people to segment space into neat, orderly compartments in much the same fashion that they carve up time. Indeed, a casual glance at the neatly drawn squares of the town layout could lead one to mistake it for a calendar page, the only difference being that the latter runs seven columns across while the bird's-eye view has nine. Both share this in common: they reduce an amorphous, disorderly, seemingly limitless entity into a bounded, repeatable, orderly pattern. Time extends backward and forward indefinitely, and we are able to experience only brief snatches of it. Mostly we engage in routine, forgettable tasks and amusements, punctuated by a few oddly spaced high points and low points that impress themselves on our memories—births, deaths, weddings, fights, car rides, accidents, ball games, promotions, injuries, blizzards, heat waves, first loves, final disappointments. What appear significant at the time and what remain etched in our memories are episodes and incidents occurring at variable intervals, often, it seems, coming together in close succession. But while the family histories that people write and the stories they tell about themselves acknowledge the unequal nature of time—concentrating on things that stand out as really important— the time that people daily experience flows past steadily, broken into equal segments, which the calendar reminds us of daily.[9]

In like manner, a map of a town like Brookings divides space into discrete, identical segments, seeming to confer equality upon every location in town. The grid system of survey, traceable to William Penn's Philadelphia, provided a quick, efficient method for platting towns; the lots were then sold to entrepreneurs and settlers scrambling to be there first.[10] What is immediately apparent in perusing the drawing done by the itinerant bird's-eye artist in 1881, a little more than a year after the town was founded, is that space, like time, confers greater privilege on some points than on others.[11] Just as certain times in people's lives are of greater importance than others, certain places in a community command more attention than others. People's activities in Brookings during the early days centered primarily along the railroad tracks and Main Street. Other places of importance included churches, schools, recreational areas, and prominent residents' homes.[12] In other words, people's lives were governed in large measure by patterns and habits dictating both when certain kinds

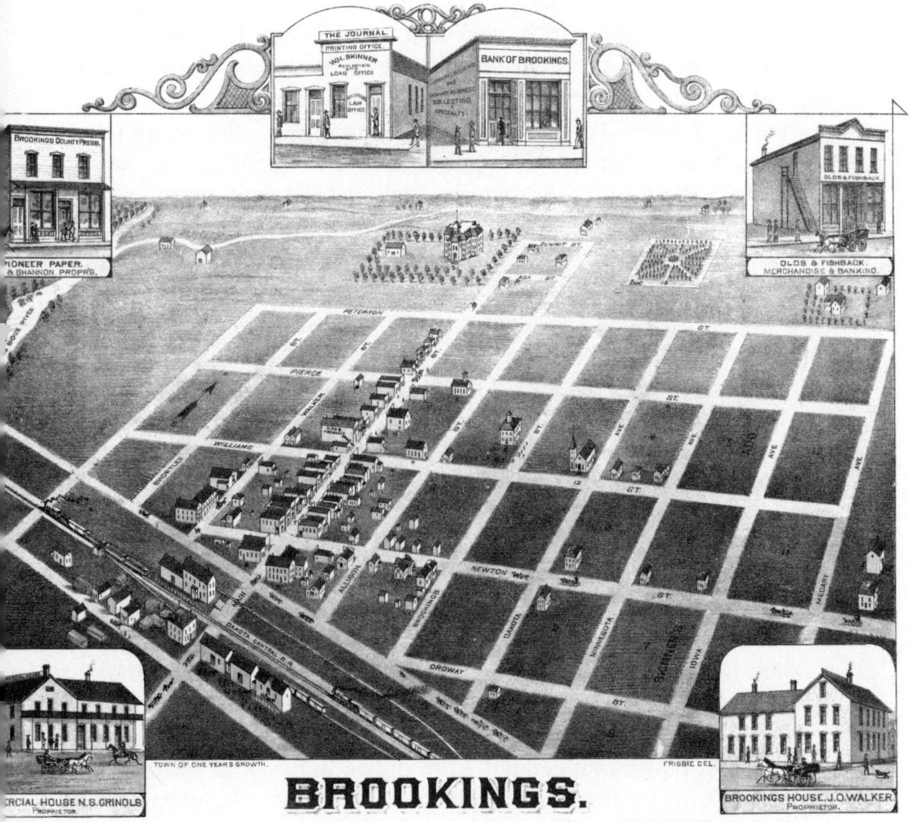

A bird's-eye view of Brookings, 1881. (Courtesy of State Agricultural Heritage Museum, Brookings)

of events happened and where they would take place. The history of a town unfolded within a matrix of time and place that channeled people's behavior, allowing for a degree of freedom but also reinforcing patterns of regulated behavior.

The bird's-eye artist, whose stay in the young village probably lasted no longer than several days, would have had only enough time to sketch the buildings and then imaginatively render them in a drawing as if observing them from a balloon somewhere southeast of town. In converting ground-level observations into an image that would be both descriptive and flattering, the artist fitted the particulars of the local situation into a stylized framework that the artist no doubt repeated dozens, if not hundreds, of times while traveling from place to place through the upper Middle West.[13] Thus, the lines of the streets did not converge, as the laws of perspective would have dictated, at a distant vanishing point on the horizon; rather, they closely resembled rectangles, which facilitated the process of drawing.

Inessential details—building decorations, trees, shrubs, outhouses, fences, garbage piles, sidewalks, dogs, cows, and so forth—were omitted. Other details, such as the neatly patterned trees around the college building at the top of the picture and the park to its right, were added for effect. In fact, the first college building was not actually built until 1884, three years later, and the artist indicated in the identifying notes that the agricultural college and Union Park were still only "prospective." Additionally, the Big Sioux River, which actually was located several miles to the west, was depicted as flowing close by the town. It must be remembered that the artist's purpose was not to render a fully accurate portrait, even if that were possible, but rather to create a likeness that would provide people with a positive impression of the town as it appeared at the time and as it was destined to progress in the future. The departure of a passenger train from the depot just ahead of an incoming freight, along with the movement of wagons and buggies on several streets, reflected a general busyness and vitality in the town, but ordinary people going about their work and daily routines were too tiny to bother with.

A 1956 aerial photograph of Brookings, taken from a somewhat different angle, indicated how much things had changed during the intervening three-quarters of a century. In place of one-story grain bins and storage sheds there towered tall, proud grain elevators. Gone were the horse-drawn wagons and buggies, replaced by diagonally parked cars filling almost every space along two blocks of Main Street. The towering smokestack of the heating plant, the spires of churches, the flat roofs of store buildings, and the arched roof of the armory-auditorium all testified to continuous rounds of construction over the years. The impressive Ionic post office near the top of Main Street on the east side reflected the influence of a member of Congress from Brookings during the second decade of the twentieth century. In place of the original plain, two-story wooden depot, a stately brick one built in 1905 reflected the good bet that the railroad made early in the century that Brookings would prosper and continue to grow as one of the major towns along its route.

Remaining constant throughout the entire period was the continuing attraction of the downtown core. Main Street stayed the center of activity, drawing people in toward it. Another magnet, a mile to the northeast, was South Dakota State College (now South Dakota State University), which enrolled 3,215 students in 1956. During the early 1960s, passenger traffic on the railroad was discontinued, and freight transportation likewise continued to decline. By the 1970s, three malls, a small one located one block north of downtown and two larger ones a mile south and a mile east of it, extended the spatial pattern of the city. Housing development drifted in a southerly and southeasterly direction,

Brookings, 1956. (Courtesy of George Norby)

and several new subdivisions emerged.

Until the mid-1950s, however, the original plat of the town provided the basic framework for its development. As population increased, new houses went up, and new businesses emerged, they fit into a spatial framework established at the outset. For a long time, then, development proceeded along well-ordered paths, highly predictable given the original layout of the town and the basic functions that the town performed.

People's contemplations of their own history fit into orderly patterns, too. The town had hardly been established before local residents started reminiscing about its past. Brookings, like other towns along the tracks, started the tradition of holding Old Settlers' picnics early on.[14] Efforts were made periodically to establish a county historical society, but that would not be accomplished until 1939. From time to time the town's two newspapers ran special stories or devoted entire editions to the history of the community and the county.[15]

The 1920s, a period of rapid change and modernization, also proved to be a key decade for promoting a historical sense among Brookings residents. Even as the town rapidly underwent modernization with the introduction of chain stores and radio and the remodeling of buildings, many of the old structures—now considered eyesores—were replaced. By then many of the old-timers who had helped establish Brookings and nearby villages during the 1870s and 1880s were aging, and some of them were beginning to die. Old-timers returning to visit during the 1920s likewise stimulated reflection on the early days. Although Old Settlers' picnics had been held before the turn of the century, during the 1920s they took on a new dimension, with crowds of more than a thousand sometimes attending. Newspaper stories on early area history became more frequent during the decade, and people were reminded of the past as old buildings were torn down to make way for more modern structures.[16]

A number of artifacts were rediscovered or handed down. In 1926 the original deed to the eighty acres used for the college was turned over to college officials. That same year Martin Trygstad, the first postmaster of Brookings County, dug out the certificate that he had been issued back in 1872. A cashbook used by the Allison brothers during the 1880s was discovered at the courthouse, and people took interest in reading the names entered in the book. Old Fiddlers' contests held at the new Brookota Ballroom, which opened in 1926, also bent people's minds to the past, and the editor of the Brookings *Register* started a column called "Our Reminiscent Corner" the following year.[17]

Another factor contributing to growing history mindedness during the 1920s was the attention being given to the decline of the small town, a focus encouraged by authors from Sinclair Lewis to Sherwood Anderson. In opposition to this line of thinking, there emerged a countertendency glorifying the heritage and influence of the small town. Additionally, as many towns in eastern South Dakota neared the fiftieth anniversaries of their founding, they were increasingly led to consider their past and to look for ways to celebrate it. A good example of this was the decision in 1929 to erect a seventeen-foot-high fieldstone monument eight miles south of Brookings at the location of old Medary, established in 1857 and one of the first three town sites in Dakota Territory.[18]

Brookings's golden jubilee celebration in 1929 reflected the tendency of people to link their thoughts about the past with their hopes for the future. Fifty years of history provided local residents with an occasion for celebrating the progress that had occurred since the railroad arrived and the town commenced as well as with an opportunity for projecting their optimistic hopes and dreams into the future. The lead article in the special golden jubilee edition of the Brookings *Register,* "From Prairie to Agricultural and Education Center in 50 Years," noted how quickly the wild, bare prairie had been converted into a community marked by fine residences and impressive brick store buildings. People in the area had witnessed the arrival of electricity, graveled roads, automobiles and tractors, rural mail delivery, extension clubs, community organizations, and radio, all of which brought city and farm into instant contact with the rest of the world. "One wonders what there is left for the youngster of today to see come into his life in the next fifty years," the *Register* enthusiastically noted.

> He will see improvements in all the existing conveniences, with many of them replaced by something better. He will see the airplane developed, as well as the radio. He will see communication bettered by many degrees over what is now. He will see the radio developed until seeing and hearing, all over the world, will be easier than hearing is now. He will step into his plane and "hop" to Europe as unconcernedly as he steps into his motor car today and drives across the country. He will sit in his home and see and hear the president inaugurated, the big league baseball games, see and talk with the Byrd who happens then to be at the South Pole, the crowning of a king in London, the digging of diamonds in Africa, the eruption of Mount Vesuvius, the beach at Waikiki. Perhaps he will talk with Mars.[19]

The economic depression that enveloped the United States after the stock market crash a few months later undercut only slightly the reverence with which people considered their past and the confidence they invested in their future. This dual glorification of past and future seems to be an enduring characteristic of local history—whether in 1929 or at any other time. A special edition of the Brookings *Register* in 1899 had observed that "from the birth of this county has sprung a wonderful development such as is rarely seen in the history of any country and rivals the wildest dreams of the imagination." History of this type blends easily into civic boosterism; building on the firm foundation of the past, the community is destined for greater and greater accomplishments. In the estimate of the *Register* in 1899, "While Brookings cannot, as yet, boast of being a metropolis of great magnitude, yet it has brighter prospects today than many of the great cities at the same period of their existence."[20]

Always, in local histories like this, the emphasis placed on past achievements and future progress is accompanied by the identification of heroic individuals who deserve credit for making improvements and reinforcing community values guiding the town's development—values such as initiative, creativity, hard work, integrity, and cooperation. The operating assumption is that people, in fact, make their own history; broad social and economic forces that place limits on their actions are generally played down. The histories focus upon individual lives. People take their own daily round of activities and elongate them in time, rendering history as a collectivity of events and actions acted out by the individuals who make up the community. Special attention goes to firsts—the first immigrants, stores, post offices, churches, schools, and so forth. Once things have been established, disasters (fires, floods, storms), famous visitors to town (Theodore Roosevelt, Dwight Eisenhower), oddities (murders, bank robberies, accidents), architectural developments (new post offices, banks, schools, monuments), technological improvements (electricity, telephone, automobiles, radio), and special local interests (college, railroad, agricultural businesses and industries) get primary attention.

The seventy-fifth anniversary edition of the Brookings *Register* in 1954 was especially long and interesting because it was largely written by Professor Parker. Full of interesting details and anecdotes, Parker's articles shared the general tendency to focus upon the early days of settlement while scanting twentieth-century developments. The newspaper's centennial edition in 1979 derived much of its material from previously published sources, such as the seventy-fifth anniversary edition, and generally boiled the material down into briefer and sketchier articles. A sixty-six-page history book on the city of Brookings written by local volunteers also placed its heaviest emphasis on the early years.[21]

This heavy emphasis on the early pioneers of an area is a cardinal feature of most local histories.[22] People are fascinated by the pioneer period and are interested in knowing about the first buildings, the first businesses, and the first churches, schools, and other developments. This natural curiosity generally meshes well with the approach of the historical chronicler, for it makes the job easier. It limits the time span the chronicler has to be concerned with, allowing the chronicler to concentrate on a specific period. Also, since people are more inclined to remember and record the first instances of anything, a rich source of materials is available. Another compelling, but less obvious, reason for emphasizing origins and for sliding over later developments is that this approach tends to avoid controversial subjects, such as debates over tax or zoning policy or conflicts between various social or economic groups, and instead allows people to appreciate and glorify the early founders who planted the seeds for later development.

Local history thus often blends into hagiography and mythology. This is only natural, since the booster spirit was central to the process of town founding, and a town's survival and development depended heavily upon maintaining the morale and optimism of its residents, not tearing the community down or exacerbating conflict within it.[23] People have a tendency to tolerate reality only in small doses; something smacking of a full, objective accounting of political issues, power relationships, and social conflicts existing in a small town may seem to them to be not only undesirable but downright subversive. Although these same people might gossip about their neighbors' faults, recording such criticisms on paper is a different matter.

The kind of history that gets written in small towns, therefore, tends to be uncritical. More than that, it generally fails to ask important questions about a community—the kind that can truly reveal its character and its development over time. History thereby blends into advertising for the town; nostalgia reigns, and local pride undergirds a myth of origins that glorifies the pioneer and the frontier period and interweaves history and the theme of progress in a seamless web.

Consider, for example, a historical sketch of Brookings included in *This Is Your Town,* a handbook issued by the League of Women Voters in 1956 (the same year as the aerial photograph referred to earlier). It consisted of a list of seventeen dates from Brookings history, thirteen of them occurring before 1900. The only information given for the dates between 1900 and 1950 were population totals showing that the city had grown from 2,346 to 7,764 residents during that period. The earlier dates were essentially a listing of firsts—the first settlement, the creation of Brookings County, the arrival of the railroad, the granting of a city charter, the opening of classes at the college, the building of the first county courthouse, and so forth.[24]

More interesting than this bare listing of important dates in Brookings was a short narrative history included in a brochure distributed by the Brookings Area Chamber of Commerce to individuals or businesses who were considering a move to Brookings. Not surprisingly, in the most recent edition of this brochure, entitled *Brookings, South Dakota: Someplace Special,* the community is praised for its "excellent quality of life and abundant opportunities in agriculture, education, commerce and industry," and for "its shaded streets, fine health care facilities and social services, modern shopping centers, fine homes, attractive parks, cultural and entertainment attractions, and many churches." In the accompanying history of the town, which runs to 350 words, no pretense is made of providing a complete account. What makes it interesting is what the essay emphasizes: the town's namesake—Judge Wilmot W. Brookings, the origins of the town during the Great Dakota Boom, and the founding of the college in 1881.

The story's mistaken observation that Brookings never visited the community that was named after him hardly matters.[25] But the devotion of more than one-third of its space to a man whose only real connection to the town is that he was one of the many territorial politicians at the capital in Yankton who had a county named after them (the county's name was then applied to the town when it was established) does seem oddly disproportionate. Such emphasis makes more sense, however, if we operate on the assumption that the essay is meant to be more inspirational than historical. Brookings, whose feet had to be amputated after he was caught in a snowstorm in 1858, serves as a vehicle for praising the vigor and optimism of the early pioneers: "His heart firmly planted in the prairie of Dakota, Brookings became involved in seeing the vast region become a state." According to the publicity writer, he personified the virtues and values that made the town's dwellers great: "Brookings, the man, and the pioneer spirit live on in the heritage of the residents. Residents have maintained the strong moral fiber and rural heritage and have developed a city representative of these values."[26]

No author for this article is listed. Who wrote it hardly matters, for it could have been written by anybody at anytime and applied to any community. This sort of boilerplate copy might offend purists who want to get their history straight, but what harm is there in it? The reader who accepts the purpose of the piece can approach it from the proper perspective. Facts are not completely lacking in such treatments and probably are only a little less reliable than those in "real" historical treatments, but mostly they come third- and fourthhand and are adapted to persuade, advertise, and inspire. What is important to observe is that this is an instance of historical material being fitted into a predetermined framework for a particular purpose. The process resembles punching buttons on a computer in order to compose a personalized form letter or checking off ingredients for a submarine sandwich at a deli; very little thought goes into it.

For those who are disturbed by all of this, it must be added that, to a considerable degree, most local history loosely conforms to this procedure (picking and choosing historical particulars to fit a preconceived framework). Let me illustrate the point with two examples: the John B. Rogers Company pageants that were performed for the celebrations in 1954 and 1979 and the Brookings County history that was written and compiled in 1989. When Brookings celebrated its seventy-fifth anniversary in 1954, it, like many other communities in the region, called on the John B. Rogers Company to create a script for and direct a historical pageant to commemorate the event.[27] Of seventeen episodes in the resulting extravaganza, entitled *Harvest of the Years,* the first eleven carried the story up to 1881, reflecting local history's tendency to concentrate upon the founders and the early stages of development. (It should be observed that the pageant dealt with the entire county, not just the town of Brookings itself.) In episodes twelve through fifteen, "The Gay Nineties," "World War I," "The Roaring Twenties," and "To the Cause of Freedom" (on World War II), almost no effort is made to key into local history; apparently the John B. Rogers Company was operating on the assumption that all areas of the country shared the same kinds of experiences during those periods. South Dakota during the 1890s, however, was anything but gay. Brookings residents certainly did fight in both world wars, but merely celebrating that fact tells us almost nothing about the impact of the war locally. And to suggest that during the 1920s prosperity abounded in Brookings County flies in the face of the facts. The script's description of the decade as "the era of flappers, bobbed hair, radio, flag pole sitters, silent pictures, and the Charleston" tells us more about American popular culture than it does about the complex realities of life in Brookings County during the period. But the pageant's producers were not really recreating history; they were staging a celebration, and in these instances they were fitting the local story into a previously formulated pattern, making almost no effort to test the fit. Episode sixteen—"Hall of Fame"—paying tribute to men and women who contributed to Brookings's greatness, fulfilled the requirement of recognizing the impact of individual heroes on local history, and episode seventeen—"Youth on Parade"—celebrated progress and looked expectantly toward the future, placing reliance on the dynamism of youth to carry on the frontier tradition: "Pioneers of the future who will push civilization forward as did their ancestors."

On the cover of the script for the *Brookings 100 Revue,* which was put on by the John B. Rogers Company in 1979, the production is called "A presentation of the historical highlights of Brookings, South Dakota," but in something like a cigarette pack warning label, it is also advised, " 'Brookings 100 Revue' is based on historical outline. Chronology of incidents, costuming and characters may have been changed to meet staging requirements. Dialogue situations and characters have been created to augment historical data and to increase the effects of this production."[28] In other words, a revue is not a review. Despite the disclaimer, the production contained some surprisingly relevant and insightful historical comments. Especially on the mark were some early scenes depicting the dispossession of the Indians by intruding white settlers, who were the heroes of the piece. "It is strange indeed that one man's dreams can be another man's nightmare," the storyteller intoned. Dakota, or Sioux, Indians had once roamed the area. An Indian chief implored the audience to "remember our identity as the landlords of America." But soon the settlers arrived, and with them the celebration began.

A surprising number of facts about the early settlement of the county fitted into the slots available for them in the script. Something of the history of the county would have been learned by the completely uninitiated on a warm summer evening under the stars at the South Dakota State University football field, where the pageant was performed. But more to the point were the prepackaged scenes, local names and facts filling in the blank spaces, local boys and girls, men and women outfitted as baton twirlers, drill team, color guards, trumpeters, court of honor, and dignitaries. In the making of everyday history, people remain the same and the action changes; in a prepackaged pageant script like this, the actions stay the same and the people move in and out of their assigned roles.

This is not to say that every local pageant put on by the John B. Rogers Company was exactly alike. Each community had to have the narrative tailored somewhat to its own particular story. What such episodes do illustrate is that the kind of history that gets served up in such historical pageants (plus Fourth of July and Memorial Day ceremonies, high school commencements, presidential campaigns, and television docudramas) is, to a large degree, fashioned to suit the purposes of the occasion rather than based upon an objective interpretation of the past. Story emerges as legend; history blends into myth. People congratulate themselves and reinforce morale by mythologizing their past. "The patterns we find in the past, whether historical or remembered," David Lowenthal observed, "are patterns we ourselves fabricate on frameworks erected by intervening generations."[29] For the most part, the process is harmless, but it is not history. At least, it is not the kind of history on which one can place much reliance.

Coming full circle, we arrive at 1989 and the writing of *Brookings County History Book.*[30] Sherry DeBoer—a Brookings mother, State Humanities Committee staffer, county commission member, and all-around go-getter—headed up the project in her usual dynamic fashion and worked with her committee to round up dozens of other volunteers and to ride herd on them. When it came time to apportion the duties of writing the text, I and several other members of the editorial committee solicited some volunteers and dragooned others. Since I teach the South Dakota history course at South Dakota State University, I wound up with the assignment of writing about the period from the first white settlements in 1857 until 1960 and also did the chapter on the university. Other authors wrote chapters on the last three decades, prehistory, the natural environment, Indians, churches, schools, art and architecture, social organizations, government, and other subjects. When the family histories came in, they filled nearly five hundred pages, adding to the three hundred pages of narrative history already written.

What did we end up with? Probably with a better product than most such efforts. To contend, however, that the book escaped the usual limits and mistakes of its genre would be claiming too much. How much time, effort, and money would it take to write the definitive history of Brookings County and compress it into several hundred pages? Merely to ask such a question is to suggest the answer. In churning out my own contribution, I was reminded once again how feeble our efforts must be to realize anything like comprehensiveness on projects like this.

The problem that seems most worrisome to many readers of local history—the possibility of getting some facts wrong—is not really the worst trap facing the local historian. Try as we might to avoid them, factual errors almost inevitably creep in. More troublesome are the failure to ask important questions, the paucity of historical evidence to answer them, and the lack of an adequate conceptual framework.

"History, at least good history, in contrast to antiquarianism, is inescapably structural," asserted Elizabeth Fox-Genovese. "By structural, I mean that history must disclose and reconstruct the conditions of consciousness and action, with conditions understood as systems of social relations, including relations between women and men, between rich and poor, between the powerful and the powerless; among those of different faiths, different races and different classes."[31] What is usually lacking in local history, and this applies to *Brookings County History Book,* is such a structural approach. I can state that confidently, because I wrote much of the historical narrative. But there were deadlines, there were other duties and responsibilities, and there were limits on what could be accomplished. What we have instead of an ideal product is a history of Brookings County that is in its own way interesting, informative, and as accurate as possible under the circumstances.

Accuracy is a virtue in such a book, but accuracy is not enough. Nor is it usually fully realized. Every day as I walk to my office, I am reminded of the hazards of historical representation. In the lobby of Scobey Hall, home of the South Dakota State University history department, hangs a commemorative plaque recognizing the deeds and contributions of John O'Brien Scobey, an early-day Brookings founder and booster whose maneuvers during the 1881 legislative session obtained the college for the town. Unfortunately, the plaque refers to him as "James O'Bryan Scobey." At least the last name is correct.

Through the windows of our third-floor offices we can view the Coughlin Campanile, built in 1929 and donated by a 1909 alumnus who went on to become a hugely successful Milwaukee manufacturer. Over each of the four ground-level doors of the tower is a block with an inscription referring to some historical event—the purchase of Louisiana Territory in 1803, the formation of Dakota Territory in 1861, the establishment of the college in 1881, and the winning of statehood in 1889. Whenever I walk past that impressive monument, I am reminded of a story about those inscriptions that I told at the end of the chapter on the

1920s in *Brookings County History Book*:

> Once the structure was built and the finishing touches put on, one local resident pointed out that the date referring to statehood was wrong. It had the words, "Admitted February 22, 1889," but in fact that was the day President Cleveland signed the bill outlining the process for obtaining statehood. Official admission did not come until President Benjamin Harrison signed the proclamation on November 2 indicating that the process had been completed and that the Territory now, in fact, was a state. Professor A. S. Harding, who taught history at the college, was consulted, and he confirmed that the November date was the accurate one. SDSC President Charles Pugsley told the newspaper that the date over the north entrance to the campanile would be changed from February 22 to November 2, but it never was.[32]

ARLINGTON

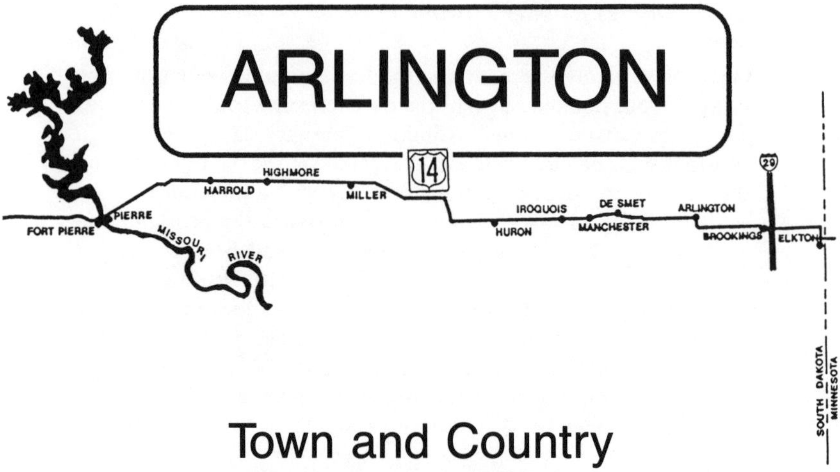

Town and Country Linked Together

A drive up Main Street in Arlington (it was originally called Nordland and later took the name of Denver for a time before obtaining its current designation in 1888) presents a picture of an active, thriving agricultural community.[1] On a busy day when no parking spaces are to be found on Main Street, drivers have to look for spots on side streets to park their vehicles. Towering on the horizon, beside the railroad tracks, stands the co-op elevator, a symbol of the town's vitality as well as of the link binding town and country together, both now and in the past. With a population of just under 1,000 in the 1980 census, Arlington ranked ninth among the thirty towns on Highway 14 between Elkton and Wall, working hard to maintain its population and vitality at a time when many of the smaller towns in the area were continuing to steadily decline. (The thirty towns between Elkton and Wall include four that used to be on the highway, which, after its rebuilding and rerouting, were left a mile or two away from it. They are Elkton, Aurora, Hetland, and Ree Heights.)

One example of that striving can be found in the city auditorium at the south end of the business district, built by the Works Progress Administration during the 1930s, now the home of the Bob Allen Sportswear factory, which produces hunting clothing, gun cases, tote bags, and other items. Across the street, in the office of the Arlington *Sun,* Bob Sturges fills the columns of his weekly paper (circulation: 1,319) with the goings and comings of people who keep a small town like Arlington on the map. Several years ago the town was accidentally omitted from the new edition of the state highway map. Once local residents got over their chagrin, they managed to capitalize on the incident by organizing a three-day festival that they called "Put Arlington back on the Map Days," featuring street dances, games, races, a variety show, and a town dinner. Stickers, buttons, and posters with the slogan "I Found Arlington" printed on them were distributed to advertise the shindig.[2]

Not much has happened to distinguish Arlington from other agricultural communities in its size range or to put it in the history books. Arlington has the distinction of having been the home of Richard Kneip, the only three-term governor in South Dakota history (and one of only four Democrats to hold the office). People today laughingly refer to the four-lane stretch of Highway 14 extending four miles south and east of town as "Kneip's Folly" or "Kneip's Interstate," because it was built during his term, presumably to link up with future four lanes of Highway 14 and Highway 81, which skirts the east side of Arlington.[3] Local folks could tell you stories about what makes the town special for them, but for an outsider what stands out about Arlington is that it is the hometown of Theodore W. Schultz, who won the Nobel Prize for economics in 1979.

"Ted" Schultz, who was born on a farm four miles northeast of Arlington on April 30, 1902, spent most of his childhood on a farm nine miles north and six miles west of the town.[4] Arlington and Lake Preston (which is located fifteen miles west of Arlington on Highway 14) were the largest market centers in the vicinity, but the Schultz family did most of its trading and other business in several smaller towns that were closer—Hetland, nine miles south and two miles east; Badger, one mile south and three miles east; Lake Norden, five miles north and three miles east; and Erwin, nine miles west and one mile south.[5] During his youth, Schultz drove those rutted dirt roads many times with horse-drawn wagons loaded with hogs or wheat or other products.[6] The family got its mail from Hetland and usually marketed its wheat and other grains there, and Schultz listed Hetland as his hometown in his college yearbook.[7] Livestock, on the other hand, usually were hauled to Badger, which sprouted in 1907 when the South Dakota Central Railroad extended a line north from Sioux Falls to Watertown.[8] Once, Schultz remembers, his father decided to drive some hogs cross-country to the railhead at Badger. The animals turned cantankerous, all seemingly bent on going in different directions. Although Schultz and his fellow "cowboys" finally managed to corral the hogs into town without losing any of them, they never tried to do that again. The family also traded at Erwin and Lake Norden. The latter boasted John Deere and International Harvester dealerships. Badger also had an International Harvester dealer. Nowadays, farmers have to drive to larger towns such as Arlington, Lake Preston, or Watertown to purchase parts for their tractors and implements.

Like the other families around them, that of Henry and Anna Schultz just grew and grew. Eventually there were eight children. Ted was the oldest. Leo (everybody calls him "Sparky") was the youngest, eleven years younger than Ted. In between came Otto ("Ott"), Henry ("Hank"), Alice, Arthur ("Skinny"), Winifred ("Win"), and Evelyn ("Pat"). It was a hardworking family, and the unremitting toil paid off. Though able to afford few luxuries, the Schultzes probably lived as well as anyone in the area, never wanting for food or other necessities. There was a piano in the parlor, which was generally reserved for company. The family bought a Victrola and often packed it into a buggy and drove over to one of the neighbors for an evening of fun. By 1916, Henry Schultz bought one of the new Model T's that were beginning to change people's lives in the countryside, but many years would pass before horses finally lost their role in farm work and transportation.

World War I affected the Schultzes' lives more than any other single historical development. Taking advantage of war-induced

The Schultz family: (*front row*) Arthur, Mrs. Schultz, Leo, Mr. Schultz, Otto; (*back row*) Alice, Winifred, Theodore, Henry, Evelyn. (Courtesy of Leo H. Schultz)

prosperity, they were able to build two big barns and to remodel their farmhouse. These buildings are visible in an aerial photograph taken of the farmstead in 1937. The house had enough bedrooms for Skinny and Ted each to have one to himself and Ott and Hank to share another. The attic was roomy enough, Skinny Schultz told me, for the boys to play football in it. Downstairs, most of the activity took place in the kitchen and the living room. They had a "great big dining room," large enough for a table accomodating ten or twelve people. They needed it when hired men were eating with them. Though large, the house had no running water or electricity. For baths, they used a washtub in the washhouse, twenty feet from the back door, where they built a fire to heat the water. Anna Schultz did her washing there with a gasoline-powered washing machine. Beyond the washhouse was the outhouse.

During World War I, fifteen-year-old Ted Schultz drove wagonloads of hogs over to Erwin and returned with lumber and cement that were used to build the new barns and silos east of the house. One of the barns was for horses, the other for cattle. By 1937, when the airborne photographer snapped his photograph, more than a dozen outbuildings were visible on the farm. The

The Schultz farm in 1937. (Courtesy of Leo H. Schultz)

monetary investment in all of this was considerable, and without money earned during the war, the Schultzes would have had to get by with a more modest operation. Behind the horse barn stood a cattle shed to protect the animals from inclement weather. Between the barns was a hay feeder. North of the house were a machine shed, a couple of toolsheds, a smokehouse, a grainery, a water tank, and a hog shed. A large rock pile testified to countless hours of lifting and hauling stones that had worked their way up through the soil to threaten plowshares and harrow tines. The trees on the north side were planted during the mid-1930s, under the federal shelterbelt program.

A major reason for the Schultzes' success at farming was that they avoided getting mired in the economic undertow of the post-war depression. Farm prices plunged during the period, and many operators slid into bankruptcy because they could not pay off loans taken to expand their operations during the frenzied wartime era. Henry Schultz was not totally debt free, but he had been careful not to overextend himself the way many others had done. Thus, when the bottom fell out of farm markets in 1920, he survived. Having five healthy boys to work with in the fields constituted another advantage. Ted Schultz vividly recalled the labor farm tasks required during the early 1900s—lifting, shoveling, pushing, and hauling. "It was extremely heavy work," he told me when I visited him in January 1989 at the office he still maintains as professor emeritus of economics at the University of Chicago. When the barns went up in 1917, things got a little easier because they could now lift hay up into the lofts in a sling rather than pitch it with a fork. Henry Schultz worked alongside his sons, and for at least part of the year they had a hired hand or two in addition. Anna Schultz joined the men in the fields when needed, running a binder to cut grain, shocking wheat, and helping wherever she could. As time went by, however, machine power increasingly replaced human muscle power.

Now on the same 560-acre farm that once required the labor of half a dozen people, Sparky Schultz's son Sandy, with the occasional help of a part-time hired man, produces two to three times as much output as they did. "It's the mechanization, it's the machinery, it's the moving of materials," Ted Schultz told me. "You don't lift many things. You don't have this physical hard work." In its place there is tension—the kind that comes from driving a $100,000 combine that could be damaged by hitting the wrong thing, a costly mistake that could occur in a second or two. "But the actual muscles—physical work—isn't there any more.

You have to go out in the evening and get some exercise," Schultz chuckled.

The family subscribed to a variety of farm journals and other publications to help keep up with the latest agricultural developments. Henry Schultz was an innovator. He seemed to be always trying out new seeds, and when South Dakota State College at Brookings started its extension service, he worked closely with its agents. During the 1910s, the Schultzes were highly progressive in taking advantage of mechanization, which became another important factor in the success of their operation. In 1914 Henry Schultz bought a large Aultman-Taylor tractor and threshing machine, one of the first outfits of its kind in the area. It cost $5,000, the same as a small farm at the time. Ted Schultz and his younger brothers were hired by farmers for miles around to thresh their grain and cut cornstalks to fill their silos. Ted Schultz dropped out of school in the middle of eighth grade because of the wartime labor shortage. After the war he continued to work on the farm, running the threshing rig from August until November or later. It was a big responsibility and a highly profitable one for a lad in his teens. The Schultz boys became well-known for their skill and dependability.

Had he stayed at it, Ted Schultz would no doubt have become one of the area's more progressive and successful farmers. His four younger brothers did remain, getting into farming with

The Schultzes' Aultman-Taylor threshing rig. (Courtesy of Leo H. Schultz)

their father's help. Sparky Schultz took over on the family farm in 1937, later buying it from his parents in 1949. Skinny Schultz ran a trucking business for several years before he went into farming. Hank Schultz operated a farm several miles west of the home place and then one a few miles south of it before getting established on another farm north of Lake Norden, where he did quite well. Ott Schultz, who died in 1988 at the age of 85, farmed in Minnesota.

The three daughters also remained in South Dakota. After graduating from South Dakota State College, Pat Schultz worked in the county extension, was married, and helped her husband run a lumber business and then manage a store at Oneida. Alice Schultz married and worked at several different jobs. Win Schultz, who has died, and her husband were in the trucking business for a while and then bought a business in Aberdeen. Something, however, drew Ted Schultz away from home, leading him in new directions that would finally take him to the University of Chicago, where he would build upon his agricultural background to become one of America's foremost agricultural economists and a Nobel Prize winner for his work on the economics of development and human capital.[9]

Even while he was working in the fields, Hank Schultz told me, Ted Schultz would practice his oratorical skills on cornstalks swaying in the wind. Giving talks at local Luther League meetings provided him with a chance to try out ideas on people, and he took advantage of opportunities to speak whenever he could. In 1921 he entered the Aggie School at Brookings (a preparatory course providing the equivalent of a high school education), attending four months a year and finishing the requirements in three years, whereupon he enrolled as a regular college student at the age of twenty-two. His fame spread locally for the Fourth of July orations he delivered in picnic groves around Badger. At South Dakota State College he became something of a celebrity, being older than most of his fellow students and being recognized as a "brain." He was a star debater and championship orator, served on student government, participated in the YMCA and other organizations, and worked as an announcer for the new campus radio station.[10]

When it came time to enroll for his senior year in the fall of 1927, his adviser Murray Benedict told him that he actually had enough credits to graduate and that there was really little point in staying around Brookings. It would make more sense, he advised, to go immediately to graduate school. He suggested that Schultz go to Madison, Wisconsin, where he had obtained his degree.

That sounded like a good idea. When Schultz arrived there and tried to enroll in the University of Wisconsin, the people working the desk were somewhat startled to discover that he carried no records with him and had not yet officially graduated from South Dakota State College. Unsure of what to do with the brash young man, they hustled him to the dean of the Graduate School, who, after talking to Schultz, told him that the situation was highly irregular and that an institution like the University of Wisconsin could not grant admission to every person who wanted to register. Nevertheless, he was going to make a special exception and give Schultz a chance to prove himself. He was to enroll for three assigned courses during the fall semester and report back at the end; if his grades passed muster, he could continue with his studies.[11] Of course, when the time came to look over the results, there was no question about Schultz's qualifications; he was one of the most brilliant students to go through the Ph.D. program. At the end of the first year he also received his diploma from Brookings, and after only three years at Madison, he became a fully certified Ph.D. in economics. He soon emerged as a rising star in the profession, first at Iowa State University and after 1943 at the University of Chicago.

Schultz's early years as an agricultural economist were an interesting time to be in the profession. The Dirty Thirties dealt a profound blow to American farmers and ushered in a revolution in governmental policy, as Franklin Roosevelt's New Deal inaugurated a program of subsidizing producers for cutting back on output to bring supply more closely in line with demand. The goal was to raise farm prices and farm income. None of this squared with Schultz's way of thinking. Such distortions of market forces would bring no long-term solutions to the farmer's problems, he concluded. A book published at the end of World War II firmly established his reputation in the field. Entitled *Agriculture in an Unstable Economy,* it notes that the wartime exodus of 5 million people from the farm population had resulted in real gains for the people who remained behind. Something that rural folk had been resisting for decades—the migration of farm youth to the cities—was in fact one of the best things that could have happened, both for the out-migrants and for those who stayed on the farm.[12]

Two trends that had been accelerated by World War II boded well for the future, in Schultz's estimation: first, increased efficiency resulting from mechanization and the resultant reduction in labor requirements; second, and even more important, the migration of people from farms and rural areas into urban areas. Salvation for the farmer would not come from resisting trends toward greater efficiency and production; rather, it would result from going with the flow of change and modernizing agricultural practices. Mechanization benefited everyone by saving labor, increasing yields, and allowing land that had been used for feeding draft animals to be converted into use for marketable crops. The key problem facing agriculture was that there were too many people living on farms: *"We have here a transfer problem, a redistribution of the working population, to relieve agriculture of the excess supply of labor engaged in, and dependent upon, farming for its income."*[13]

Schultz himself was a good example of a former farm dweller who had migrated to the city to engage in more productive labor. If his brothers were to make a go of farming back in South Dakota, they would have to get bigger. The exit of surplus farm population and the increase in farm size were the flip sides of the same coin. "Many thousands of family farms in the United States are too small as operating units to make efficient use of modern farm technology and to earn a return for labor and capital inputs that are at all comparable to returns in other fields," Schultz asserted in his 1945 book.[14] He repeated those themes eight years later in another book, *The Economic Organization of Agriculture.* In it he noted approvingly that approximately 50 million people left agriculture between 1920 and 1949, representing a net movement of approximately 17.5 million people from farm to nonfarm areas. The book includes a graph projecting further decline in farm population to a point in 1975 of less than 20 million people. Schultz would increasingly sound the trumpet for investing in human capital; this included making sure that the population that remained on the land was highly educated and fully capable of utilizing the resources of the land to the best advantage. Logically, he contended, the only way to eliminate the need for out-migration was simply to stop economic development. That, in his view, was totally unacceptable.[15]

During the 1950s, Schultz turned his attention increasingly to poverty and rural development in the Third World. He focused much of his attention upon social and cultural factors that interacted with economic ones to promote or inhibit economic development. When I visited him in Chicago in January 1989, I wanted to learn what kind of a future he saw in store for small rural towns like the ones near where he had grown up, such as Hetland, Badger, Erwin, Lake Norden, and Arlington. We also talked about Frankfort, the town near the farm where his wife grew up, and Redfield, a larger town a few miles farther away from it. Did he see any salvation for small towns like these, and if so, how were they going to survive?

"I think the hard-boiled answer," he replied, "is that if they aren't as efficient as larger places are—if people can do better by going to Redfield rather than Frankfort—why shouldn't they go to Redfield? There's a beautiful road. It's a matter of twelve minutes from where Esther [his wife] grew up, fifteen minutes at most." The point he emphasized was that the concept of community in such circumstances had not disappeared but rather had changed.[16] With distance obliterated, the boundaries of the community have greatly expanded. Driving twelve or fifteen miles to the larger town of Redfield today is easier than it was in the 1910s to drive five or six miles over dirt roads into Frankfort.

As in everything else, Schultz is clear-sighted and hard-headed on the matter of rural community. He retains wonderful memories of the kinds of social interaction his family participated in when he was young, but he also realizes that those days are long gone. He ticked off for me the kinds of bonds that tied people together during his youth. First, there were the ones formed by the one-room country school he attended. The District 19 schoolhouse was a two and a half mile walk every day. The Schultz children were heavily outnumbered there by Norwegians, although there sometimes were other students also of German background. During World War I, they were referred to as "Huns" and "Kaiser Bills," but more often they felt close bonds of affection and neighborliness to the other children and their families, most of which were as large as their own. Ted Schultz retains a special place in his heart for Edna Lund, a teacher who encouraged and inspired him to accomplish great things in life.

A second kind of community centered around the North Preston Luther League that Ted Schultz and his brothers belonged to. The family attended a little German Lutheran church located just a mile west of the farm, but the boys preferred English language services and the meetings of the predominately Scandinavian North Preston congregation and were involved in it even though it was several miles farther away. They also enjoyed playing baseball for the North Preston baseball team against rival teams in the area. Hank Schultz told me that his older brother was a pretty good fastball pitcher, but Ted Schultz averred that his own talents were never very great. Except for Skinny Schultz, who did not go in for baseball, all of the boys were involved in this network combining religion and sports. In 1925, the family quit the German church and joined with several others in establishing an English Lutheran congregation in the town of Badger. The continuing importance of this organization in the Schultzes' lives was demonstrated in October 1988, when two hundred people gathered in the church parlor for a birthday party on Skinny Schultz's eightieth birthday.

Third, Ted Schultz enjoyed being a member of a ubiquitous fraternity of hunters and fishermen. Frequently his expeditions led him over to the farm of P. R. Crothers, about two miles away from the Schultzes'. Crothers, indeed, was an extraordinary person, according to Ted Schultz. He had been involved in politics and served two terms in the South Dakota House of Representatives.[17] He possessed an inventive turn of mind and was constantly experimenting with new agricultural methods. One of his sons later became dean of the College of Engineering at South Dakota State College, while the other eventually took over the family farm. Crothers took a special interest in young Ted Schultz and always had the time to talk to him, which drew the youth back again and again for more conversation. Crothers's proposal to help get Schultz into politics apparently left a big impression on him. A group of men in Kingsbury County offered to get him the uncontested nomination for a seat in the legislature, but while considering this proposition, it dawned on him, he told me, that he didn't know very much and that he had better get some more education. Had he not gone on for degrees at South Dakota State College and the University of Wisconsin, perhaps a political career would have been in the offing.

Later on, as a college student, the young scholar brought several of his professors from Brookings and Madison out to Kingsbury County to go hunting. He smiled as he told the story. "I always say I got my Ph.D. by corrupting the major professors at Wisconsin, as I told them how many pheasants we had on the farm, and they liked to hunt, and my folks liked to have them come." When Murray Benedict, the head of the Department of Agricultural Economics at South Dakota State College and only several years older than Schultz, came out to the farm, the results were rather hilarious. Sparky Schultz was around twelve at the time and had a short-barreled shotgun with which he had become quite accurate. When the hunters reached the end of a field, a pheasant took to the air, and Benedict managed to get off three shots at it with his fine gun without even coming close. Then little Sparky Schultz took aim and fired, and down the bird plopped, right by their side.

Trapping provided another kind of community for Ted Schultz. Good money could be made at it with luck and perseverance. He and his brothers offered a nearby farmer $30.00 for the right to trap in his slough for a season. At the time pelts were selling for $.35 or $.40; by the end of the season, the price had climbed as high as $3.50. They trapped muskrats, foxes, minks—even skunks—and made good money at it for several years.

Along with school, church, and sports, Schultz noted family ties and threshing rings as other evidence of the kinds of community links that drew people together while he was growing up. One of the benefits of belonging to a large family was that economic storms were more easily weathered. Family members were able to help each other out in getting started in farming; eventually everyone came out all right. The family was both a close-knit social unit and a hard-working economic unit. Each depended upon the cooperation of everyone else. To a high degree they were self-sufficient, growing vegetables in their garden and canning them, butchering hogs and cattle, digging potatoes and storing them in their cellar, milking cows and churning butter, tending to plums and apples in the orchard. Without everyone playing his or her role, the family could not have prospered as it did.

The changes that occurred in farming and the resultant impact on small towns and surrounding rural communities were mostly a postwar phenomenon. Until the late 1930s, many South Dakotans were still farming with horses. Major trunk highways did not get hard-surfaced until 1936 or 1937. Massive increases in agricultural productivity, stimulated by the use of fertilizers, insecticides, and new machinery, occurred in the 1940s and 1950s. What became fully apparent at that time had been only a dim apparition earlier. But perceptive observers might have been able to pick out some trends that portended what was to come by the 1920s. The spread of the telephone, the growing popularity of the movies, and the rise of the automobile caused considerable comment even before World War II. By 1920 there were 120,000 motor vehicles registered in South Dakota, and in per capita automobile ownership the state ranked among the leaders. More than anything else, the automobile transformed rural culture. With more cars and better roads, people quickly saw the advantage of driving longer distances to towns that offered wider varieties of goods and services. Once the process had begun, it was almost impossible to reverse. The smallest towns were easily bypassed, as farm dwellers drove beyond them to the larger towns and cities. Many towns in South Dakota peaked in population in the 1920 census. Most of the rest did so by 1930.

Accentuating this trend was the declining population in the rural countryside. Population decline accelerated in response to two inexorable processes: the growing size of farms and the declining size of the farm families that lived on them. The Schultz family had eight children. When they grew up and were married, they averaged about three of their own. Ted Schultz has three children, a son who teaches economics at Yale University and two daughters who are also teachers. None of them finds it practical to hold on to the land that he owns. Schultz's own life personifies the conclusions he drew early on about agriculture: the best solution for the agricultural problem in the United States was for a large part of the farm population to leave the countryside and for those who remained behind to get bigger and more efficient.

When Hank Schultz started farming in the 1930s, he knew a neighbor who was making a decent living on 60 acres of land; they agreed at the time that 80 acres was enough for somebody to get by on. Today Hank Schultz's son Russell farms three miles northeast of Badger, working as many as ten quarter-sections, some of them rented. Hank Schultz used to plant corn with a two-row planter. Now one of the big operators in the neighborhood uses a rig that plants twenty-four rows at a time. This man hires a lot of help and uses a helicopter to check on how the work is going.

Sparky Schultz's son Sandy now runs the farm that has been in the family for more than eight decades.[18] During the 1920s, the Schultz farm comprised 560 acres; these days the younger Schultz's operation covers 1440 acres, some of which is wasteland. Henry Schultz and his sons ran about twenty-eight horses sixty or seventy years ago. The grandson manages more than twice the acreage with a couple of tractors and some part-time help. The old barns and most of the other outbuildings were torn down long ago, replaced by newer, modern ones. Some, like the machine shed, still stand. In place of the farmhouse is a modern ranch-style home. The old tractors have been replaced by huge new ones. Gone are the chickens and the pigs. A modern farm family no longer lives self-sufficiently like Sandy Schultz's parents and grandparents did. There is more income, but there are more expenses, more complications, and more headaches, too. Loan rates, interest rates, government programs, machine parts, commodity prices, inflation, marketing evaluations—the business of farming increasingly overwhelms the husbandry of farming.

Many of the surrounding places have disappeared. The one that Ted Schultz's mother grew up on half a mile south of the District 19 schoolhouse is long gone. The school itself was torn down several years ago. Sparky Schultz told me that in the sixteen miles between his place and Lake Preston he can remember two dozen farmsteads that have disappeared. When he served on the Badger Township board a decade ago, they were losing an average of three to three and a half farms a year. What has happened to the number of farms in Badger Township constitutes a microcosm of the state and, indeed, the nation. Since the early 1930s, farm numbers have declined from eighty-four thousand to thirty-four thousand in the state.[19]

Last year the German church that the family used to attend was sold and torn down for lumber. (The pulpit went to a museum in Lake Preston, and the old bell now is displayed in front of a church in Willow Lake.) The landscape itself is, in a sense, reverting to nature. Now the works of man that mark the landscape are not so much churches and schools as they are fields cultivated by three-hundred-horsepower tractors with air-conditioned cabs that take a field in twenty passes that once required two hundred. The questions that arise are: What has been lost in the process and what has been gained? And what can a knowledge of the process's history do to help us understand what is going on?

The story of the Schultzes reminds us that looking for history on Highway 14 sometimes requires that we turn off the main route and reconnoiter the surrounding countryside. It is here where we will discover the dynamics of economic and social change that are transforming these small towns, and it is here where we will find some of the most interesting aspects of rural culture.

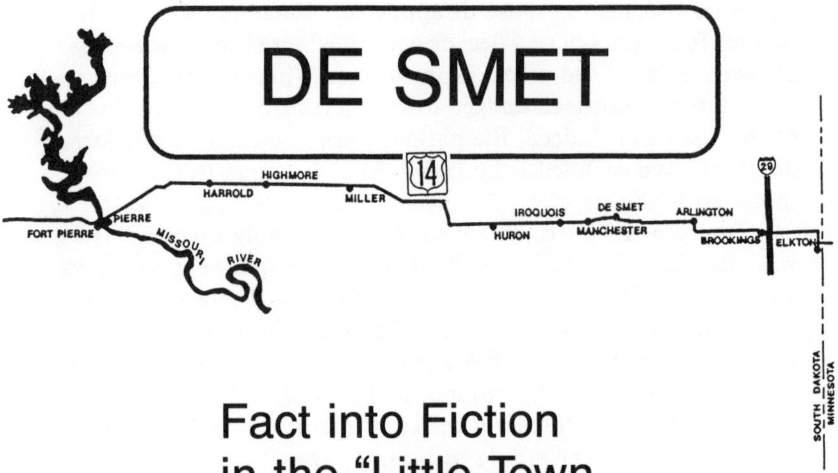

Fact into Fiction in the "Little Town on the Prairie"

People in search of history in small town America could choose no better place to visit than De Smet, South Dakota. As the "little town on the prairie," the setting for five of Laura Ingalls Wilder's books (one of them published posthumously), De Smet could claim to be the quintessential American small town.[1] Sinclair Lewis's Gopher Prairie is too unrelievedly narrow and dull and Thornton Wilder's Grover's Corners tends too much toward syrupy nostalgia to be truly representative of American small town life. Robert and Helen Lynd's Middletown, with its population of 36,524 in 1920, is more a small city than a small town.[2] For many readers of Laura Ingalls Wilder's books and viewers of the television program inspired by them, "Little House on the Prairie," De Smet came to represent what small town life was all about.

The trouble is, people who only watched the television program think that Wilder's "little town" is Walnut Grove, Minnesota, not De Smet, South Dakota. The Ingalls family did, in fact, live for a short time near Walnut Grove before moving on to De Smet, and the Minnesota location provides the setting for one of the books, *On the Banks of Plum Creek*.[3] Perhaps the television producers considered the name "Walnut Grove" to be more euphonious or picturesque-sounding than "De Smet." If so, they relied on their imaginations throughout the series, for their scripts bore little resemblance to either the books or the lives on which they were based. Caroline and Charles Ingalls and their four daughters—Mary, Laura, Carrie, and Grace—were the central characters in the program, but beyond that just about anything went. An adopted brother became part of the family group, Mary was married and had a child who died in a fire, and Laura and her husband Almanzo Wilder took a niece into their household. Adopting children seems to have been a popular plot device. But none of this had anything to do with the life that Laura Ingalls Wilder and her family led and that she later wrote about.[4]

For millions of "Little House on the Prairie" fans, however, the television plots became the reality, so when they visit De Smet to observe firsthand the place where the Ingalls family actually lived, they are sometimes disappointed. There aren't any mountains in sight, and the buildings don't look much like the ones on the studio set. While listening to the tour guide at the Surveyors' House Museum in De Smet during the summer of 1989, I overheard a high school student whisper to her friend, "That's not the way it was! And I ought to know; I watched all the programs on TV!" Outside the museum afterwards I asked her what she thought about the exhibits. She replied that while taking the tour she had wanted to ask a few questions. For one thing, in the television shows Laura met Almanzo in Minnesota, not De Smet, as the guide had mentioned. In addition, she heard a woman who had bought a copy of *Little House on the Prairie* say that the action in the book occurred in Kansas. To her all of this information was confusing. "Like it's really weird," the high schooler told me, "because they said Laura moved *here* and lived with her parents *here,* and so it's really different. It's *totally* nothing like . . . like it's *opposite!*"

Although the residents of De Smet dislike the liberties taken with the books by the producers of the program, they have taken advantage of the television-generated curiosity to attract tourists to their town. In 1968 they opened up the old surveyors' shanty, the building where the Ingalls family lived during the winter of 1879–80, and which later was moved into town. Five years later they made a museum out of the home on Third Street that Caroline and Charles and Mary Ingalls lived in from the late 1880s until Caroline died in 1924. (Mary died in 1928).[5]

Some of the furniture and artifacts in these houses were actually used by the Ingalls family; the rest are as historically authentic as possible. The chest of drawers in the surveyors' shanty was built by Charles Ingalls, and the drawer pulls were carved by him. The lace doily atop it was used by the family, too, and the picture hanging on the wall above it of Charles and Caroline Ingalls was taken from a tintype made when he was forty-five and she was forty-one.

I asked the tour guide, a student at De Smet High School, if many children have questions about the television programs.

"Sure," she smiled. "Older people, too. Everybody."

"Are they surprised to hear how it really happened?" I asked.

"Yes. They'll say, 'Oh, wasn't Mary married? Didn't she have a son who died in a fire or something?' "

"Do they seem disappointed?" I asked.

"Sometimes. When they see the pictures of Ma and Pa, they just about die!" she laughed. Charles and Caroline Ingalls were rather plain when compared with the glamorous Michael Landon and Karen Grassle, who portrayed them in the television series.

In 1986, the Laura Ingalls Wilder Memorial Society purchased the house next to the surveyors' shanty and converted it into a gift shop and tour headquarters. The tour includes stops at the city library, which contains some Ingalls memorabilia and several original Harvey Dunn paintings, the store and home of Daniel Loftus (one of the characters in the books), the town's first school building (now used as a home), and several other spots. Actually, De Smet doesn't much resemble the way it looked during the early 1880s, the period depicted in the books. The oldest buildings have either been torn down or remodeled and modernized. The owners of the old Daniel Loftus store recently installed a sign on the front of the building identifying it as such, and they also advertise their store with a sign near the Wilder museum. But most of the stores and homes in De Smet resemble those in any other town, with nothing to identify them as being anything special. Around twenty thousand tourists a year visit the Wilder sites, helping to support the local economy.[6] For some people, a stop in De Smet is part of a pilgrimage taking them to all of the locations associated with the Ingalls and Wilder families, from New York to Kansas, Wisconsin, Iowa, Minnesota, and South Dakota.

Three weekends each summer, townspeople put on a pageant based on one of the books. After five years of doing *Little Town on the Prairie,* they started using a new script in 1989 based on the next book in the series, *These Happy Golden Years.* The play was written by Marian Cramer, an author who lives nearby and who has written extensively on historical subjects for regional newspapers and magazines.[7] My twelve-year-old daughter and I came well equipped with bug spray on a warm Sunday evening in July when we drove over to watch the pageant, which is performed on a gently sloping hillside several hundred yards from the quarter-section claim the Ingallses lived on when they first came to De Smet. A brisk wind kept down the mosquitoes and cooled things off as twelve hundred spectators chatted amiably on benches and lawn chairs, waiting for the 9:00 performance to begin. Before the show began, the public address announcer invited spectators to stand when their home states were called off—twenty-seven in all, including Massachusetts, Virginia, Florida, Texas, New Mexico, California, and Oregon.[8] The smiles and chatter were reminiscent of oldtime community picnics and outdoor band concerts where almost everybody knew each other; for a moment, people from widely separated places were affiliated with a larger community.

In its nineteenth season, the Laura Ingalls Wilder Pageant had successfully worked most of the kinks out of its operation, but it remained a low-budget volunteer effort, making no pretense to being a Broadway production. Receipts from the $4 tickets ($2 for children twelve and under) go into equipment, sets, costumes, and other expenses. The actors—adults and children alike—are all volunteers. Some of them have done it year after year; Milo

The home of Caroline, Charles, and Mary Ingalls.

Apland, a local policeman and farmer, has played Pa Ingalls from the very beginning.

In the distance beyond the stage, in relief against the purples and pinks of the sunset, stood four tall cottonwoods that Charles Ingalls had planted on the claim when the family first arrived. During the performance, several cars stopped and the passengers took a quick look around. A stone marker identifies the site, but none of the buildings remain. After a time, the car lights ceased, and the play had my undivided attention.

Most of the scenes were familiar from reading the book. The playwright had added a few items here and there and contributed some dialogue for continuity and emphasis, but the basic story line came from Wilder. Fifteen-year-old Laura spends several weeks teaching at a one-room school south of town, later continues her own studies in De Smet, attends a singing school, listens in the evenings to Pa playing his fiddle, and falls in love with and eventually marries a local bachelor farmer, Almanzo Wilder, although not before entertaining some doubts and second thoughts about it.

The genius of Wilder's books, and what has made them immensely popular for half a century, lies in the concrete images she created of frontier life, the authenticity of the emotions she attributed to her characters, and the simplicity but believability of the stories she told.[9] Wilder's capacity to make her readers actually *see* what was happening on the pages of her books was no doubt greatly enhanced by her having to serve as her sister Mary Ingall's eyes when scarlet fever robbed Mary of her eyesight. As a child, Wilder tended to identify more with her father than with her mother: father and daughter were impulsive, poetic, and free-spirited. Wilder, however, learned to rein in her impulses and to conform to societal expectations and family necessity. She sewed to earn money for sending Mary Ingalls to school, although she hated doing it; she taught school, also hating it; she played the ladylike role, although her inclination was to be a tomboy. Through it all, she carefully observed and reflected on people's feelings and behavior.

Her storytelling ability was no doubt inspired by stories she heard over and over again at home and by songs she and the rest of the family joined heartily in singing when her father brought out his violin, which was often. In an era before movies, radio, and other forms of mass media, storytelling was a major form of entertainment as well as a means of making sense of experience. In telling stories people revealed the things they considered important, the values they lived by, the dreams they clung to, and the meanings they attached to these. Stories converted the raw material of daily experience into something both meaningful and reassuring for them. Historian David Lowenthal observed that the "contingent and discontinuous facts of the past become intelligible only when woven together as stories."[10]

The Wilder books, therefore, are more than simply children's literature, although they have deservedly won many awards for that. They also constitute a window on the history of the frontier experience, providing a detailed and accurate picture of small town and rural life. In a talk at a Detroit book fair in 1937, soon after the publication of her fourth book, *On the Banks of Plum Creek,* Wilder observed, "Every story in this novel, all the circumstances, each incident are true. All I have told is true but it is not the whole truth." There were some stories, she said, that were not fit for children's literature, such as the one about the children who froze to death in a blizzard on Plum Creek and the grisly tale of the Benders who killed people who stopped at their house in Kansas and buried the bodies in the garden.[11]

What many readers don't realize is that most of the characters in the books about De Smet were real people; the places were real places. Daniel Loftus, whose store was just across the street from that of Charles Ingalls, became a highly successful, well-liked businessman, running the largest ad in the local newspaper,

Spectators at the Laura Ingalls Wilder Pageant can see the cottonwoods planted by Charles Ingalls in the background.

helping organize the state Retail Merchants Association, and eventually rising to its presidency.[12] Banker J. H. Carroll, whose bank was on the north corner across the street from Charles Ingalls's store, served as the town's first mayor, went on to become speaker of the South Dakota House of Representatives, and wound up selling real estate in St. Petersburg, Florida.[13] Ben Woodworth, whose birthday party in the railroad depot flustered Laura Ingalls because she didn't know how to eat an orange, had an older brother, Jim, who went on to become a high-ranking railroad official.[14] Lawyer V. V. Barnes, who handed Charles Ingalls some firecrackers to give to the girls on the Fourth of July, did "go in for politics," as Charles Ingalls had predicted he would, emerging as a prominent leader in the territorial temperance movement during the 1880s.[15] A bird's-eye view of the town drawn by an itinerant artist in May 1883 and a business and residential map printed in the newspaper several months later identified many of the people and places described in the books.[16]

The authenticity of the people and places described in the books is not in question, and the episodes recounted therein are quite plausible, if not always literally true. In asserting the historical value of the Wilder books, we need to keep in mind that she was a writer, not a historian. As such, she shaped her material to her own purposes, foreshortening time, rearranging details, and filling in gaps where memory failed.[17] For a woman who waited until she was almost sixty-five to start writing her books, Wilder's memory served her remarkably well. Visits to De Smet with her husband Almanzo in 1931, 1938, and 1939 helped refresh her memory.[18]

While considering herself a storyteller in the tradition of her father and calling herself an author of children's literature, Wilder was very much aware of the historical significance of her work. The overwhelming response to her first book, *Little House in the Big Woods,* helped her to realize the degree to which she had seen and lived every phase of frontier life, from the time of the earliest pioneers to the arrival of farmers and the towns. "Then I understood that in my own life I represented a whole period of American History," she reflected. "I wanted the children now to understand more about the beginnings of things, to know what is behind the things they see—what it is that made America as they know it."[19]

Wilder's experiences were not unusual. In fact, their very typicality contributed to the popularity of the books. But it is easy to underestimate her achievement in converting these experiences into art. A comparison of her accounts with the reminiscences written by other pioneers of east-central South Dakota for a Pioneer Days contest sponsored in 1948 by the Huron *Daily Plainsman* is revealing.[20] The events recounted in the letters that were submitted to the newspaper resembled and sometimes were identical to the ones that Wilder wrote about, such as the hard winter of 1880 and 1881. But the bare recital of events that was given by most of the respondents revealed only a small part of their historical significance. The stories fell into patterns, since people tended to focus their attention upon similiar kinds of events—changes of seasons, festivals, disasters, community gatherings, weather phenomena, and so forth. These materials became part of the folklore of the region. In an artist's hands, information like this is converted into something denser, more dramatic, and more memorable. Both types of narration, in their own special ways, constitute useful perspectives on local history.

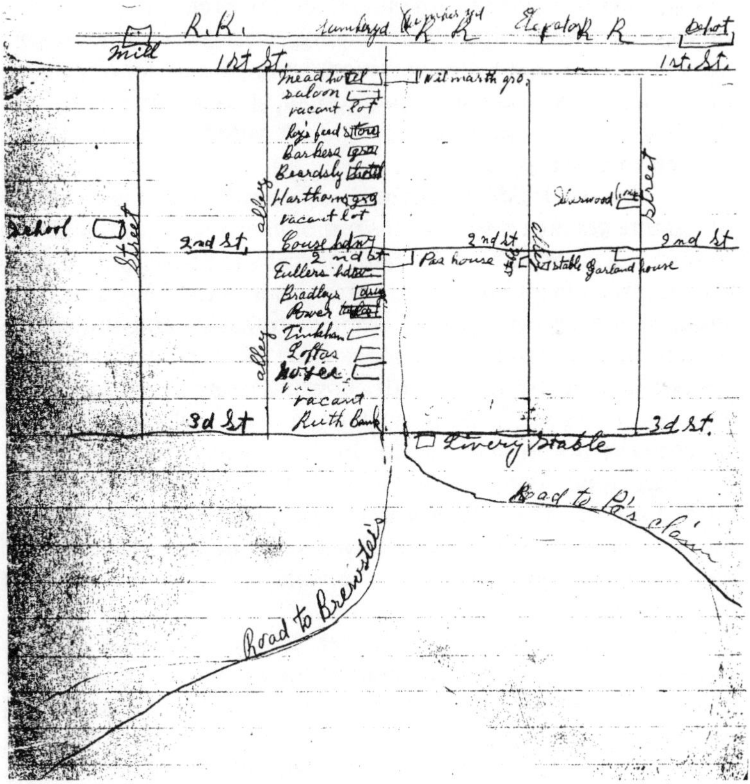

A drawing of De Smet done by Laura Ingalls Wilder to assist her in writing her books. (Courtesy of Rare Book Collection, Detroit Public Library)

We should keep in mind that the books about De Smet that were published during Wilder's lifetime deal with her adolescent years—the time when she was maturing from a child into a young woman. Adolescents then, as now, were bundles of emotions and full of hopes and dreams. Wilder, who had been trained to carefully hide her own feelings, became a careful observer of other people's feelings and emotions and faithfully captured them in her writings.[21] Only twelve years old when the family rode out to Dakota Territory, where her father had obtained a job as bookkeeper and timekeeper for a railroad construction crew, she married at eighteen, assuming adult responsibilities before she was out of her teens. It is no coincidence that the books she published stop at that point. A final, posthumously published book describing the first four years of her marriage to Almanzo Wilder has quite a different tone from the others and deals with much different subject matter—the trials and tribulations of trying to wrest a living from recalcitrant soil under attack from drought, high winds, and prairie fires. The dreamy, nostalgic childhood perspective, full of hope and ambition, gave way to the wide-eyed calculations of a doubtful young woman, skeptical about her husband's continual refrain that prosperity would be achieved with the next good crop.[22]

No wonder Wilder chose to store her manuscript about these frustrating years in a trunk. It is out of character with the earlier books, which, despite their wealth of realistic details, fail to convey fully the magnitude of the hardships and challenges encountered on the Dakota prairie. Though tragedies and difficulties appear in the adolescent books—deaths, suicidal impulses, drunken sprees, fierce blizzards, howling wolves, and larcenous businessmen—good generally triumphs over evil, and pleasant memories crowd out the sordid. In these books, Wilder focused primarily upon what novelist William Dean Howells called "the smiling aspects of life," even if few people today would readily choose to return to a time requiring such unrelenting labor for such meager material rewards. The wolf was never far from the door, literally or figuratively.

The First Four Years, however, makes clear that Laura's dreams of flight and birdlike independence will never be fulfilled. Like Pa, Laura yearns for freedom, imagining herself like a bird, swooping wildly over the Wessington Hills to the west, unencumbered by everyday worries and limitations.[23] In *These Happy Golden Years,* while riding through the countryside in a buggy with Almanzo on a quiet evening under brilliant stars, she softly sings:

In the starlight, in the starlight,
Let us wander gay and free,
For there's nothing in the daylight
Half so dear to you and me.[24]

The tone shifts in the last, posthumously published book, *The First Four Years.* Starlight gives way to daylight. The first sentence describes the heat and a strong wind blowing up from the south. "They were to be expected: a natural part of life,"

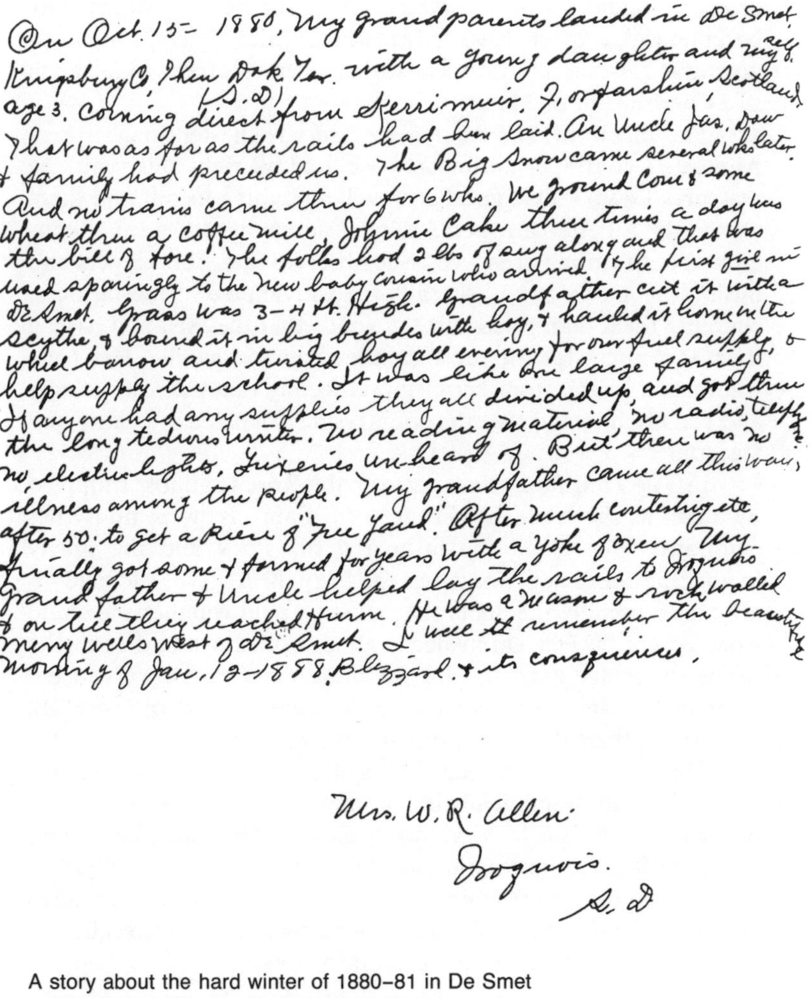

On Oct. 15 – 1880, My grandparents landed in De Smet.
Kingsbury Co, Then Dak. Ter. (S.D) with a young daughter and myself.
age 3. coming direct from Kerrimuir, Forfarshire, Scotland,
That was as far as the rails had been laid. An Uncle Jas. Dow
& family had preceded us. The Big Snow came several wks later.
And no trains came thru for 6 wks. We ground Corn & some
wheat thru a coffee mill, Johnnie Cake three times a day was
the bill of fare. The folks had 2 lbs of sug along and that was
used sparingly to the new baby cousin who arrived. (The first girl in
De Smet. Grass was 3–4 ft. High. Grandfather cut it with a
scythe & bound it in big bundles with hay, & hauled it home in the
wheel barrow and twisted hay all evening for our fuel supply, &
help supply the school. It was like one large family
If anyone had any supplies they all divided up, and got thru
the long tedious winter. No reading material, no radio, telephone
no electric lights, luxuries un-heard of. But there was no
illness among the people. My grandfather came all this way,
after 50: to get a piece of "free land". After much contesting etc,
finally got some & farmed for years with a yoke of oxen. My
Grandfather & Uncle helped lay the rails to Iroquois
& on till they reached Huron. He was a mason & rock walled
many wells west of De Smet. I well remember the beauty
morning of Jan. 12–1888. Blizzard. & its consequences.

Mrs. W. R. Allen
Iroquois.
S. D

A story about the hard winter of 1880–81 in De Smet submitted in a Pioneer Days contest. (Courtesy of Dakotaland Museum, Huron, S.Dak.)

Wilder wrote. But the rest of the book records how the hot, dry winds along with blizzards, hail storms, mortgages and high interest rates, low farm prices, prairie fires, and disease all conspired against the homesteaders who were trying to make a living on the land. The book describes the debt that Laura and Almanzo Wilder ran up in their farming operation, the sale of their homestead (leaving them a 160-acre tree claim to farm), the destruction of their farmhouse by fire, the death of their newborn son, and the destruction of their crops by hail on one occasion and hot winds on another. It was their misfortune to begin farming when the wet seasons of the early 1880s ran out, to be replaced by drought conditions in the latter part of the decade, which only became worse after 1890. Meanwhile, farm prices fluctuated downward, while interest rates varied from 8 percent to as much as 24 percent on one loan.[25]

The theme of *The First Four Years* is the tension between Almanzo's continual optimism ("We'll be all right this year," he reassures Laura. "One good crop will straighten us out and there was never a better prospect.") and Laura's hard-headed skepticism about farming prospects. She observes that storekeepers and businesspeople in town generally take advantage of the farmers, charging them high prices for the goods that they sell and paying them low prices for the products they buy and handle. Her frustration is a switch from her girlhood feeling that the town is ugly and constricting and that the countryside is a place of beauty and freedom.[26]

In *The First Four Years,* after baby Rose is almost trampled by a colt as she is playing in the yard, Laura is swept up by her emotions: "She hated the farm and the stock and the smelly lambs, the cooking of food and the dirty dishes. Oh, she hated it all, and especially the debts that must be paid whether she could work or not."[27] Her ambivalence about both town and farm life seems to resolve itself toward the book's end in the wish to become one of the townspeople who live easier lives than farm folk and escape their financial burdens and worries.

The difference between the earlier books and the last one comes through dramatically in the songs Wilder quoted at the end of them. She finished *These Happy Golden Years* with Laura and Almanzo lovingly gazing at the stars on their wedding night at their new home on the claim. "It is a wonderful night," Almanzo says. "It is a beautiful world," Laura replies as she recalls the sound of Pa's fiddle and the echo of a song:

> Golden years are passing by,
> These happy, golden years.

The song that echos through *The First Four Years,* on the other hand, is less an elegy than a hymn of encouragement for those in distress who might be inclined to pack up and move away. Sundays on their new homestead, Laura and Almanzo drive through the countryside belting out their favorite song from school days, "Don't Leave the Farm, Boys."

> You talk of the mines of Australia,
> They've wealth in red gold, without doubt;
> But, ah! there is gold on the farm, boys—
> If only you'll shovel it out.
> Chorus:
> Don't be in a hurry to go!
> Don't be in a hurry to go!
> Better risk the old farm awhile longer,
> Don't be in a hurry to go![28]

Of course, what happened in the end is that Laura and Almanzo Wilder did go. After living for a while with Almanzo Wilder's parents near Spring Valley, Minnesota, and then for a time in Florida, they left De Smet for good in July 1894. They packed all of their belongings in a wagon, carefully hiding a $100 bill in a portable writing desk, and headed off to an apple farm in Missouri.[29] That is not how the book ends, however. While she was growing up, Wilder had frequently heard her father say that homesteading in Dakota was the equivalent of making a $14 bet with the government that you could stick it out on the farm for at least five years.[30] The claim is humorous in Wilder's books because the reader realizes that Pa will eventually win his bet. By the time Laura and Almanzo Wilder set out to try to repeat that experience, however, the odds had changed. Try as they would, they could not make their farm pay. Instead of ending her book realistically, however, Wilder concluded it on a note of hope. Charles Ingalls always dreamed of new horizons in the West where life was better. For Almanzo and Laura, salvation will be found not farther to the west but further down the road in time. Something is *bound* to show up, given enough hope and confidence: "The incurable optimism of the farmer who throws his seed on the ground every spring, betting it and his time against the elements, seemed inextricably to blend with the creed of her pioneer forefathers that 'it is better farther on'—only instead of farther on in space, it was farther on in time, over the horizon of the years ahead instead of the far horizon of the west."[31]

The book ends by repeating the words of "Don't Leave the Farm, Boys," but knowing what we know—that the Wilders *did* leave the farm—renders this ending ironic.[32] It reverts to the dreamy hopes and expectations of the earlier books, but now Laura and Almanzo are caught up in a web of circumstances that does not allow escape. Laura is no longer a girl, but a woman; her options are no longer open, but limited. Dreaming on a star is one thing; calculating one's finances in broad daylight is another. The arithmetic of farming quickly caught up with the brave young couple. Actually, it didn't take a lot of fancy figuring to compute what 3 percent a month interest would do to their prospects. The lush, verdant Dakota prairie—what had appealed most to Wilder as a young teenager—turned brown and unyielding when she entered her early twenties. Like thousands of other Dakota farmers, the Wilders reaped only bitter disappointment from their efforts.

Our understanding of the underlying economic forces that affected people's lives during this period of history receives little illumination from the "Little Town" series. Descriptive as the books are about social mores and institutions, architectural features and material culture, individual motivations and emotions, the books published during Wilder's lifetime picture all of these through the eyes of a teenager. She was a curious and perceptive teenager, to be sure, closely observant of a multitude of details. But of the structural forces that shaped daily life and were undergoing profound transformation during the period—of these significant influences we learn very little.

The First Four Years ends in August 1889, just a few months before South Dakota became a state. In June 1890, an Independent party was established at Huron—the first of the farmers' parties that would fuse into the Populist movement the following year. For a time the Populists would take over the state government during the 1890s, a major departure from traditional Republican domination.[33] About this we learn nothing in the Wilder books. Perhaps it is unfair to blame the author for not discussing something that occurred after the period she was writing about, but her failure to mention the developing forces in the 1880s that contributed later to the rapid rise of the Populists does tell us something about the books. The Populists emerged directly out of the Farmers' Alliances, which were active in Dakota Territory by the mid-1880s. But Wilder's attention was directed at individual lives and social interactions, not at the broad political and economic forces that were reshaping the rural environment.

Breaking off the final book at the end of 1889 is therefore revealing. After that date, politics insistently intruded upon Dakotans' lives. But Wilder was not interested in politics.[34] The struggles she described were with nature. Laura and Almanzo

Wilder were defeated by windstorms, hailstones, drought, and other natural forces. She did take note of low farm prices and high interest rates, but what for Alliancemen and Populists constituted a political issue was for her essentially another force of nature, unpredictable and unfathomable. While Laura and Almanzo Wilder were battling the elements, however, Alliance-backed legislators in the territorial capital at Bismarck passed laws creating a railroad commission to regulate railroad rates and others to bring the intermediary dealers under control. They did not prove to be very effective, but they did contribute to a growing belief on the part of many farmers that the villains that were oppressing them consisted of more than natural disasters: their oppressors were people situated in high places who used their power and influence to rob the farmers of their hard-earned income. High finance and Wall Street were conspiring to keep them in a slavelike status.

All of this, which is central to the history of the period, is omitted from Wilder's books, and thus the books must be judged exactly for what they are—wonderfully evocative accounts of prairie and small town life written about a particular time (the years of the Great Dakota Boom) and from the perspective of a highly perceptive, albeit naive and innocent, adolescent whose viewpoint would change after she married and moved beyond her teen years. Wilder seemed to have recognized this when she hid away her manuscript about the first several years of her marriage. Life for a married person is much more complicated than it is for a romantic teenager. Conditions during the hard years of the late 1880s likewise posed far more complications than did the heady, expansionist years at the beginning of the decade. That Wilder's marriage coincided with the end of the Great Dakota Boom was sheer happenstance, but a happy one it was in the sense that we have her beautifully rendered stories of frontier life in Dakota Territory during the early 1880s. They constitute a major contribution to our historical understanding of that time and place, but they provide only a partial perspective. Among the many mansions of history, her novels constitute an important, but only one, little house.

MANCHESTER

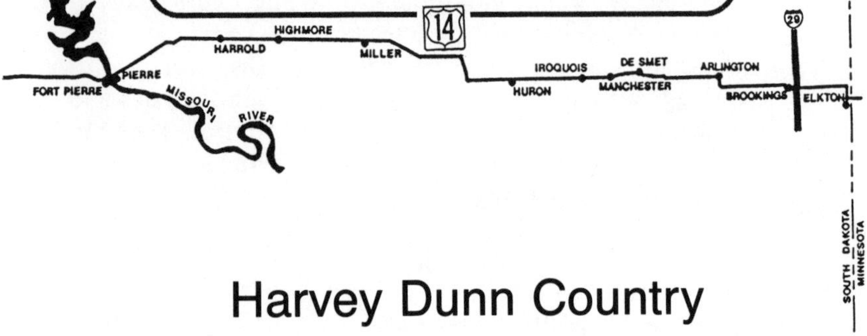

Harvey Dunn Country

This is Harvey Dunn country—eastern South Dakota—and Manchester is Harvey Dunn's hometown. Born on a homestead three miles south and one east of the tiny railroad town, young Dunn grew up next to Redstone Creek and an old buffalo trace that ran by it, enjoying the wildlife and wildflowers and the clouds that arched over the virgin prairie that was his playground. Years later, after gaining recognition as one of America's foremost magazine illustrators, he would return almost annually to those haunts to sketch and refresh his memory in order to capture remembered images on canvas. Today, Harvey Dunn is South Dakota's most beloved and most famous artist, and arguably its best.[1]

Little could his parents, Thomas and Bersha Dunn, have realized what lay in store for their secondborn child when he came into the world before daylight on March 7, 1884. They were typical young pioneers—he twenty-seven and born in Canada, she a Wisconsinite six years his junior—determined to make a go of it on the challenging Dakota prairie. He had arrived with a party of home seekers in November 1880 and had filed a claim close to the railroad soon after the arrival of the tracks and the platting of the town of Fairview. (Upon discovery that there already was one "Fairview" in the territory, the name was changed to "Manchester," after a local settler.) Tom and Bersha Dunn were married in Dekorra, Wisconsin, on Christmas Day, 1881, and arrived in Dakota the following spring to begin their prairie adventure.[2]

With the arrivals of Caroline in 1882, Harvey in 1884, and Roy in 1885, their family was complete. In 1888, Tom Dunn sold the homestead, and they moved to a new place three miles down the buffalo trace to the south, transporting their little house on four wagons pulled by oxen. Here, amidst the slightly rolling terrain of tallgrass prairie and under the bright canopy of open sky, which would figure so prominently in his later paintings, young Harvey Dunn spent the next thirteen years of his life attending school through the ninth grade, filling out his frame as he walked behind the plow, and drinking in the sights and sounds around him. So great was his enthusiasm for drawing likenesses of animals and flowers and train locomotives on the blackboard that the teachers at the nearby Esmond Township school found it necessary to hide the chalk box from him so they wouldn't run out of chalk too quickly. His mother, who possessed some artistic talent of her own, encouraged her son, but Tom Dunn seemed to consider it all foolishness and a distraction.

Thus, it was something beyond the usual when seventeen-year-old Harvey Dunn broke away from the confines of home to enroll in the preparatory department at South Dakota Agricultural College (now South Dakota State University) in Brookings in the fall of 1901. Bersha Dunn had persuaded her husband to permit him to do so. For the artistic soul, there was much to beckon the young plowman beyond the world in which he had grown up. Forty years later, Dunn would recall, "When the glimmering along the horizon got too much for me, I set out to find the shining palaces which must exist beyond it somewhere."[3] At Brookings, the encouragement of a young art teacher named Ada B. Caldwell, recently arrived on the college campus, provided Dunn with the confidence and inspiration he needed. He acknowledged later that it was she "who opened vistas for me. For the first time I had found a serious, loving, and intelligent interest in what I was vaguely searching for. She seemed to dig out talent where none had been, and she prayed for genius. She was tolerant and the soul of goodness. With my eyes on the horizon, she taught me where to put my foot."[4]

Caldwell encouraged him to enroll in the Chicago Art Institute. After a year at South Dakota Agricultural College and two years in Chicago, Dunn received his most important training at the hands of the famous illustrator Howard Pyle at his Wilmington, Delaware, studio. Dunn quickly established himself as one of Pyle's most gifted students. Later, when he in turn began to pass his knowledge on to others, he considered teaching to be his most important activity. Almost immediately after setting up his own studio in 1906 in Wilmington, Dunn became a popular success, doing illustrations for the *Saturday Evening Post* and other large-circulation magazines. During World War I, he was one of eight artists commissioned by the U.S. government to portray the combat activities of the American Expeditionary Force.

The war seemed to work a permanent change in Dunn, for afterwards he appeared to friends to be unhappy and dissatisfied. After the exuberance and excitement of the front, the return to peacetime illustrating seemed rather tame, and it showed in his work. Now his attention focused more and more on his teaching. His thoughts, moreover, increasingly strayed back to the Dakota prairie of his youth. Having married into wealth and earning a comfortable income from his illustrations, Dunn could afford to pursue his intense desire to do significant work—something that would last. He considered it more important to please himself than to please his clients.

A European trip with his wife Tulla in 1925 returned him to the wartime battlefields he had known. Two years later, he toured the Southwest with his son Robert and Arthur Mitchell, a former student. A turning point came in 1930 when he traveled back to South Dakota, where he attended the annual Old Settlers' Day celebration in De Smet on June 10.[5] Dunn was so taken up with the people and the countryside that for the rest of his life he would return almost every year to relax and visit with people and sketch. Seldom would he do a painting on the spot. Instead he made his sketches and used them back in his studio in Tenafly, New Jersey, to aid his memory when painting scenes of homesteaders in the place of his childhood.

People still remember those visits of his in the 1930s and 1940s, invariably mentioning the size of the man, his geniality, and his lack of pretense. Eunice Moore, who grew up south of Manchester but now lives in a farmhouse a couple of miles north of town, reminisced, "On the tenth of June he would come back from New Jersey. He had such broad shoulders and he looked so erect and so tall. There was something about him that made him great—just his stature, his big build—but he was the most common person when he came back here to visit." Harvey and Lucille Marx, who moved to Manchester as young marrieds in 1933 and are two of its dozen or so residents today, remembered when he'd come into their store on Main Street to buy groceries and stop to chat. "He usually smoked a pipe," Harvey recalled. "He was just an ordinary guy. You'd think he was a farmer out there."

Dunn loved the prairie, and by all accounts, he loved prairie people. This eastern sophisticate, who had studied his craft with the best and in turn had himself trained some of the best illustrators of the day, who pursued his work most of the year within the orbit of the New York City art world, and whose published thoughts about the role of art and artists verged on the profound, seemed perfectly at home in rural South Dakota and appreciated the toils and triumphs of the people there. His sister Carrie Reiland had moved back from Oregon and bought the old Dow place, two miles south of town and near the family's original homestead on Redstone Creek. Dunn generally stayed with her for three or four weeks during the summer.

He'd bring his sketchbook along and often drive his big automobile into the country to sketch. Laura Sherwood, whose husband Aubrey did more than anybody else to educate South Dakotans about their native son, recalled him drawing a straw stack on a sketchpad resting on his steering wheel.[6] Many people in and around Manchester professed to recognize the people in his paintings or enjoyed speculating about their identities and about the locations of various scenes. For instance, Alferd Wallum, whose family sharecropped on several farms south of town before moving to Manchester in 1931, told me that he had seen the incident which had inspired Dunn to paint *Patience,* depicting a farmer milking his cow.

Several people suggested to me that the house in the background of Dunn's popular painting *The Prairie Is My Garden* is a rendering of Carrie Reiland's house as it stood near Redstone Creek. The creek itself also resembles the one in the painting, but in fact it did not run that close to the house. "On account of the way it is cut out, it is the Redstone Creek," Eunice Moore averred. But she readily conceded that Dunn probably manipulated the elements in the painting for effect and that his purpose was not to depict any particular place at any particular time. "Harvey Dunn did not want to specify what he had in his mind when he painted those pictures," she told me, "because he wanted everybody to think that this was his place. He wanted everybody to think that maybe they knew of a place like that."

Moore went to the same Esmond Township school that Harvey Dunn attended during the 1890s. Her mother, Annie Curley, had gone there before her and later taught there. There was no pump at the school; parents had to haul in water as well as fuel. At the time that Moore attended it, there were two outhouses, one for the boys and one for the girls. In Dunn's painting, *After School,* only one outhouse is visible; by it several children are heading home after school. Moore said that her mother, who went to school with Dunn, might have been one of them. Since Carrie Reiland was a year older than Dunn, it is tempting to infer that they could have been the models for the two children heading home down the hill in back of the school. One can run into problems, however, by reading paintings like this too literally. The school was originally located near Redstone Creek before being moved west half a mile to the section-line road, and the incline behind the school could be the one leading down to the creek. But the school fronted on the south, while in the painting, since the sun is going down, the school must be facing north. Today the old school is used as a storage shed on Eldon Whites's farm, several miles northwest of Iroquois.

Dunn, were he to return to Redstone Creek today, would no doubt brush aside such speculations about what or whom he was depicting in his paintings. While he was deeply interested in particular people, places, and events, his art was universal. He sought to capture the truth, but that to him consisted of more than surface appearance. It included the inner drama and spirit of the people and places that possessed so much meaning for him. "Look a little at the model and a *lot* inside," he told his students. "Paint more with feeling than with thought."[7]

Dunn was passionately devoted to the truth. "The first square inch you cover on that canvas should be significant—so full a statement of truth that you'd be willing to take an oath on it," he emphasized. "That first inch of truth will be an anchor to windward to which you can return and refer." And again, he'd admonish, "Be a sound honest workman and tell the truth." But photographic reproduction did not interest him in the least. "We have got to be dramatic," he taught. "A cobweb or a trainwreck are dramatic. You can't paint a picture with intellect alone. You know the thing that makes picture making the hardest work in the world is the fact that you can't acquire all the knowledge you need and then turn it out in assembly line fashion."[8]

Dunn thought hard and profoundly about art and life and the relationship between the two, and the wisdom he acquired he passed on to his students, several of whom recorded his remarks in the classroom. "He taught art and illustrating as one. He taught it as a religion, or awfully close to such," Dean Cornwell, one of Dunn's most successful students, recalled. "He taught dramatic viewpoints based on the truth of human existence, as against artificial, theatrical effect. 'Take liberty,' he used to say, 'but not license.' In his teaching he was more concerned with the essential spirit of the work than technical procedures."[9]

As an artist, Dunn had integrity, eschewing the false, the stylized, the artificial. He encouraged his students to pursue work that was significant. It was not the subject itself that made a work important, but the way in which it was conceived that conferred

After School, painted by Harvey Dunn during the early 1950s. (Courtesy of South Dakota Art Museum Collection, Brookings)

The Esmond Township school that Harvey Dunn attended as a boy. Smokey Wallum, shown here, attended the school during the 1930s.

importance upon it. *Any* subject, approached in the right spirit, could achieve the kind of significance he urged his students to aspire to. "You have to go back to what you are, what you know, what you believe. You have to be true to the inspiration or whatever it was that drove you to art school," he told them. "If you ever amount to anything at all, it will be because you were true to that deep desire or ideal which made you seek artistic expression in pictures."[10]

The work that made him famous in the years before and during World War I, however, seldom allowed Dunn to paint from his own experience. Pirates, cowboys, woodsmen, armored knights—subjects like these depended upon imagination or historical research, not direct observation. Even his war scenes, despite his insistence upon actually getting to the front to observe the action, only incompletely capture the gruesome, brutal aspects of combat. Doing the prairie paintings allowed him to paint what he knew most intimately. That he loved the prairie and admired the people is obvious in his work. That he sought to depict the hardship and the difficulties as well as the beauty and the compensations is also evident. In a real sense, Dunn was painting history. By recapturing experiences on the Dakota frontier, Dunn left a valuable historical legacy. The family arriving in a prairie schooner, the plowman breaking sod, the mother at the pump or cutting wildflowers, the children playing by the creek, the cattle grazing in the meadow, the chickens pecking in the yard, the wildflowers emblazoning the landscape in a kaleidoscope of color, the wispy clouds—these are the scenes that make Dunn so popular with his fellow plains dwellers, who hang copies of his paintings on school, elevator office, and living room walls. "Art," he liked to say, "is the music to which the common facts of life are played."[11]

But if Dunn, in fact, was a historical painter, the history that he chose to portray is incomplete. It encompasses the daily experiences of the farm boy that he had been. But almost entirely missing are train locomotives, improved agricultural machinery, grain elevators, Main streets, cornet bands, pool halls, oyster suppers, and church services. We know they were all present; the newspaper stories and personal accounts of the period tell us they were. Dunn's prairie vision is set outdoors, where most of a farm family's life was spent. But where are the interior scenes, around the table, at the fireplace, in the rocking chair, by the pump organ? With the exception of a burial scene and a threshing vignette or two, Dunn omits the community gatherings that provided relief from the lonely existence of individual families on the prairie.

Certainly what he did he did well, and the legacy of his more than twoscore prairie paintings is a national treasure. But the question that intrudes is why he focused so much upon individuals or small family groups and excluded so many possible subjects. Perhaps his conservative Republican way of thinking inclined him to concentrate upon the rugged individualism of the pioneers rather than upon their social and political activities. It could also be that by the 1930s and the 1940s, when he made his visits to home territory, the automobile, new powerful train locomotives, and other forms of modern technology had obliterated the culture of the 1880s and 1890s, except in the rural countryside. Unlike his fellow regionalists of the 1920s and 1930s, such as Grant Wood and John Steuart Curry (a student of Dunn's for a time), who concentrated—often critically—on contemporary rural society, Dunn portrayed a historical rural scene that had existed a generation earlier. He stuck almost entirely to prairie and farm panoramas, hardly ever rendering a town scene.

It is the vast skies and prairie landscapes that initially capture our attention in most of his paintings, but upon reflection it becomes obvious that these magnificent physical settings serve as mere backdrops for the human drama being depicted in the pictures. Always it is the people who stand out, whether in the foreground or almost invisible in the distance. They appear stolid, hardworking, tough, and persevering—the women as strong as the men. The drama being depicted is human being against the environment—sometimes single individuals, usually families, isolated on the prairie, united in their determination to make a go of it and determine their own destiny. As a child Dunn lacked the opportunity or ability to observe and understand the social dynamics of towns. As an adult, he avoided painting those kinds of scenes. Dunn, who constantly preached the virtue of directness and simplicity in painting, did not want insignificant details to detract from the central message. "Don't fuss around with it—don't niggle," he advised. "Paint significant values that will sparkle."[12] That approach is much easier to follow in the country than in town. Depicting Main Street stores or social gatherings almost automatically multiplies detail—more buildings, more people, more things to incorporate. Dunn enjoyed visiting towns and chatting with the people there, but when it came to expressing his art, he stuck to the countryside.

One of the only town scenes he did helps to illustrate this

point. It is a drawing of Manchester reprinted in an article about him by Ernest W. Watson in *American Artist* in 1942. Talking about his hometown, Dunn told the interviewer, "It is much the same as it was, except that the whiskers have grown a little longer."[13] More than most of the towns along the railroad, tiny Manchester had remained as it had been. In his drawing, telephone poles run the length of Main Street, and though not discernable in the sketch, there was an electric generating plant to light people's homes. But most people still drew their water from the old town pump, which may be seen toward the left side in the middle of Main Street. At the end of the block, looking toward the south, is a small building, probably the filling station that had gone up on the south side of the tracks during the early 1930s. Several people living today in and around Manchester can identify most of the buildings in the drawing. The large false-front store building on the right (west side) of the street with the awning over the sidewalk is the Maxwell store, which Harvey and Lucille Marx moved into after running restaurants in two other places along the block. Beyond that were a private residence, a pool hall, a cafe, a garage, a bank, the Manchester town hall, and Woodall Produce. People who lived in town during the early 1940s when the sketch was made can't quite make out all of the buildings; several places seem to have been omitted and two or three possibly combined. All agree that the grain elevator in the drawing is situated too far over to the right (it was actually farther east along the tracks) but that Dunn probably moved it over that far so that he could get it into the picture. Verisimilitude was not Dunn's primary goal, however. He explained it this way: "If you paint what you *see,* you won't have a good-looking thing. . . . Paint a little less of the facts, and a little more of the spirit."[14]

Until she died a couple of years ago, Olive Toberman lived in a house at the south end of Main Street on the east side. On one of his visits, Dunn did a couple of drawings of Manchester from a distance and gave them to her, both picturing the town on the horizon, one from about a mile to the southeast and the other from about the same distance to the southwest. He told her to hang on to them because someday they would be valuable. Her son Noel, who now lives in the house alone, has them locked away in a safety deposit box in Huron.

One wonders if Dunn ever intended to do a painting of his hometown, and if so, how he would have executed it.[15] There appears to be a reason for his failure to tackle such a project. If he had treated the town like he usually did the rural countryside,

Harvey Dunn's pencil sketch of Manchester. (*American Artist,* June 1942, p. 118)

Manchester's Main Street today. The town hall is third from the end on the right.

he would have used the townscape as a background for the drama of human figures in the foreground. Dunn pitted men and women in the country against natural forces, but he might have found conflicts within the town much more complicated: storeowner against storeowner, town dweller against rural dweller, Catholic against Protestant, Republican against Democrat, northsider against southsider, teetotaler against saloon keeper, local business owner against outside corporation. Townspeople, while they tried to maintain harmony and promote the interests of the community as a whole, were inevitably divided among themselves by opinion, interest, and circumstance. Dunn's world is a world of individuals, families, and small groups possessing similiar purposes and goals. The town, on the other hand, small as it may be, is always driven as much by conflict as it is by community, and it is just this sort of conflict that Dunn felt incapable of, or was uninterested in, depicting.

Dunn's paintings tell an important story, therefore, but only a truncated one. In later years, much of the life of the community centered on the Manchester town hall, a concrete block structure put up after the frame building burned down. "If the walls could only talk!" John ("Whitey") Woodall laughed as we poked our heads into the hall, still the scene of many an event in town. Just thirty feet wide and about a hundred feet deep, with a stage to the front, it has survived for more than half a century, while most of the other buildings on Main Street have decayed and been torn down. The scene of dances, elections, basketball games ("We skinned our shins running past the chairs set up along the walls," said Alferd Wallum), chicken pie suppers, all-county school Christmas programs, traveling theater productions and home talent plays, and a dozen other events, it remains the center of community activity in town. One might expect that there would not be much of that with only a dozen residents left, but potluck suppers three or four times a year during the winter months still draw crowds from the surrounding countryside and from nearby towns, and every five years or so school reunions are still big events. Even as the town steadily disappears (the two remaining grain elevators were set on fire several years ago to clear space for widening the highway; earlier part of one of them had been torn down and the weathered boards hauled to California to be sold for people's basements and picture frames), the Manchester town hall stands as a reminder of what the community once was.

One person who remembered the activities that went on there was Whitey Woodall, whose family lived in the back of its produce business on the corner just south of the hall. His mother operated a cafe at the front for several years, feeding travelers on the highway as well as farmhands and locals. The big barrel out front, which was used to replenish thirsty car radiators, was supplied from the town pump in the middle of the block. The pump was depended upon by most of the town's residents since well drilling was a chancy business around there.

Another Manchester resident during the 1930s who remembered activities in the hall was Alferd Wallum, the oldest of five brothers in a family that, like many others, went broke during the Dirty Thirties. Listening to him recall the days when he unloaded carloads of coal in Manchester by hand with a big scoop shovel brought to mind the exertions of the pioneers, breaking sod and hauling stones and engaged in other kinds of hard physical labor in Dunn's paintings. Somehow, Alferd, after a stint in the Civilian Conservation Corps in the Black Hills and a number of poorly paying jobs in the area, managed to get started in 1937 with a filling station on the corner a half-mile east of Manchester. He was twenty-one years old at the time, and he called it "Wallum's Corner." When he pulled out a camera to take a picture of the first car that drove in to buy some gas, the driver, apparently not wanting his picture to be taken, stepped on the gas and sped down the road. The station itself was the old office of the Atlas Lumber Company, for which Alferd paid $125 and another $15 to have it hauled a half-mile over to the corner. For a little while, while he was repainting the sign on the building and before he painted out the "Atlas," some people drove up thinking it read, "At Last a Service Station."

Dunn stopped in frequently at the station when he was back in South Dakota. He had to drive past it every time he drove into town from his sister Carrie Reiland's place. Interestingly, the sons of Alferd and his wife Muriel both became professional artists. Dunn died before they ever had a chance to show him some of the childhood works of their older boy, Galen. Like Dunn, Galen as a child was much more interested in drawing than in schoolwork. Once, when his father brought some plywood home, he soon had it filled with western scenes. Cowboys and westerns were his passion; when some neighbors mentioned that they were going to a funeral, little Galen exclaimed, "Who shot him?" Encouraged by a high school teacher in De Smet, Galen studied art at Oklahoma State Tech in Okmulgee, graduating in 1973, and brother Craig, who specializes in portraits, followed in his footsteps several years later. They both now live in Beggs, a small town south of Tulsa. Just like the great Harvey Dunn, they both have many of their pictures hanging on walls in the area around Manchester.

Noel "Toby" Toberman has a painting hanging in his living room that Galen did of him sitting on a horse. Eunice Moore has portraits Craig did from photos of Dunn and Laura Ingalls Wilder underneath her bed, waiting to be given to her daughter. Four or five of Galen's western scenes hang from the walls of the Farmers and Merchants Bank in Iroquois, which also for years had three Harvey Dunns, until they were packed and shipped to the South Dakota Art Museum in Brookings.

Walk into Wallum's Corner today and you will see two of Galen's large western canvases on the wall, side by side with ads for the Laura Ingalls Wilder Pageant in De Smet, a clipping from the Huron *Daily Plainsman* about the history of Wallum's Corner, Coke ads, pizza warmers, and potato chip racks. The paintings are a reminder that art is prized here. That an area with a diameter of three or four miles could produce three artists is rather unusual. Who would have predicted it? Dunn's prairie paintings are works of love, offerings to the people who begot him and the place that nurtured him. They constitute a regional and national treasure—artifacts that freeze in color and line a place and time that are part of our heritage. Galen Wallum's western paintings capture the independent and individualistic spirit of a people and reflect the dreams of a boy growing up in a postwar environment where he imagined himself riding along with Hopalong Cassidy, Roy Rogers, and the Lone Ranger and performing brave deeds. What documentary qualities his western scenes possess derive from what he learned later, after he left home, as he traveled across the West in search of his dream.

Dunn's dream lay right where he was born, where he lived the first seventeen years of his life. He left home in search of a glimmer beyond the horizon; he returned home again and again when he discovered that nowhere else had anything more to offer him, visually or communally, than the rolling prairies around Redstone Creek and the old buffalo trace. As he observed in a letter to the librarian at South Dakota State College in 1941, "I find that I prefer painting pictures of early South Dakota life to any other kind, which would seem to point to the fact that my search of other horizons has led me around to my first. May I garble a very old saying: 'Where your heart is, there is your treasure also.' "[16]

IROQUOIS

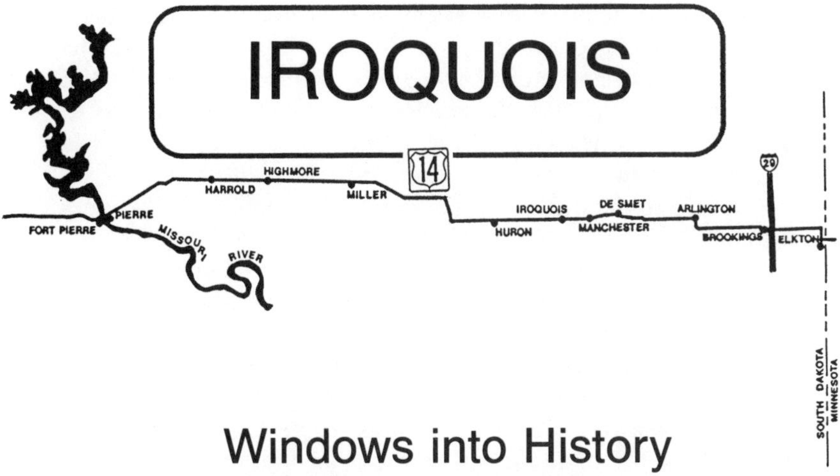

Windows into History at the Local Cafe

If you want to find out what's happening in a small town like Iroquois, the place to go is the cafe. Thirty or forty years ago a town its size (population 348 in 1980) would have supported two or three cafes or restaurants; today, more than one would be unusual. Empty buildings and vacant lots furnish evidence of the difficulties confronting people trying to make a go of it in towns like Iroquois nowadays. The dwindling number of small town cafes has made them unique, making them grist for journalists' and scholars' mills. Several years ago, the *Wall Street Journal* ran a front-page feature on them, and National Public Radio recently interviewed a professor from the University of Northern Iowa who is writing a book about the cultural significance of small town cafes, based on his travels around the upper Midwest.[1]

The Countryside Cafe on Highway 14 draws mostly local people, along with a few people traveling on the highway. Entering it for the first time, one notes nothing particularly unique or surprising. In neat handwriting on a chalkboard above the grill, sizzling with steaks and burgers, are the specials of the day: "Hot Beef—$2.50," "Steaktips in Mushroom Sauce on Noodles with Carrots—$2.85," and "Ham Sandwich and Pea Salad—$2.25." Six circular stools line the counter in the front; in the larger dining area to the rear are two booths and five tables that could accommodate about forty people. The breakfast rush begins the daily rhythm, followed by groups coming in for coffee from about 9:00 to 11:00. From 11:30 to 1:00 or so the place hums as a highway construction crew swells the usual tourist and local crowd, filling almost every seat in the place. By midafternoon the second round of coffee drinkers returns. Velma Leichtenberg and her helper work quickly and efficiently, getting people's orders to them in short order without ever seeming overly hurried or too busy to listen to a joke or acknowledge a compliment.[2]

Tacked to the wall by the restroom is a calendar with "Homesteading Scenes from Dewey and Corson Counties, 1910–1920." This was one of the main projects of the Timber Lake and Area Historical Society, which Velma's daughter and son-in-law are actively involved in. One quickly surmises that her daughter's historical interest came naturally, for hanging on a wall in the dining area are a dozen neatly framed photographs showing scenes of Iroquois taken over the years. The minigallery provides a brief historical sketch of the town. Without an interpreter, however, the story remains truncated, suggestive enough for a lively imagination, but like a song whose words are half-forgotten.

When I asked about the photographs in the summer of 1988, Wes Rounds and John Woodall came to my rescue. Wes, a retired rural mail carrier, has lived within a few miles of Iroquois all his life. "Whitey," as Woodall is known to everyone, grew up in nearby Manchester and moved with his family to Iroquois in 1934 when he was eighteen. He worked in the produce business with

Velma Leichtenberg points out the band concert scene on the wall of the Countryside Cafe.

his father, buying cream and eggs and chickens. As these two longtime residents reminisced, the pictures of street scenes that chronicle the town's progress from the age of the horse through the age of the automobile took on new meaning. Especially striking was a photograph of a band concert taken on a summer evening in 1950. Cars are parked three and four deep around a portable bandstand moved into the middle of the town's main intersection. The scene is alive with people—men perched on car fenders or straddling the stoops in front of stores, women sitting in car seats or casually chatting through open windows, children running around while the band plays on. Interspersed among mostly postwar model cars are old Model A's. In 1968 the *Dakota Farmer* magazine ran the picture with a story on the decline of the traditional small town Saturday night.[3] The photograph perfectly

The 1950 band concert on Main Street in Iroquois.
(Couresty of Velma Leichtenberg)

captures the ambience of the Saturday night experience, when people piled their families into the old jalopy and drove into town to sell their cream and eggs, buy a few groceries and other needed items, and stay to chat and relax for several hours at the end of another hard week of work.

For close to half a century, Saturday night was the quintessential communal experience for rural South Dakotans and neighboring midwesterners and plains dwellers. Issuing from economic circumstances—the centrality of the cream and egg economy and the inability of farm families to get to a town more than once or twice a week—it gradually emerged as more than an economic phenomenon. For years it was the most significant cultural happening in small town life, commensurate with Sunday church services, baseball, chicken pie suppers, and Fourth of July celebrations. Not everybody played baseball, people went their separate ways to attend church services, and towns took turns celebrating the Fourth of July. But when people recall Saturdays in rural America, what they remember is that almost everybody came into town to do their business and catch up on the doings of friends and neighbors. It was a virtually universal experience.

The pleasure of searching for history is recapturing significant moments like small town Saturday nights and finding explanations of origins, functions, and meanings. A problem with history, however, is that its recorders can make mistakes, and always its truths reside in the realm of probability, not certainty. Thus, the *Dakota Farmer* had it right when it called Saturday night "the best night of the week," and it utilized good artistic judgment in illustrating its story with a picture of the Iroquois band concert. But it almost certainly was wrong in linking the two together, because everybody from Iroquois who remembers those lazy summer evenings will tell you that band concerts there were always on Wednesday nights, not Saturday nights.

An Iroquois band was organized in 1930. After World War II, when the Rural Electrification Administration (REA) began to light up the countryside in eastern South Dakota, Iroquois had an REA band. It obtained the designation of *national* REA band—the only one of its kind in the country—and its leader was an experienced band man, Floyd Aughenbaugh. He was a local farmer who had been a band member while in the navy; before him his father had conducted bands in Iowa. So many Aughenbaughs played in the REA band that it almost seemed like a family band. There was also a large group of Ekmans from Cavour, nine miles west of Iroquois.

The concerts usually started around eight; by the time they

were done an hour and a half or two hours later (with time out for a pop break), the last rays of sunlight had faded, and it was time for parents to get their children home to bed and to get some rest themselves for another hard day's work. The streets were roped off—north and south, east and west—in the afternoon, and the cars getting there first obtained the front row. People who wanted to leave early were out of luck; had there been a fire, it would have been a mess. Fortunately, no fires or major disasters ever marred the enjoyment of the concerts, but fires did play a major role in the history of small towns like Iroquois over the years. A comparison of the 1950 photograph with a current one of the same corner vividly underscores this.

Several years after the 1950 picture was taken, a fire destroyed the two buildings on the left, housing a grocery store (it has a Coca-Cola sign), a drugstore, and an electric light and appliance business. Around 1956, as the town celebrated its seventy-fifth anniversary, several local citizens built a permanent bandstand on the now vacant lot next to the meat market on the corner. People would come and sit on chairs or on the grass to listen to the concerts, but things were never quite the same as before, when they could pull up in their cars around the bandstand on Main Street. Not long thereafter, the meat market building, which by then had been converted into a restaurant and supper club, went up in flames, too. At one time in the life cycle of small towns, fires had been taken in stride, and people had simply rebuilt, usually on a larger and more elaborate scale than before. By the 1950s and 1960s, however, replacement costs for burned-out buildings were increasing and business owners had to measure carefully the probable future returns against the very concrete and steep current costs. As a result, many lots remained vacant.

Driving down Main Street in Iroquois today, you will discover an attractive one-story brick bank building, the Farmers and Merchants Bank, on the corner where the meat market once stood. The only business building on the west side of that block, its presence symbolizes the continuing economic viability of the town. On the corner across the street to the north stands the only other building in the two-block business district built in the last quarter century—the new post office, constructed in 1987. It stands on the site of the old Knecht store. Charles Knecht arrived in Iroquois early and built his store there in 1881. For many years it was Pete's Home Store, and then Robert and Velma Leichtenberg had a store there until he died in 1975. Then it was a ceramics shop for several years until it, too, burned to the ground.

Now nothing occupies the three lots north of the post office. Beyond that are three old store buildings, two of them empty and one housing Scott's Tavern, the only business on the west side of that block. At the end of the street is an old hotel, a hopping business during the years when travelers could walk right over from the depot. Now it is empty, a visible reminder of the days when the railroad was the lifeblood of the town. Across Main Street on the east side of the block one business, Wonderland Ceramics, operates out of an old lumberyard. Besides the fire hall, the rest of the block is vacant lots. South, on the block across from the bank, are another vacant store building, a locker plant, an antiques store, and the American Legion hall.

The antiques store, called the "New to You" store, is located in the old Fischer and Grier hardware store. Like most store buildings in towns along the highway, this one has lived several lives, serving, among other things, as a furniture store under several different proprietors. It had been vacant for several years before being taken over by Nila Ondricek and her husband, Myron. She grew up in Huron, he in a Czech community near Highmore. They spent a decade in Kansas before returning to Huron, where they started an antiques business in a stable near the fairgrounds. Needing a bigger building, they moved into the old lumberyard in Iroquois in 1985, and after just a few months there they moved their "stuff" (Nila prefers that term to "junk") over a block into this solid old brick building. Wonderland Ceramics moved into the lumberyard when they moved out.

You can find almost anything imaginable in Ondriceks', and several dozen of each, at that: plates, pipes, lamps, mirrors, radios, coat hooks, jars, bottles, pots, pans, glasses, tobacco cans, boxes of every description, books, chairs, beds, washboards, roller skates, mugs, player piano rolls, and knickknacks. It is a nostalgia-seeker's paradise, everything laid out and neatly arranged. Myron attends lots of sales, sometimes running over to Minnesota, but most of the items (probably 90 percent of them) are from around this area. Thus, the New to You store contains a treasure trove of eastern South Dakota's material culture. If you want to discover how people lived around here during the past century, this would be a good place to start. If you understood or could imagine what people did with all of these artifacts, you could reconstruct their daily lives.

But what if you were looking for things from Iroquois itself? I asked Nila Ondricek how much Iroquois history could be found in the store. "Well, there isn't anything," she replied, perhaps overstating the case a bit. "Because Velma—if we've got it, she buys it!" Aha, I thought, so that's where Velma gets her stuff—at least some of it. Besides the pictures on the wall, Velma had dug out a box of mementos and historical items for me to look at in her cafe. Among other things it contained a decorative plate illustrated with the picture of a store building interior, compliments of J. B. Dickey, M.D., Drugs and Stationery, Iroquois; a shoe shine brush from Pete's Home Store, Dry Goods and Groceries, Iroquois; several thermometers, one in the shape of a plastic key advertising Vogelman's Blacksmith, Welding and Repairing, Iroquois; ink blotters from the Home Insurance Company, New York, "the largest fire insurance company in America," D. F. Wilmarth, agent, Iroquois; an ashtray with messages on four sides advertising "Clean Comfortable Rooms, Hotel Iroquois / Soft Drinks, Meals, Lunches / I Swiped This From American Cafe / Iroquois, So. Dak. on Trail 14, The Hunters Paradise"; a keychain distributed by Woodall Produce, Iroquois; a button announcing "Bicentennial '76, Iroquois Celebration, June 15 & 16"; another for the Iroquois centennial, 1880–1980, June 17–28; and several other items. Here in a box in Velma's cafe is contained, in part at least, the history of the businesses that have made Iroquois a going community for more than a century.

On one of my visits to the cafe, Velma dragged out a ledger that I only briefly glanced at and set aside after noticing that it contained the proceedings of old court cases. In my conversation with Nila Ondricek, she told me that her husband bought the ledger at an auction and that when Velma learned about it she just had to have it. The Ondriceks reluctantly parted with it. They, after all, are really Huron folks, and it means more to Iroquois residents like Velma. A closer look at the volume revealed that it is the docket book from 1912 to 1914 of justice of the peace court cases, which broke down mainly into public intoxication, debt collection, petty theft, and, increasingly during this period, automobile speeding (going over twelve miles per hour). Thus, the history of the community floats about, hidden away in attics until the houses are sold or someone dies and they are auctioned off to the highest bidder—someone from Iowa or California who is merely curious and likes to latch on to old things, or someone from around town who knows or knew someone who did know the people whose stories are recounted in the memorabilia.

Toward the front of the New to You store is a box with several hundred snapshots and studio portraits of people, young and old, male and female, fat and thin, well-dressed and shabby, happy and dour-looking. Some of the faces are intriguing; most are nondescript. All are unidentifiable. These are pictures that meant something to the subjects themselves and to their families, friends, and neighbors. Now, after years hidden away in albums, drawers, boxes, bins, and attics, they have lost their human connection. Now and then someone recognizes a familiar or identifiable face and purchases the photo as a keepsake. Mostly, however, these are generic photographs—meaningless to the viewer except that they might illustrate some general insight into people and the human personality. Nila Ondricek whimsically has taped a little sign to the box with the words, "Instant Relations—25¢ each." Once these pictures told a human story, embodying biography and history. Now, except as curiosities, they are lost testimonies of place and time, except in rare instances where someone is able to make a connection.

The precariousness of our memory of, and connection to, the past came home for me once again as I left the antiques store and went next door into the American Legion hall. The Senior Citizens have their get-togethers here, and potlucks, socials, and community events are usually held here, too. I was drawn to the framed pictures hanging on the walls, especially a wonderful bird's-eye photograph of the town taken in 1912 from atop one of the trackside elevators. Such views were commonplace in the early 1900s; towns of a few hundred people could be captured in a single wide-angle photograph. In the great majority of towns around here, most of the houses and businesses were located on one side of the track. Josephine Stroub, who as a child of two arrived here with her parents in a railroad immigrant car in 1909, remembers the days when people living on the north side of the tracks literally were on the wrong side of the tracks. "It used to be that when you were on the north side of the tracks you were nobody," she said. "You had to live on the south side of the tracks to be somebody. Now the new houses or the nice houses are north of the tracks!"

Stroub has lived in and around Iroquois nearly all her life. I asked her to tell me what happened in some of the buildings in the picture. She worked in the post office for thirty-four years and can recall the days when six mail trains a day went through Iroquois. The depot was a busy place. The hotel across from the depot, after closing its regular operations, would open up for hunters during pheasant season, which was a great boon for the local economy. The opera house used to be the place where most of the town's social events took place. The Modern Woodmen of America and the Odd Fellows had their meetings upstairs. Traveling troupes and local talent groups staged their plays downstairs, which also served as a basketball court for many exciting, hard-fought games. During the great flu epidemic around the end of World War I it served as a hospital, and a lot of people died there. Of course, dances were held in the opera house, too, as was the case in opera houses and halls up and down the line. But now, like the old brick school across the street, which had just been completed when the bird's-eye photograph was taken in 1912, the opera house is gone, the depot is gone, and most of the stores are gone. What remains are memories and photographs like this one. It's a picture that conjures up a town that on the surface may seem sleepy and slow but over the span of years has been constantly changing.

There are reminders, however, of what the town once was—in these pictures and in the ones down at the cafe, in scrapbooks and photo albums in people's homes, in the stories people tell and the memories they retain, in physical artifacts like the old movable bandstand, and in the buildings themselves. Here are people who remember their past, naturally and usually unselfconsciously, and they are proud of that heritage. Once in a while they go out of their way to leave the imprint of the past in a visible way. The old bandstand now is in a vacant lot on the east edge of town. The Methodists saved the bell that had rung in their original frame church, which was moved to Osceola many years ago. When the Osceola congregation disbanded, the bell was brought back to Iroquois as a memento and put up on a standard in front of the ornate brick church the Methodists constructed in 1920. Then, when they tore that down several years ago and built a third church across the street, the bell was moved and is a reminder to the congregation of their past.

The old bandstand, with a fresh coat of paint.

Down the street a couple of blocks, the bell from the old school (the one in the 1912 bird's-eye photograph) was preserved and placed under a protective cover on a pedestal in front of the new school. Maynard Sweet, who's been a schoolteacher, silo salesman, real estate broker, and sheep farmer, among other things, over the course of his seventy-five years, had persuaded people to save it, but it was in the lumberyard for a time before it was put on display several years ago. The bell in the Catholic church tower can't be seen, but it rings out for church services the same way it used to in the bell tower of the old Catholic church in town (originally a Congregational church, the edifice now stands abandoned on Main Street).[4]

Bells are appropriate historical reminders of where small towns have come from; in the beginning they announced that a town had "arrived." One of the first things the Congregationalists did in De Smet after building their church was to order a bell from a Baltimore foundry. "This is the first church bell in Kingsbury County," local newspaper editor Mark Brown enthused, celebrating the occasion. "So, one after another the institutions, the refinements, the social, intellectual and religious privileges of America's Christian civilization become naturalized and at home where only four years since was but a vast wilderness of prairie grass, whitened by the bones of the bison and the poles of Indian wigwams still standing, but now filled with a population of intelligent, moral and enterprising people."[5] A century ago bells symbolized for the settlers the distinction between savagery and civilization. Now the bells in Iroquois celebrate a history and a community spirit that its residents hope will help maintain a viable community and stave off the oblivion that comes to towns unable to withstand the economic pressures threatening their existence at the end of the twentieth century.

HURON

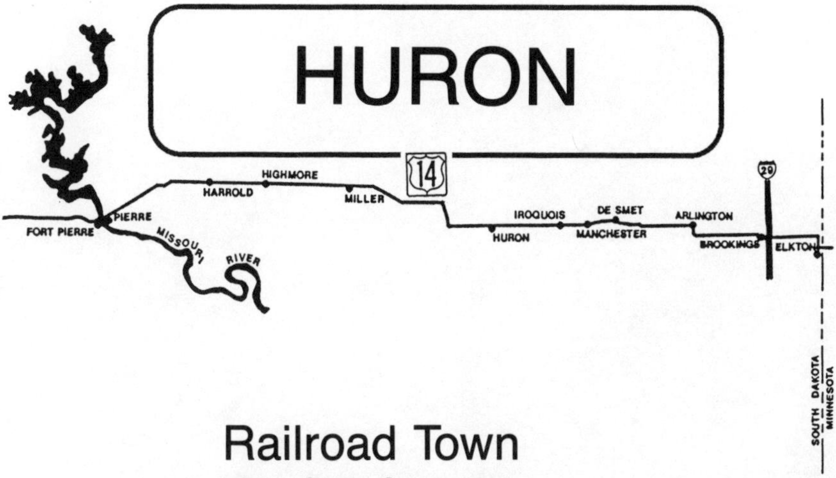

Railroad Town on the James

All of the towns highlighted in this study are situated along the route of the old Chicago and North Western Railway, but Huron was truly a railroad town in the sense that the railroad dominated its daily activities and defined its character. The railroad's decision in 1877 to establish a division point where its projected line into Dakota Territory would cross the James River immediately guaranteed that town's dominant status (at least in the beginning) among the towns to be located along the route and fixed its early lines of development.[1]

Huron, as a result, was blessed by its location—doubly so, in fact. Not only did its position on the river grant it a special status but it was also centrally placed in the East River region of southern Dakota Territory.[2] Its location in the middle of a large agricultural hinterland sparked visions among Huron's early-day entrepreneurs of a regional commercial center capable of rivaling Omaha, Denver, and maybe even Minneapolis. The history of Huron, in large measure, is the story of how those extravagant hopes and dreams were short-circuited. Though Huron was and is one of eastern South Dakota's more vital and progressive towns, its growth was stunted and in recent years its population has hovered around 13,000. In the tension between its residents' aspirations on the one hand and their need to accommodate themselves to more limited realities on the other lies the dramatic plot of Huron's history.[3]

Visible evidence of these disappointments and accommodations awaits travelers who slow down and turn off Highway 14 for

Chicago and North Western train crossing the James River bridge in 1911. (From Dorothy Huss et al., *Huron Revisited,* Huron, S.Dak.: East Eagle Co., 1988; courtesy of Dakotaland Museum, Huron)

a drive through Huron. As you head south along the main street—Dakota Avenue—looking to the right across the railroad tracks you will observe the old Chicago and North Western depot. Just beyond it the old Great Northern depot stands empty now, a picturesque reminder of the golden days of passenger travel. The much larger Chicago and North Western depot is now in use as a furniture and tire warehouse. Directly north of it across the tracks is the old Swift and Company packing plant, windows broken here and there, a monument to the days when business along the track was humming.

On the east side of Dakota Avenue, an antiques shop now occupies the old brick freight warehouse that used to be busy, and farther down the tracks a couple of hundred yards are the old shops and roundhouse. Most of the roundhouse bays have been torn out, and a handful of employees now are sufficient where once several hundred employees worked. The Dakota, Minnesota and Eastern Railroad purchased this branch line from the Chicago and North Western in September 1986 and runs the operation as cheaply and efficiently as possible. If it didn't, it would not be in business at all.[4]

South along Dakota Avenue are several blocks of stores, eating places, a theater, post office, and other buildings. Standing tall on the horizon at the corner of Dakota and Fourth Street is

Chicago and North Western depot today.

the eight-story Dakota Plaza Building, with stores and offices on the first floor and apartments above. Until the 1970s it was the Marvin Hughitt Hotel, named appropriately after the great Chicago and North Western executive whose vision was responsible for the location of Huron in the first place. In 1877 while driving across the Dakota prairie in a buckboard to reconnoiter the area, he chose this location for a railroad division point. When the hotel, which was built by Huron Elks Lodge 444, opened in 1921, it stood as the most imposing structure (except the state capitol) along the whole line of the railroad in eastern South Dakota.[5] Ironically, despite its name it soon became a witness to dramatic postwar transportation changes that radically diminished the railroad's importance. Picture postcards printed in the 1920s show automobiles parked around it, presaging the day when rail passenger traffic would drastically decline, causing the older hotels located conveniently near the depots in various communities to close their doors. Eventually large, modern hotels like the Marvin Hughitt that catered to automobile traffic were forced out of business, too, victims of the auto motels strung out on the approaches into towns.

Farther south along Dakota Avenue for half-a-dozen blocks or so extends a strip catering to the drive-in crowd. Filling stations, grocery stores, convenience stores, and half-a-dozen fast-food places serve the fast-paced, automobile-oriented life-style of today. Lying between this strip and the downtown business section is a park with a large bandshell at one end where concerts, Memorial Day ceremonies, and other community get-togethers are held. The park, which is two blocks long, is only half a block wide on the west side of Dakota Avenue. I wondered aloud about its width when our family was in town for the state fair during the fall of 1985 and stopped for a picnic lunch near the bandshell. None of us had a clue, but the answer soon emerged when I began to inquire into the history of the town.

It turned out that this was once part of the "Capitol Square" that had been set aside as the site for the state capitol, which Huron boosters hoped to obtain once statehood was achieved. The four-square-block area stands out clearly in an 1883 bird's-eye drawing of the town done by William Valentine Herancourt of Dubuque, Iowa.[6] Dakota Avenue would have had to detour around the square had a capitol building ever actually gone up there. The sun on the horizon in the drawing forecasted the ultimate fate of this aspiration. Being located in the west, it is a setting sun, not a rising one. Huron's capital dreams died aborning. For several years, the town was in the thick of the battle for the capital. In the process of trying to attain it, however, Huronites actually damaged rather than enhanced their chances for growth and development.

The year 1883 witnessed several major developments in Dakota Territory. This was the heyday of the Great Dakota Boom, which saw southern Dakota Territory's population explode from 82,000 to 249,000.[7] Huron found itself ensconced in the middle of the action; waves of homesteaders flooded through the region in search of an ideal patch of ground that would make them their fortunes—or at least provide decent livings for themselves and their families. Huron obtained a federal land office in 1882, as the line of settlement rapidly proceeded westward toward the Missouri River.[8]

It was also in 1883 that Governor Nehemiah G. Ordway teamed up with Alexander McKenzie of Bismarck, in the northern part of the territory, to engineer the removal of the capital from Yankton to Bismarck. During the early maneuvers in the legislative session that winter, a bill was introduced to move the capital to Huron. Designed as a trial balloon rather than seriously aimed at picking a specific location, it was quickly buried. A nine-person capital commission was later established to choose a site. Huron's appetite had been whetted, however, and it made a bid of $100,000 and offered to donate 160 acres of land for the capitol grounds in its effort to sway the commission.[9]

The nine commissioners visited all of the towns in the running to listen to their arguments and observe their locales. The dark and gloomy weather prevailing in Huron on May 9 when they arrived there accurately forecasted the town's chances in the balloting. When the time came eventually to vote, only G. A. Mathews, a lawyer from Brookings whose partner J. O'B. Scobey was serving as chairman of the Territorial Council at the time, cast his ballot for Huron. But not for the town's lack of trying. The commissioners were treated to a lavish banquet at the Wright House, one of Huron's several hotels, where they listened to glowing tributes regarding Huron's many assets, including a telephone exchange with sixty patrons, two daily newspapers, an agricultural journal, a board of trade, and eighteen hundred industrious citizens.[10] The secretary of the commission, Ralph W. Wheelock, a newspaper editor from the rival town of Mitchell, was considerably impressed by the appearance of Huron. "It is booming (if the term is permissible in this western country)," he wrote, "and while it has not very many substantial business buildings, it is compactly put together, and its residences inside and out surpass anything I have yet seen in Dakota. Still there is a feverish atmosphere about the place, and its rapid growth reminds me of the swift, uncertain motion of a steam engine when the governor belt has snapped."[11] The town's most valuable attributes, and the points its boosters fixed on during the early, heady days of development, were its central location in populous eastern Dakota Territory and its railroads—already in place and soon to be built (they hoped).

Although preliminary moves were made as early as 1879, the

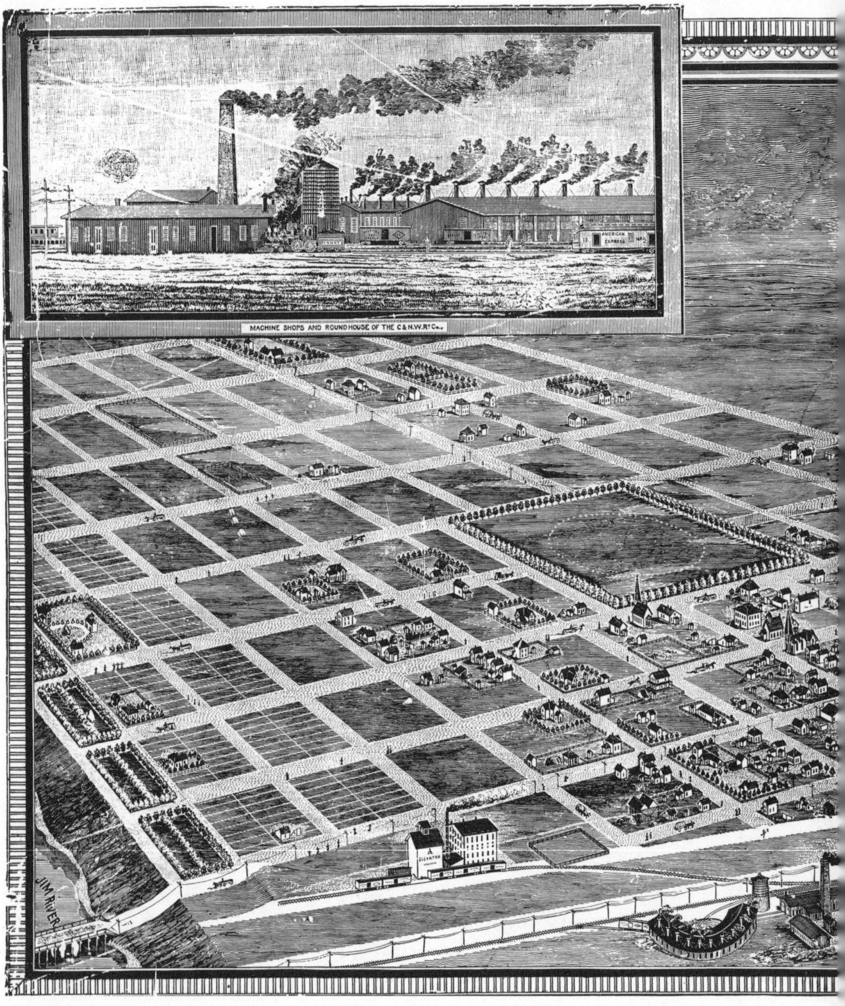

An 1883 bird's-eye view of Huron. (Courtesy of Dakotaland Museum, Huron)

effective beginning of the South Dakota statehood movement can be dated to a mass meeting held in Huron on June 19, 1883.[12] Acting under authorization of a bill passed over Governor Ordway's veto during the legislative session, a group of pro-statehood delegates convened and proceeded to call a constitutional convention to meet in Sioux Falls in September. These activities failed to obtain any response from Washington, so two years later the process was repeated. An almost identical constitution was

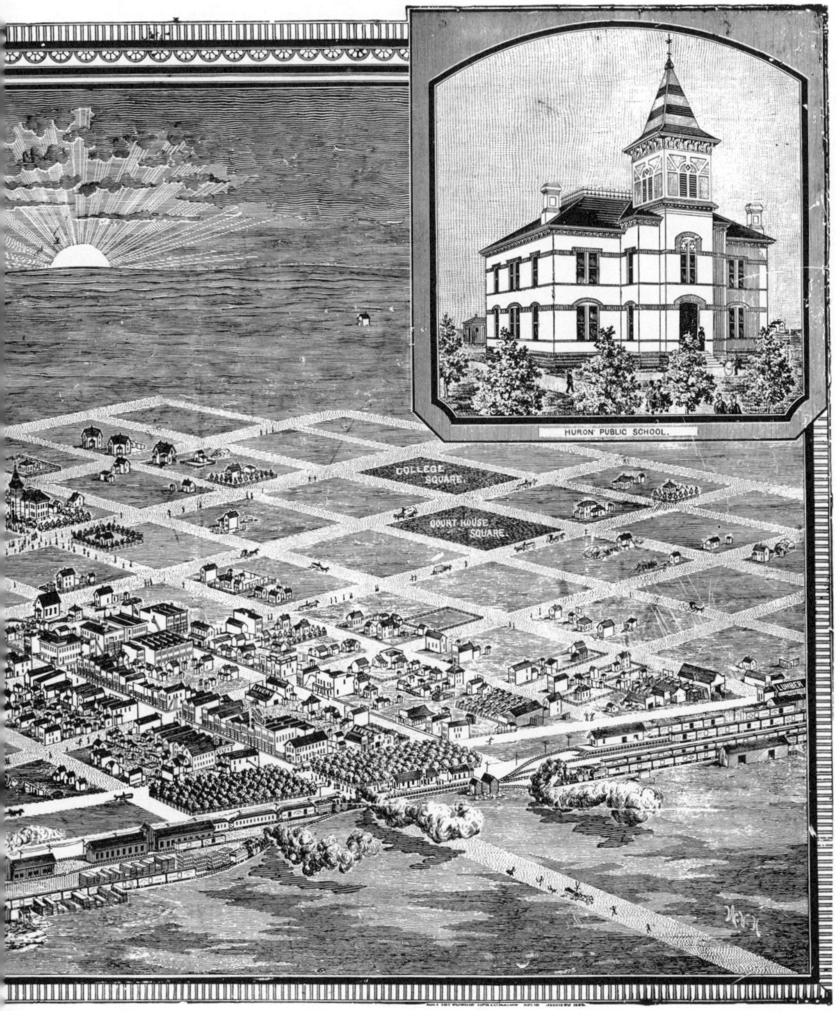

written, but in 1885 the statehood seekers went a step further. This time they actually conducted an election and went through the motions of choosing two U.S. senators, a slate of state officers, and state legislators as well as a location for the new state capital. In this balloting, Huron was selected over five other candidates, obtaining 12,695 votes, with Pierre as its nearest rival with 10,574 votes.[13]

Huron's victory in the straw poll greatly encouraged the town's go-getters. If they could capture the capital, they believed it would guarantee Huron's future greatness. For the next four years, until the arrival of statehood in 1889, Huron retained its unofficial designation as capital of the prospective state of South Dakota, something it hoped it could convert into official status once all the legal hurdles were negotiated. That prospect at least partly compensated for the hardships the town shared with its neighbors in the region after 1886, when drought and declining agricultural prices depressed the economy, halted population growth, and put most new construction projects on hold. The stage was being set for the Populist protest of the 1890s, but for Huronites depressed economic conditions were partially offset by grand dreams revolving around the capital they hoped would someday be theirs.[14]

Depressed economic conditions scuttled most of the seemingly limitless railroad schemes that were in the planning stage during the mid-1880s. One line actually did build to Huron in 1888—the Duluth, Watertown, and Pacific Railroad (later the Great Northern)—linking with Watertown and from there with Minneapolis.[15] While the others had to be put on hold, local citizens continued to be hopeful that at least some of them would eventually get translated from paper into reality. Huron could still argue that the rail lines would someday be theirs, and their favorable geographic location was unalterable fact. Central location, however, was to some degree a matter of opinion. One had to ask, central with regard to what? Huron's probable rival for the capital was Pierre, 110 miles to the west and virtually equidistant between Dakota Territory's eastern and western boundaries. During the 1885 session, in fact, just two years after the capital had been moved to Bismarck, Pierre managed to get a bill through both houses of the legislature to move it once again, this time from Bismarck to Pierre. However, Governor Gilbert Pierce, who was disturbed by rumors that Pierre lobbyists had bribed several legislators and who did not want to make the capital location a perennial political controversy, vetoed the bill.[16]

When statehood arrived in 1889, along with choosing state

officials, South Dakota's electorate also were required to designate a temporary capital that would serve for a year until a permanent capital site would be determined in a second vote in 1890. The contest quickly settled down to a battle between the two rivals on the Chicago and North Western line—Huron and Pierre. Both campaigned vigorously. Huron tried hard to capitalize on its designation in 1885 as temporary capital. Many of the two towns' activities were all in fun and aboveboard—buttons, banners, newspaper articles, rallies, parades, songs, even little boxes of dirt to demonstrate the superior qualities of the land in the surrounding region. Some, however, were highly questionable.[17] "To say that it was a campaign of wholesale corruption of voters is to put the matter in its mildest form," state historian Doane Robinson wrote later. "Practically every newspaper in the state was subsidized in the interest of some candidate, and many voters were subsidized by all of them."[18]

Both towns touted their railroad connections and predicted more lines would soon be built to them. Their propaganda suggested each would soon be a rail hub. The Pierre *Free Press,* for example, ran a map showing seven railroads running out of the city, including two going west to the Black Hills.[19] In these assertions they let their dreams and aspirations run away with them. Maps showing such rail lines were distributed. Pierre's weightiest asset—its central location in the state—drove Huron advocates to develop a map demonstrating, at least to their own satisfaction, that Huron was actually the center town in the state. Already Huron touted itself as the convention center of South Dakota, with good reason. At least seven major conventions, including both the Democratic and Republican state conventions, were held there in 1889.[20] In the first place, Huronites argued, Huron lay in the center of the populated parts of the state. Secondly, they asserted that Pierre was located on the edge of a desolate, forbidding wilderness west of the Missouri River that would never attract many white people to it. The opening for settlement of nine million acres of former Sioux Indian reservation land through the Sioux Land Cession of 1889 prevented Huronites from claiming that the land was totally unaccessible, but in their viewpoint things remained virtually unchanged. They even went so far as to argue that people living in the Black Hills region would find Huron easier to get to than Pierre, because they would prefer to take the train through northern Nebraska and then cut north to Huron, rather than travel by wagon across desolate West River trails.[21]

Especially innovative were several land schemes initiated

during the capital contest. Huron's number one go-getter, real estate dealer William T. Love, sold lots on the southwest edge of town on a contingency basis, requiring one-fifth down and the remainder of the purchase price only after Huron won the election. Imitators concocted similar plans, setting off a "veritable mania" of land speculation, according to one historian. The West Side Addition Company offered choice lots for $20 apiece, requiring an additional $30 payment if Huron won the election but nothing more if it lost. Most noteworthy were the activities of the Woonsocket Investment Company, named after a town twenty miles south of Huron. Its sole purpose being to realize a profit from the capital contest, the company offered to trade 10,000 votes in return for choice city lots from one of the capital contenders. It sold shares to investors, which it said would be redeemed in lots in the winning city, promising the plungers that the lots they thus obtained would rise substantially in value once the city the company gave its backing to obtained the capital. It expected its choice to become a self-fulfilling prophesy, since the announcement of its decision would signal everyone associated with the scheme to vote for that town for capital. After Huron and other towns failed to cooperate with the company, Pierre came around and deeded it a number of city lots. When the company announced a month before the election that it was placing its bets on Pierre, Huronites rose up in righteous fury. But there was nothing they could do about it. The fact of the matter was Huron had been outmaneuvered.[22]

In the end, Pierre's central geographic location probably more than anything else carried it to victory in the final balloting (by a vote of 27,096 to 14,944), but Huron was not content to let it go at that.[23] Balloting on a permanent capital would occur in 1890, and this time Huron's boosters decided to let out all the stops. First, they persuaded Watertown, a town seventy-five miles to the northeast, to drop out of the fray so that residents of east-central South Dakota would not split their votes between the two. A group of local businesspeople formed the Capital Investment Company, headed by Mayor Harvey J. Rice, to coordinate their activities. A $60,000 campaign chest—enough for starters—was collected after a petititon had been signed by most of the town's businesspeople, and before the year was out, several times that much apparently was spent. A three-story State Capitol Hotel costing an estimated $75,000 was built for hosting legislators during semiannual legislative sessions. William T. Love returned with another land scheme, this time the sale of lots fronting an artificial lake south of town that was to be constructed by building a thirty-foot dam across a creek called Stony Run. A plush resort named Lincoln Park was to be part of the development. In addition, the Farmers' Alliance, which had grown dramatically since its founding in the territory six years earlier, announced shortly before the balloting that it was planning to build a new four-story office building in town.[24]

A heavy propaganda effort designed to insert favorable stories in local newspapers around the state achieved considerable success. While building up the virtues of Huron, the stories and editorials denegrated Pierre as an isolated town situated on the edge of a desolate Indian reservation with no realistic hopes of further railroad building to it in the future. The cost of these and other activities engaged in by the Huron propagandists ran to far more than the original $60,000 allocated. Before it was over, the city council sold off its waterworks—valued at $100,000—for only $45,000 in order to help finance its efforts. The city also sold $14,000 worth of "public improvement" warrants to conduct the capital fight. Even the board of education got into the act, selling $60,000 worth of school bonds, with proceeds turned over to the capital committee.[25]

All of Huron's efforts were in vain, it turned out, for in the final tally Pierre hung onto the capital with 41,969 votes to Huron's 34,610. Unfortunately, Huron's drive not only failed, it seriously undermined the town's efforts at growth and development in later years, for it had run up a considerable debt, which took the town many years to pay off. In addition, political strife and bitterness, otherwise containable within reasonable limits, were greatly exacerbated by continuing debates over the wisdom of the failed capital scheme, and in the wake of these controversies prospective business enterprises hesitated to locate in Huron during the early 1900s.[26]

For dedicated town boosters, however, failing to obtain the capital constituted only a temporary setback. The town continued to be the division point on the Chicago and North Western Railway and remained the largest town on the route for many years. Several hundred railroad employees contributed to the town's economy, as did company expenditures for supplies and materials. Over time, a number of small industries dependent on the railroad developed, including produce houses, packing plants, mills, wholesale distributors, a Standard Oil warehouse, and several small manufacturing plants.[27]

Huron capitalized on its railroad connections and favorable geographical location to promote itself as the center city of South Dakota, even if it could not be the capital. "Huron is unquestionably the metropolis of Central Dakota," the *Dakota Huronite* had asserted in 1884.[28] From early on, and up to the present, Huron has promoted itself as an ideally located convention center and headquarters town. "Hardly a week passes throughout the year that Huron is not host to one or more district or state gatherings," noted an advertising brochure put out by the Chamber of Commerce in 1930. "The city's accessibility and its hotel accommodations make Huron an ideal convention center."[29] In fashioning their publicity, Huron boosters demonstrated considerable ingenuity in devising maps designed to prove that Huron was, in fact, the center town of eastern South Dakota.

More than any of its competitors along the railroad, Huron's boosters envisioned greatness for their community and aspired to growth and influence. The first city directory, published in 1883, observed that "from the day the first stake was driven to the present time her progress has been unceasing, rapid and substantial. Springing into existence like the magic mining towns of the West she has not the dangers of as rapid a decay, for her wealth is all 'in sight,' and will pan out for years to come, increasing as they pass."[30] Until World War II Huron remained comfortably ahead of its two major rivals—Brookings and Pierre—for dominance along the Dakota Central branch line, with a population more than double either of theirs. As the decades proceeded, however, it became increasingly apparent that spectacular growth was not in store for the town. Its aspirations had to be downsized to fit reality. Gradually, Huron's citizens accommodated themselves to their status as a modest-sized town, drawing its sustenance from an area that was unable to support a city as large as Omaha or even Sioux Falls.

Huron remained a railroad town, full of activity around the train yards, the squeal of flanged wheels rubbing against the rails, creating a symphony of sound at any time of day. Bars, restaurants, and pool halls were full of railroad talk as engineers, brakemen, conductors, and machinists congregated there during their off-hours. Local union halls brought workers together for recreation as well as business, and the camaraderie of railroad families penetrated the community. Railroad workers and their families made up a large segment of the population. Of 1,860 adults listed in the 1905–6 *Huron City Directory,* 271 of them were employed by the Chicago and North Western Railway as engineers, conductors, timekeepers, dispatchers, machinists, carpenters, and boilermakers and in other occupations.[31]

During the fall of 1989 I had an opportunity to lead a series of discussions at the Huron Senior Center based on a book of readings put out by the National Council on the Aging called *We*

Got There on the Train.[32] For six weeks, between a dozen and two dozen people joined our discussions. Many participants had either worked for the railroad themselves or came from railroad families. Most of them retained vivid and fond memories of working or riding on the trains and action around the depots and the train yards. Ninety-six-year-old Phoebe Bard, whose coal-miner father moved his family in 1906 from Streeter, Illinois, to try his hand at farming just north of Huron, recalled the bumpiness of the train ride as her family rode out to South Dakota. On their farm every morning they could hear the 6:00 whistle from the roundhouse as it blared across the prairie.

Reuben Funk, a former section foreman who worked for thirty-four years on the railroad, recalled that as young men in the 1930s he and his buddies would catch free rides on freight trains, hoboing it to the grainfields of North Dakota, Minnesota, and other states. Once, while riding from Rapid City to Huron on top of a train, he took a wide belt and ran it underneath the walkway on the boxcar and through his belt loops so that if he drifted off to sleep he wouldn't fall off the train. Such belts were necessary items, especially when passing through tunnels where the air might cause the men to pass out.

Railroad workers were highly conscious of time. Otto Erickson, who worked as a brakeman for fifteen years and then as a conductor for another twenty before retiring in 1975, told me, "One of the most important things to a railroad man was his watch, and it would be *exactly* on time, not to the hour or minute, but to the *second.* In other words, if it was 8:14, the engineer and the conductor would compare times, and they'd say 8:14 and twenty seconds before each trip. And the engineer would compare it with his fireman. And the conductor would compare time with his brakeman. So there really would be four watches on the train." People compared watches upon reporting for work, and every hour the dispatcher in the roundhouse would obtain naval observatory time from the telegraph wire so they'd have it right to the second. For railroad workers, time was of the essence. Its primary importance intruded incongruously into a small town culture that was used to moving to the pace of the horse and the rhythm of the changing seasons and for which seconds, minutes, and even hours were of less-than-crucial concern.

Norvin Brown, retired now for a little more than twenty years, told me he was a charter member of Lodge 859 of the Brotherhood of Railway Clerks. He attended union meetings secretly during the early days when the lodge was being organized for fear he might lose his job. He kept time for the crews in the roundhouse and was responsible for calling in workers as they were needed and for getting crews together for trains that were sent out in both directions on the line. His duties varied over a long career that eventually lasted more than fifty-one years. He was born in 1903 and started with the railroad at the age of thirteen, working on and off for three years before quitting school and going to work full-time at sixteen. His father, a switchman for the railroad, had been killed—crushed between two cars in the train yard where he was working—when the boy was only seven years old. But that trauma did not prevent Norvin from taking a job with the railroad himself when he became old enough to do so.

During the harvest season, hoboes arrived from all directions to work in the grainfields, Norvin told me. Once when a train pulled into Huron, the county sheriff, Verne Miller, climbed up on top of a boxcar and, gun in hand, cleared them all off, yelling, "OK, boys, this is the end of the line!" Such tactics never stopped the hoboes for long, however; they merely waited and grabbed another train out of town after the pressure slacked off. Railroad workers like Norvin can sit and tell you stories for hours. He grew up just a block away from Muriel Buck, whose future husband, Hubert Humphrey, worked in his dad's drugstore on Dakota Avenue.

Norvin's wife Irene also has stories to tell, because she worked at the Union News dining room in the Chicago and North Western depot for twenty years. It was a fancy place, with finger bowls and linen tablecloths and napkins. The tables occupied the south side of the depot on the west end, and there were several waitresses on duty most of the time, because things sometimes got hectic when trains stopped for a meal break. It was a good restaurant; some folks claimed it served the best food in town. Roast beef, steak, raw oysters on platters with ice, hamburgers, sandwiches—there was something for every taste. A lot of townspeople ate there too, especially on Sundays. Irene especially looked forward to railroad officials coming through town. All the waitresses wanted to wait on them because they'd often leave $1 tips.

The depot was a hot spot of activity in the railroad town of Huron. Noise and the bustle of activity kept things hopping. And always there was change. The original Chicago and North Western depot that went up when the town originated in 1880 was replaced three years later by the Depot Hotel, or Kent House: a Queen Anne-style building that was the most ornate and architecturally interesting of the depots along the line. Frederick Kent, who ran the restaurant and the hotel that were attached to the depot, took great pride in his operation, and for the town itself the depot constituted an ornament to show off to the world.[33] By

1910, however, it was becoming increasingly apparent that the Depot Hotel was getting too small for all the business in Huron, and demands for a modern replacement grew insistent. A fire that leveled it in February 1913 finally forced the railroad's hand, and a large brick depot was quickly built.[34] For the next half-century people came and went through it, but during the early 1960s, as passenger traffic was discontinued, it fell into disuse. Today, as mentioned earlier, it serves as a furniture and tire warehouse.

The glory days of the railroad have long since ended. Now freight trains ease their way down the tracks at reduced speeds. Passenger trains are no more. The hobo jungles are only a memory, and the old freight warehouse now stores antiques. Weeds grow between the sidetracks, and only a few stalls in the roundhouse remain. One Huron railroad buff has moved an old caboose into his backyard. Observant visitors to Huron can detect traces of its railroad past. It only takes a few conversations with oldtimers like Norvin and Irene Brown, Phoebe Bard, Otto Erickson, or Reuben Funk to recapture some of the spirit of Huron's glory days when the railroad ruled supreme. There in the physical remnants, in pictures, museums, and memories, a whole different world is discernible, bound up in the scream of the train whistle and the tick-tock, tick-tock of a railroad clock.

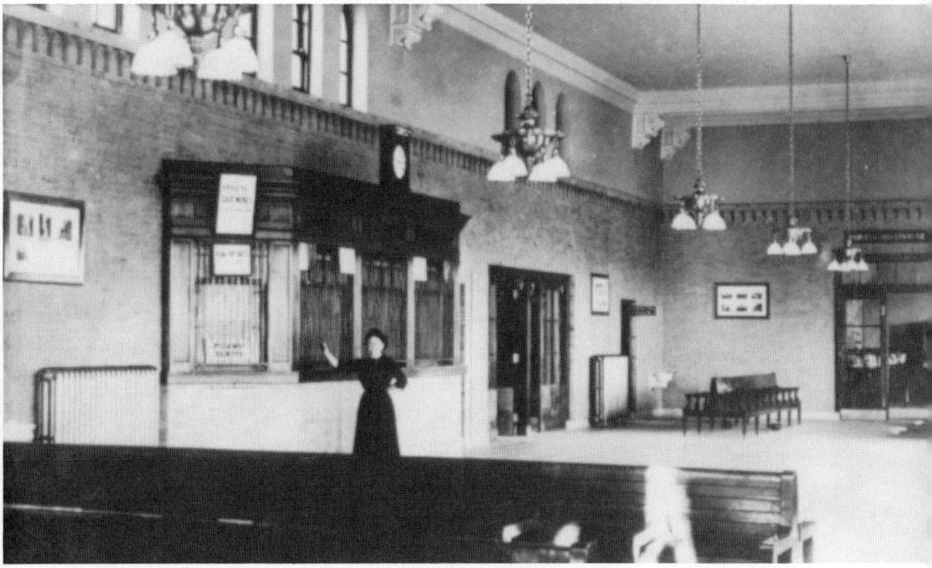

Interior view of the Chicago and North Western depot in 1914. (From Dorothy Huss et al., *Huron Revisted,* Huron, S.Dak.: East Eagle Co., 1988; courtesy of Dakotaland Museum, Huron)

MILLER

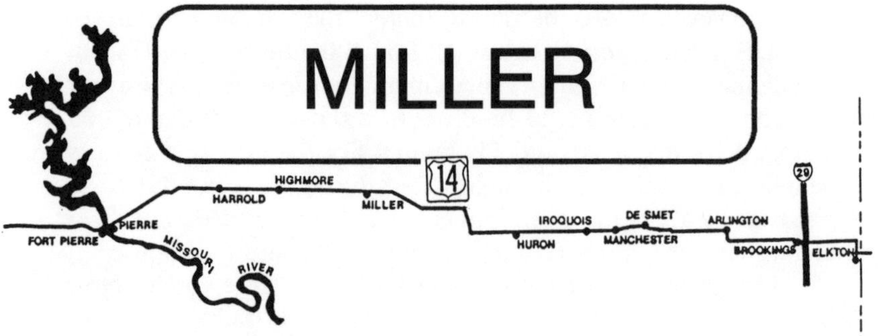

Guardians of Local History

Miller, with a population of 1,931 in 1980, is the largest town on Highway 14 between Huron and Pierre. Things needn't have turned out that way. People who are inclined toward the notion of historical inevitability should look at the story of Miller's victory over its rivals to become the premier town in Hand County. The exercise should cure them of the malady.[1]

The evidence of Miller's local supremacy lies visible on the landscape as one drives along the highway. Travelers heading west out of St. Lawrence will observe a sign on the edge of town announcing that Miller is just one mile down the road. Immediately the question arises, "Why would there be two towns located so closely together out here on the wide open prairie?" The ready reply is, "It wasn't meant to be that way."

In the beginning, the Chicago and North Western Railway, as it extended its tracks westward to the Missouri River in 1879 and 1880, located a series of nine sidings west of Huron along its right-of-way.[2] Originally consisting merely of blue rectangles on surveyors' maps, they would later contain the depots, water tanks, and other facilities necessary for rail traffic, and around them would be platted the towns that would serve the farmers using the railroad to ship their products to market. Had everything gone according to plan, towns at Siding No. 3 and Siding No. 4 would have emerged and probably contested with each other for the Hand County seat prize within short order. Elsewhere in the region, something like that generally happened.

But people have a way of complicating the best-laid plans. Enter now into the picture Henry J. Miller, a successful farmer, mill owner and lumberyard proprietor from Blairstown, Iowa, who was fifty-six years old in 1881 and interested in the prospects of his eight children (three others died in infancy). Only one was a girl; the other seven were boys and in need of a livelihood. Miller had already gained some experience in town site promotion, having unsuccessfully attempted in 1862 to interest a railroad in purchasing 360 acres of land he owned in Benton County, Iowa, for the purpose of starting a town there. Eight years later he failed in an effort to establish a settlement on 5,000 acres of land he had purchased in Texas. In 1879, however, his twenty-two-year-old son William set up a law practice in the new town of Audubon, Iowa, on a branch of the Chicago, Rock Island, and Pacific Railroad, and another son, Eudell, only twenty, joined William in establishing a furniture business there. They witnessed directly how the railroad influenced the choice of Audubon as the new county seat, and their stories about the process undoubtedly had an impact on their father.[3]

By 1881, the area around Blairstown was already beginning to seem crowded to some, and Henry J. Miller decided to give town promotion another try. Success at it would mean not only financial security for himself but also greater opportunity for his sons to get ahead. They were arriving at the age where they could help him in the project; four of them—William ("W. H."), Eudell ("E. J."), John, and Charles—eventually settled in the new town of Miller, which was located just two miles west of Siding No. 3 and twelve miles east of Siding No. 4 on the Dakota Central branch of the Chicago and North Western Railway. Personal acquaintance with the company's president, Marvin Hughitt, could not have hurt Henry J. Miller when he made a request for a new siding to be added between St. Lawrence (the town at Siding No. 3; its original name had been Rex) and Ree Heights (at Siding No. 4), which were somewhat slow in getting started in 1881. By quickly relocating themselves in Dakota Territory and booming their upstart town over its competitors, the Millers were able to create opportunities where none had appeared to exist before.

Henry J. Miller and his son E. J. first reconnoitered the area west of Huron in a team and wagon in July 1881, before settling on a location. On September 8, they returned to the spot with another son, John, and about two dozen friends and neighbors from the Blairstown and Audubon areas, laid out the town, and drew lots for locations in the town that the day before had been nothing but bare prairie. They had something going for them that their competitors to the east and west lacked—a ready-made population all set to come and to work together to promote the town.

In October a post office was established, with W. H. Miller taking over as postmaster. The following January 4, having traveled to Chicago to buy a printing press, he published the first issue of the Hand County *Press,* which he then used to boom the prospects of Miller and to encourage more settlers to come and take advantage of the opportunities to be had on the wide open prairies. Free copies of the paper were sent to people back East to advertise the virtues of the Dakota climate and soil.

That fall, Miller and St. Lawrence fought it out for designation as county seat in a battle not unlike scores of others waged all over the West during the period. For a town that had not originally been planned to be there at all, Miller started out with the advantage of the energies and skills of the Millers and the families they had brought along with them from Iowa, but the outcome of the county seat election was by no means foreordained. Charges and countercharges of fraud and bribery furiously flew back and forth. Both sides hurled every weapon they had at their disposal. In the end, the margin of victory may have resulted from Miller's greater success in importing "thirty-day voters" to support its cause (a thirty-day residence was required to be eligible to vote). St. Lawrence partisans allegedly hired an entire surveying crew from the Huron area to come in temporarily and pretend to stake land claims so they could vote for that town, while their Miller antagonists purportedly brought in between "thirty and forty cattle thugs from Fort Pierre" to vote for them. "Folding money" also allegedly was distributed in Ree Heights to influence votes, but the people there, who favored Miller by a ratio of about six to one, probably were more impressed by the fact that Miller was the closer town. The final tally showed Miller the victor, with 352 votes to 282 for St. Lawrence and 32 for Ree Heights.[4]

To the enterprise and drive of the Millers and the fateful vote for county seat several other factors must be added to account for Miller's relative success and growth while St. Lawrence and Ree Heights faded as competitors in succeeding years. Miller's businesspeople and professionals continued to push hard for their town. At one time five newspapers were operating there. The Hand County *Press* continued to be the most important of these, being taken over in 1883 by John A. Bushfield, the father of a future state governor. In 1882 Metropolitan Hall, which was used for dances, celebrations, school classes, and other community activities, was built. Four years later a large opera house went up and became the main community center. Crucial to the growth of the town was the tapping of a gushing artesian well in 1886. Not only did St. Lawrence fail in its effort to dig its own well, the expenses and increased taxes incurred drove many of its residents to Miller. A devastating blow to the prospects of both Ree Heights and St. Lawrence in 1889 was the disastrous fires that destroyed almost all of Ree Heights and much of St. Lawrence's business district. Drought and economic depression during the 1890s inflicted severe setbacks on Miller but were even more damaging to its two neighbors.[5]

Population of Hand County and three of its towns, 1890–1980

	1890	1900	1910	1920	1930	1940	1950	1960	1970	1980
Hand County	6,546	4,525	7,870	8,778	9,485	7,166	7,149	6,712	5,883	4,948
Miller	536	544	1,202	1,478	1,447	1,460	1,916	2,081	2,148	1,931
St. Lawrence	320	115	305	390	413	297	261	290	249	228
Ree Heights	(unincorporated)				339	258	254	188	183	88

Having established itself as the major town in the county, Miller maintained its dominance as the decades ticked by. The results are written clearly on the roadscape as one travels down Highway 14. Today St. Lawrence's Main Street consists mostly of boarded up buildings and vacant lots, while Miller sports two full blocks of business establishments. Ree Heights, which saw the highway relocate one mile north of it in 1936 and witnessed the death of railroad passenger service in 1962, now boasts only a grocery store and an implement business on its Main Street.

For someone wishing to learn something about Miller's history or about South Dakota and regional history, no better place could be found than the home of John and Ellebeth Pugh, who live at the west end of town. Enter their basement library and you'll be excused if you confuse it with a section of the public library downtown. In fact, on the subject of South Dakota, the Pughs' collection far exceeds that of the Miller Public Library, where Ellebeth recently retired as head librarian. The public library's several hundred books on South Dakota (many purchased because of Ellebeth's interest in the subject) pales in comparison to their personal collection, which contains approximately five thousand books. On a recent trip to Seattle, during which they may be exaggerating only slightly when they claim that they "stopped in every town that has a used book store," the Pughs picked up several dozen books on South Dakota history and literature and books by South Dakota authors to add to their collection. Such journeys enable them to strike many items from their want list, which now numbers "about twelve or thirteen hundred items," but they continue to add to the list almost as rapidly as they augment their collection, so its length remains relatively stable.

Visiting in August 1988, I perused the five stacks of shelves lined with books from floor to ceiling and I asked the Pughs what their principle of selection is. "Anything we can get our hands on," Ellebeth laughed. They insisted that they *do* set limits on what they will purchase, but when I asked what they are, they only shrugged and replied that they couldn't think of anything offhand. History, biography and autobiography, poetry, fiction, county and local history, church anniversary booklets, high school yearbooks, state government reports and documents, legislative journals, session laws, planning reports, county atlases, and a variety of other books and publications fill their shelves. Ellebeth, good librarian that she is, has catalogued most of the collection (it's hard to keep up with the task) on standard three-by-five-inch library cards, which are neatly filed away in drawers, arranged by author and title as well as by position on the shelf. She uses a memory typewriter to duplicate the cards for the different entries but sticks to the old Dewey decimal system of classification, which she feels comfortable with. Her husband John, a retired electrician, has his own system that he uses to enter each item separately into a computer. On their trips they take along his computer-generated lists to remind them which books they need and which ones they already have.

The evening I stopped in to talk to them, they had another visitor—Professor James McLaird of Dakota Wesleyan University in Mitchell. Like them, he does some book collecting and selling on the side. That night he brought along a large box full of items he thought they might be interested in. They picked out a dozen or so things to add to their collection. When I suggested that they might well have the best collection on South Dakota history anywhere, McLaird readily admitted the possibility. While the South Dakota State Historical Society and the state library possess good collections, they, like other state agencies, work with limited funds for making purchases and miss some things that get published. Nor do they have employees like the Pughs, who are able to roam the country from coast to coast combing used book stores for finds. They are quick to pick up any bibliographies that are published and integrate them into their own lists. One of Ellebeth's current projects is to construct an annotated bibliography of books on South Dakota by South Dakota authors. Other collections, like the Herman Chilsen Collection at the University of South Dakota or the one at the Center for Western Studies at Augustana College in Sioux Falls, contain many high-quality books but probably not as many overall as the Pughs' collection.

The Pughs' collection began when their daughter, a student at Black Hills State College in Spearfish, came home on vacations to visit. She'd stop at Wall Drug and pick up books to give to them, and they became enthused. Soon they were on the trail of South Dakota books. "The thing just grew," according to Ellebeth. Once, after making a big purchase at an auction, they began filling a rented truck with their loot. The weight of the books so flattened the tires that they had to remove some of the books and make another trip. McLaird let out during our conversation that he recently came across a person who told him about a takeoff on *The Wonderful Wizard of Oz,* set in the Black Hills. Ellebeth immediately responded, "I have to have it!" (The author of the original Oz books is L. Frank Baum, a onetime resident of Aberdeen.)

John pulled out one of their many maps, and we began perusing the old route of Highway 14. This was a 1930 Hand County map showing clearly where the highway used to go before it was hard-surfaced and rerouted a mile farther north on the section of the road west of Miller in 1936. Previously the highway had run directly through Miller and west of town about a mile before dipping south of the railroad tracks and then shooting west to Ree Heights and Highmore. Our discussion reminded John of the terrible accident that occurred at Death Curve, or Dead Man's Corner, about fifty years ago. Where the road curved to the south to cross the tracks, the turn was rather gradual, but once across the tracks motorists had to negotiate a hard right—virtually a ninety-degree angle—onto the stretch running parallel to the railroad. So many people had been injured, and some even killed, at the corner that a large concrete standard had been set up just off the side of the road and topped by a blinking red light to warn motorists about the turn.

One Saturday evening, a car at Ree Heights missed the turn and crashed into the concrete post, killing two of the passengers. The other two miraculously escaped death, although they suffered severe injuries. As townspeople tell the story, the men had been enjoying themselves that evening when they challenged the driver of another car to race back to Miller. They bet that they could get back to town faster on the old (gravel) highway than the others could make it on the new (blacktop) one, which ran a mile to the north and required an extra mile or two to get to Miller. They never made it home. John and Ellebeth were unable to remember just when the accident occurred, so she phoned their friend George Niederauer to ask about it.

In about five minutes George had the answer. It was on the evening of December 9, 1939, but he thought the race started in Highmore, not Ree Heights. Further asking around the next day engendered debate also about the size of the the concrete abutment (was it four feet square or six feet square?). Some further interesting information emerged. The flashing light atop it had been turned off after Highway 14 was rerouted to the north; with so few people traveling the old gravel road, it was thought it wouldn't be necessary anymore. The local paper provides facts about the people in the death car and about funeral arrangements, but it tells nothing about the real circumstances leading to the accident.[6] To learn about them we had to tap people's memories.

George Niederauer, the local history expert, has a unique storehouse of information on the buildings in Miller. If you want to know something about any business building in Miller, he's the guy to go to. He can also fill you in about many private homes in town. He moved a lot of them himself. After World War II he spent seven years in the business, moving, he guesses, five hundred buildings. About a tenth of them were houses he moved into Miller, four of them located together on a single block. With lumber expensive and in short supply and with many vacant houses and farm buildings standing empty on farms that had been consolidated into larger holdings, it made sense for people to make use of them on other locations.

George was six years old in 1924 when he moved to Miller with his parents and older brother and sister. He's lived there most of his life, although he and his family moved south of town for a while in the late 1920s and he worked for a while in Aberdeen in the late 1930s and then in Californian aircraft factories and shipyards during World War II. So, like other Millerites, he has memories of many of the buildings in town, such as the city auditorium, which replaced the old opera house in 1924 as the main gathering place for plays, Memorial Day services, and other community events; the Princess Theatre, where a dime would get you a show and a bag of popcorn on Saturday night; and the Vanderbilt Hotel, hard by the railroad tracks, with its fancy mansard roof, where traveling salesmen and saleswomen and others coming through town could stay in what for a town like Miller was elegant comfort. But what really got George going on the subject was the celebration of the town's centennial in 1981. He had missed out on most of the festivities of the diamond jubilee in 1956, since he was doing construction work at the time in another town.

To help celebrate the centennial, a local committee planned to have historical displays put in all of the store windows on Broadway. George helped with the research, and once he began, he found it irresistible. The centennial came and went, but he continued to wade through old abstracts and newspapers, carefully noting each transaction and change in the buildings and copying information from the newspapers about people who owned them and worked in them. Retirement left him with plenty of time, and he accumulated thousands of cards filled with details about each building on Broadway and all the major buildings in the rest of town. He bought a computer to help with the work but discovered that three-by-five-inch note cards worked better for him, so the new machine was left unused in the basement. By now there are ten shoe boxes full of cards on his desk in the dining room, and neatly stacked on shelves nearby are ten large three-ring binders containing hundreds of pictures of the town that were taken over the years. George scoured Miller for pictures and also copied photographs held by the South Dakota State Historical Society and anybody else who happened to have some. In this he cooperated closely with John and Ellebeth Pugh, who also made a set for the town library.

For the past couple of years, George has been content to go

George Niederauer with his research materials.

back and check dates and facts that he's already researched in the newspapers and deed abstracts. He's plowed his way through the Miller *Press* from its first issue on January 4, 1882, up to September 3, 1950. He has a file on every building he has researched, so if you want to find out something about the Princess Theatre or the Scenic, the Vanderbilt Hotel or Henshaw's or the Miller Hotel, the old opera house or the auditorium or Roll's Rink or the Metropolitan Building, or if you want to check out something about a pool hall or a grocery store or a filling station or the county courthouse, just ask him. It won't take him long to find the answer. I shouldn't have been surprised that it had only taken him about five minutes to tell us the date of the accident at Death Curve.

As we perused some of his photographs, we came across one taken by local photographer J. N. Templeman in early 1887 of two buildings that had just recently been completed. George knew from his newspaper research that they were constructed in late 1886. A paragraph in the Hand County *Press* on November 11, 1889, related, "Emmons and Pyle buildings getting the finishing touches. The best buildings in town. Dr. Pyle's drugstore is the Artesian." The building on the right, located on lot number three in block one of the original town site, was on the west side of Broadway (the town's main street) near the north end of the two business blocks that constituted the town then—and now. Like many of his fellow physicians, Levis Pyle, a practitioner of homeopathic medicine, also operated a drug business. (Today he is remembered primarily as the father of John L. Pyle, who served as state attorney general, and as the grandfather of Gladys Pyle, the state's first woman legislator, first woman secretary of state, and for a brief period of time a U.S. senator.) In 1882, Levis Pyle had built an office one block south. In 1886, two buildings were constructed simultaneously on lots three and four, probably by the same carpenters. From the photograph, one can observe that they are of the same design, with identical windows, doorways, and trim. Both were twenty-two feet wide, leaving just enough space on the side of the standard twenty-five-foot lot for a narrow walkway or stairway. The door of Dr. Pyle's first-floor office is visible to the rear on the north side of the building. He and his wife lived in the apartment upstairs.

Located on lot four, to the south of Pyle's building, was the Emmons Block, housing A. J. Kuenster's boot and shoe store. It sported a retractable cloth awning, unusual during a period when awnings or sunshades were mostly made of wood. Shoes hanging in the doorway advertised themselves to potential customers.

A. J. Kuenster's boot and shoe store and Levis Pyle's drugstore, constructed in 1886, on lots three and four. (J. N. Templeman, photographer; courtesy of South Dakota State Historical Society, Pierre)

The buildings on lots three and four in the 1950s. (Courtesy of George Niederauer)

Lots three and four in 1988.

George had a quotation from the March 10, 1887, issue of the *Press:* "Will have the best stock of boots and shoes in the Emmons Block." By referring to his deed abstract files, binders of pictures, and shoe boxes of note cards George can recapitulate the history of every building on Broadway. The Emmons Block, for example, later housed the post office for about thirty years and also had a jewelry shop and then a Coast to Coast hardware store, which George's son John purchased in 1980. He extended the back of the building to the alley for additional storage space and later tore down the front and remodeled it as part of an expanded store that also fills lot five to the south.

Around 1898 an unidentified photographer walked up and down Broadway taking pictures of buildings along the street while people posed in front of them. (A fellow named Matt Holman traipsed along with the photographer and got himself included in many of the pictures.) By this time, the store on lot three had become a millinery store, run by Mrs. E. E. Trinery, who is shown in a photograph with her three children and a friend. Before that, Levis Pyle had temporarily moved north of Third Street for a short time and then moved back to lot three again. After his death in 1895, Mrs. L. T. Young had operated a dry goods store in the building for a year or two, and Fitzgerald and Redmund had briefly tried a drugstore there.

During the early 1900s, the building on lot number three housed the Miller *Gazette* and a job printing office for a number of years. In a photograph of Broadway taken in 1909, the sign identifying the office is clearly visible. Two doors south, on lot five, was the Scenic Theatre, catering to the new fad, watching moving pictures. Next to it, on lot six, was a brick veneer building, the first brick building in town, originally a bank but at that time a meat market. A fire insurance map printed in 1904 indicates that it continued to be the only brick building on Broadway at that time.[7] Within five years, the First National Bank and the Hand County State Bank, anchoring opposite corners at the intersection of Second Street and Broadway, provided brick edifices that instilled pride in the town's residents. By the time the 1925 map came out, every building south of the movie theater down to Second Street—about two-thirds of the block—was constructed of brick.

It is good to keep in mind that the faces that towns like Miller presented to the world were constantly changing. To the casual observer, the town depicted in the photograph of Broadway taken in 1909 might appear to be rather quiet and unexciting, what with its wagon tracks crisscrossing the dusty street, horses and buggies tied up at hitching posts, bicycles left lying haphazardly along the sidewalk, and men sauntering down the sidewalk. The electric lights now strung across the intersections, the telephone poles and concrete sidewalks, and the new brick buildings, however, all indicate that times, indeed, have changed. The evidence contained in George Niederauer's card files reminds us that buildings were constantly undergoing new owners and functions. And his later career as a house mover provides many examples of how often buildings were moved from lot to lot and even from town to town. Many of the buildings standing in Miller today were transported there from St. Lawrence many years ago, some as far back as the 1890s, when it and many other towns were severely squeezed by drought and economic depression.

In 1950, another photographer, Jack Jones, walked the length of Broadway taking pictures of the storefronts. In his binders George has juxtaposed these snapshots with the earlier ones taken in 1887 and 1898, and the comparisons are interesting. While several obvious changes stand out in the pictures of lots three and four—the striped awning of the Coast to Coast store, concrete sidewalks in place of wooden ones, a new window cut into the upstairs wall, double brackets replaced by single ones on the left—the buildings are still easily recognizable. When I visited the town in 1988 and took a snapshot of George standing in front of his son's remodeled Coast to Coast store, I saw that the process of modernization had continued. By now the Emmons building was gone. Levis Pyle's structure remained, now housing a radio station and a gift shop, but as with other buildings that go back to a town's first decade or two, it was virtually unrecognizable.

As long as people like George Niederauer and John and Ellebeth Pugh carry on their work, the history of towns like Miller can be brought to life. Without folks like them, our knowledge and understanding of local history would be much impoverished.

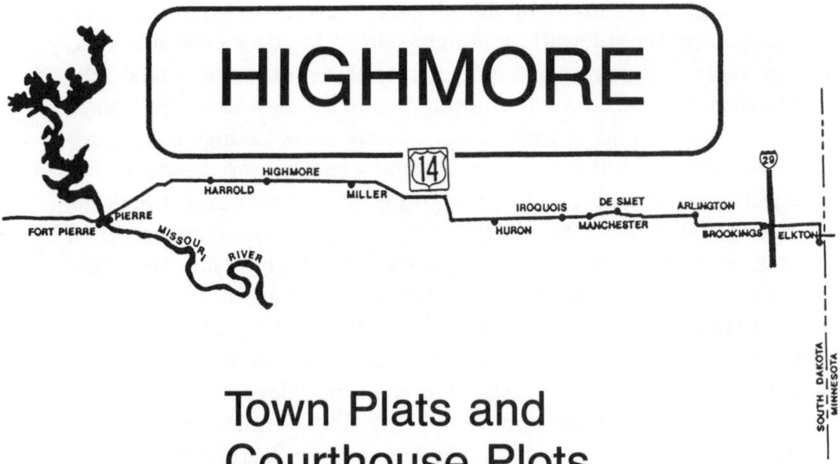

Town Plats and Courthouse Plots

An argument could be made for county courthouses as the supreme architectural achievements of the towns situated along Highway 14. In opposition, one could point to a number of outstanding church edifices, such as First Methodist Church in Pierre, First Lutheran Church in Brookings, and American Lutheran Church in Huron, the last designed by the accomplished architect F. C. W. Kuehn.[1] Post offices following classical lines in Brookings, Huron, and Pierre, built between 1906 and 1914, also stand out. In many towns, to varying degrees, banks achieve considerable distinction. Besides the state capitol itself, two of the largest and most impressive architectural gems in the towns along the highway were hotels—the St. Charles, just down the street from the capitol in Pierre, and the Marvin Hughitt, on Dakota Avenue in Huron. Fine brick railroad depots ornamented Brookings, Huron, and Pierre. In addition, attention should be given to a number of opera houses, schools, college buildings, and private homes. Nevertheless, aside from the state capitol, the county courthouses hold a collective claim as being the most impressive architectural achievements in towns along the highway.[2]

Public buildings everywhere provide clues about the cultures that build them, and county courthouses are especially suggestive. In addition to the practical functions they perform, courthouses project images of solidity, stability, and even grandeur that are meant to impress people with the legitimacy and strength of governmental institutions and also to generate community solidarity and support. Beyond that, each county, in its desire to compete with its neighbors, sought to make a statement about its own prosperity and position and, within the constraints of its financial resources, constructed as elaborate a definition of that achievement as it could afford.[3]

The Hyde County Courthouse in Highmore, which was dedicated on September 30, 1912, provides an attractive and highly satisfactory expression of these impulses. Its classical Greek pediment and Doric columns lend it beauty and dignity. Constructed of cement blocks and stone, it is two stories tall with a basement underneath.[4] Brookings County, building its granite courthouse in the same year, chose similiar classical motifs, but its larger population base and budget allowed it to obtain a larger structure and to adorn it with an impressive dome. Kingsbury County was eclectic in building its two-story brick courthouse in 1898. Possessing several wings and topped by a small dome, it provided a relatively simple but attractive building. For Hand County's third courthouse in Miller, built in 1925, concrete forms closely resembling stone were used, resulting in an impressive building at relatively small cost. By the 1930s, when Beadle County and Hughes County constructed their new courthouses, architectural styles had moved toward simpler, more functional lines. Impressiveness in their cases was achieved through sheer size and the use of attractive building materials rather than through ornamentation or stylistic elaboration.[5]

The courthouses in use today are second- or third-generation structures. As with banks, churches, schoolhouses, and other buildings, they proceeded through regular stages, from early wooden frame constructions to brick or stone replacements and, in a couple of cases, to larger, more elaborate, or more modern buildings. Always, functional needs interacted with formal considerations in fixing their designs. In addition to the courtroom, judge's chambers, and office of the clerk of courts, a courthouse needed space for the auditor, treasurer, register of deeds, and other officials. Sometimes jails were included in the courthouses, and in later years jail additions sometimes were attached in ways that undermined the architectural integrity of the courthouses.

At Highmore, as elsewhere, before the courthouse was built, court sessions had to be held in a rented building. Records were stored and business transacted wherever space was available. Hyde County voters rejected a courthouse bond issue in May 1885 by a margin of 114 to 342, but six months later they changed their minds and voted 263 to 184 to issue $7,000 worth of bonds for the construction of a courthouse-jail. Costing $4,475—the furniture came to $216—the resulting two-story wooden structure might have been mistaken for a schoolhouse except for the ornamental tower above its front entrance. After this building burned down in June 1892 (arson was suspected), county officials purchased the Phoenix Hotel, a three-story, mansard-roofed building, which served as the courthouse until the current structure was built in 1912.[6]

Highmore's selection as county seat in the first place did not come without a fight. During the early days of settlement, conflict among county seat aspirants frequently erupted, for ambitious town dwellers recognized the advantages that might be reaped by the victor.[7] It is no coincidence that the six largest towns on Highway 14 in East River South Dakota were usually the six county seats. Early settlers knew exactly what they were doing when they avidly sought county seat status. Benefiting from their early head starts, the county seats continued to maintain the advantage they held over their commercial rivals.

All over the frontier, county seat wars contributed color and excitement to the early history of settlement.[8] While none of the contests in counties along the Dakota Central branch of the Chicago and North Western generated the degree of drama and intensity that, for instance, the notorious Spink County war occasioned, there did occur some heated tussles, including the one in Hyde County. In Brookings County, enterprising businesspeople combined forces with newspaper editor George Hopp to capture the prize for Brookings against challengers from Volga and Aurora within two months after the railroad made its appearance. In Kingsbury and Beadle counties, De Smet overcame a challenge from Lake Preston, and Huron deflected aspirants from Altoona. The battle between St. Lawrence and Miller in Hand County was a heated one, matching towns situated only two miles apart. St. Lawrence's defeat doomed it to perpetual satellite status in the shadow of its victorious rival. Even in Hughes County there was some sentiment to elevate Blunt above Pierre as county seat, but that prospect never stood a chance of fulfillment.[9]

Along with the Miller–St. Lawrence rivalry, and perhaps even more dramatic in its playing out, the battle for the county seat of Hyde County stands out as the most interesting of the six counties along Highway 14 in eastern South Dakota. Until 1882, the year that Hyde County was created, few settlers ventured into the area. With population picking up in 1883, the county was officially organized when Governor Nehemiah G. Ordway was presented a petition certifying that 150 inhabitants resided there. In accordance with territorial law, the governor proceeded to appoint three commissioners who would be responsible for locating a temporary county seat and naming temporary county officials to serve until elections could be scheduled.[10]

The governor, however, was not merely a disinterested observer. Like many other territorial officials in post–Civil War America, he accepted a federal appointment largely in order to milk it for financial gain. Long experience in New Hampshire politics and twelve years as sergeant at arms in the U.S. House of Representatives had educated Ordway about opportunities for graft and influence.[11] His apparent intention in Hyde County was to name commissioners who would locate the county seat at Holabird, a town site on the railroad eight miles west of Highmore. According to Highmore newspaper editor John B. Perkins in his 1908 history of the county, "The governor had made some deal whereby he was to be benefited by the location of the county seat at Holabird, and to carry out that deal he was to appoint as commissioners L. E. Whitcher, John Falde, and A. E. Van Camp, giving the Holabird location two commissioner votes, for, as Mr. Van Camp was the owner of the Highmore townsite, his vote was not expected for Holabird, nor was it needed." Holabird, with hardly a resident in it, was not much of a town yet. Neither was Highmore, for that matter, but it was bigger than Holabird, which it derisively referred to as "Gumbo Holler."[12]

Postcard view of the Hyde County Courthouse. (Courtesy of South Dakota State Archives, Pierre)

At some point, the governor changed his mind and switched his preference to a site two miles east of Holabird, on land owned by J. S. Harris, expecting his henchmen to rubber stamp his whim. When he learned that Falde intended instead to vote with Van Camp for Highmore, Ordway attempted to revoke Falde's commission and replace him with George W. Dunham, whom he believed he could count on to vote correctly. This action precipitated a court case challenging the governor's authority. Meanwhile, two separate boards began to meet—one with the governor's men, Dunham and Whitcher, the other with his opponents' representatives, Van Camp and Falde. The Ordway group held its meetings on the west side of town in the office of E. O. Parker.[13]

Each of the boards proceeded as if it were the rightful government of the county, holding regular meetings, purchasing supplies, locating roads, establishing schools, and naming county officials. A. E. (Abram E.) Van Camp's brother, A. N. (Andrew Nelson) Van Camp, was named county superintendent of schools by the Van Camp–Falde board. During that first year, according to Perkins's history, "there was no other town in the county except Highmore and during that time there was little else to do except to join one faction or the other, each mingling with the other with such smiles and blandishments as they could command and carry upon their faces under a real feeling of hatred and dislike, which, however, never culminated in an outbreak of personal warfare, and after all the real humor of the situation would appear upon the surface, and show itself in various ways."[14]

Finally, in September 1884, after Falde and Dunham exited the scene, all of the temporary officials resigned, and the remaining commissioners—Whitcher and A. E. Van Camp—made a whole new set of appointments, which included Parker as register of deeds. By this time, Governor Ordway apparently had turned his attention to more important things. His role in changing the territorial capital from Yankton to Bismarck in 1883 had stirred up a hornet's nest of opposition, and with public sentiment rising against Ordway, President Chester Arthur refused to reappoint him in June 1884. Voters went to the polls on November 4 to name permanent county officials and gave Highmore a 159-vote majority in the balloting on the county seat. To change that decision and remove the county seat to another town after this would require a two-thirds majority under territorial law. The tiny village of Holabird never grew to more than a few houses and businesses, although for a time it did boast a newspaper and a bank and there was even a talk of a Christian college locating there. During the 1920s, the school served about eighty students and offered two years of high school. The town never incorporated, so the population can only be estimated, but it probably never rose to much more than 100.[15]

Highmore's victory at the polls in 1884 settled the county seat question, but another issue remained to be resolved—the competition between A. E. Van Camp and Parker over the future development of the town itself. Highmore was unusual among the towns along the railroad in being composed of two separate town sites owned by two different energetic boosters who possessed differing agendas for the town's development.[16] East of Huron, once the Chicago and North Western Railway had determined where the towns would go, the Western Town Lot Company, a subsidiary of the railroad, had been primarily responsible for platting them out and selling the first business and residential lots. As the towns grew in size and expanded beyond the railroad's holdings around the depots, people who owned the surrounding land extended the plats with their own additions. West of Huron, where settlement and town building occurred a little more slowly during the early 1880s, the railroad located sidings—nine in all—between the James River and the Missouri River. Each of these eventually became the nucleus of a town. Wolsey was located at Siding No. 1, Wessington at Siding No. 2, Rex (later St. Lawrence) at Siding No. 3, Ree Heights at Siding No. 4,

A. E. Van Camp. (From John B. Perkins, *History of Hyde County, South Dakota,* 1908)

E. O. Parker. (From Perkins, *History of Hyde County,* 1908)

Highmore at Siding No. 5, Harrold at Siding No. 6, Blunt at Siding No. 7, Canning at Siding No. 8, and Rousseau at Siding No. 9. Several other towns—Miller, Bramhall, and Holabird—were added later.[17]

Siding No. 5 attracted little activity until the summer of 1882. All that distinguished it from the wide open prairie surrounding it was a railroad section house, where the section men stayed while they were working on the tracks in the area. By May people began to trickle in, and the last day of the month saw the arrival of A. E. and his brother A. N. Van Camp from Muscatine County, Iowa. The former was twenty-nine, the latter two years older. A. E. Van Camp had spent three months at an academy in Iowa City before following his father into farming. A. N. Van Camp had finished a law course in Iowa City, graduating in 1871, and continued practicing law in Highmore while simultaneously tending a farm he homesteaded a mile outside of town. During the early 1900s, he organized and became general manager of the Hyde County Telephone Company.[18]

A. E. Van Camp used Valentine Scrip to obtain forty acres of land adjacent to Siding No. 5 in the southwest quarter of section 12 in Township 112, Range 72 (Highmore Township), intending to make it into a town site. At almost the same time, Parker secured the right to the quarter-section immediately west of Van Camp's claim. He had the same goal in mind—to locate a town site on his land. Parker, who had served during the Civil War as a musician in the New York Volunteers, became a charter member of the Highmore unit of the Grand Army of the Republic when it organized in 1883. The rivalry between the two men was apparently friendly enough. They both were members of the local Masonic Order, Van Camp serving as senior warden and Parker as treasurer. They were charter members and on the original boards of trustees of the Methodist and Congregational churches respectively.[19]

After the decision to build a courthouse in 1885, each entrepreneur offered to give the county a block on his town site for its location, Van Camp's on the east side of town, Parker's on the west side. By accepting the former's offer, the county board encouraged development along Commercial Avenue. The original courthouse was located on that street and, after it burned down, so was the second one, which was housed in the old Phoenix Hotel. The third courthouse, still in use today, was built on the original site in 1912. Meanwhile, a bank, a large mercantile store, and several other business establishments went up along the avenue. Paralleling it a block to the west, Iowa Avenue ran along the section line dividing the two plats and was the westernmost street of Van Camp's town. It was also the easternmost street of Parker's town and constituted Highmore's other, larger Main Street. Over time, it attracted most of the business concerns, and in 1912, when the highway locaters came through town, they routed the Black and Yellow Trail right down the middle of it. With a considerable amount of business continuing to center on Commercial Avenue, however, Highmore emerged as a town with two Main Streets.

A casual visitor today, however, would hardly infer any of this, since the surveyors hired by Parker and Van Camp joined the two plats just like a dressmaker fits a seam. The plans each man used were almost identical. In fact, all along the route of the railroad, towns were laid out in repeatable fashion. The rules originally followed by surveyors for the Western Town Lot Company in Brookings County continued to be applied in the towns west of Huron. Today, these plans can be studied in the platbooks located in the register of deeds office in each courthouse.[20] The original surveys, conducted in 1879 and the early 1880s, provide a tangible link to the history of the towns.

The first surveys in Brookings County all had streets with 80-foot widths. There were two exceptions—Main Street and Front Street (the street bordering the railroad right-of-way)—both of which were 100 feet wide. Alleys were 20 feet in width. Business lots on blocks facing Main Street had 25-foot fronts, residential lots 50-foot fronts. In a few cases, business lots with 25-foot fronts were placed along other streets, too, but variations like this were few. Almost always, lots were 165 feet deep. With blocks being 350 feet square, seven residential lots or fourteen business lots fit along their lengths. A 200-foot gap separated Front Street from the railroad tracks. Across the tracks, on the other side, were warehouse lots for railway-related facilities. Each warehouse lot was 80 feet by 100 feet. In every town from Elkton to Pierre, the Main Street ran perpendicular to the tracks (or at a slight angle, if the tracks did not run straight east and west or north and south). As a result, there were two main axes of development in every town—one along the railroad tracks and the other along Main Street. In the smaller towns, businesses stretched only one block down the street from the depot. Larger towns might have two blocks of businesses, the largest ones three or more.[21]

Consequently, variations existed within set parameters in the towns along the railroad. Many different kinds of structures could be built on a 25-by-165-foot lot. One did not have to fill up the whole lot. Double lots allowed frontages as wide as 50 feet, and occasionally lots were divided up into odd fractions so that they would include one whole lot and part of another. Nevertheless, the 25-foot single-lot frontage or 50-foot double-lot frontage tended to channel the designs of buildings into identifiable patterns. Hotels, opera houses, and the like could express greater individuality, but ordinary store buildings generally were long and narrow. Interior photographs of these buildings tend to resemble each other, making it appear as if the viewer is looking down a long box or tunnel. Yet if the basic boxlike dimensions of the interiors did tend toward similarity, opportunities existed for variations in furnishings, decoration, rooflines, windows, and paint schemes. When brick and stone structures began to replace the earlier wooden frame ones, more variations occurred. The resulting mélange can be observed in photographs of Main Streets that have been taken over the years. They do bear interesting resemblances.[22]

The likelihood that some other kind of developmental pattern would emerge in the towns was slim but nevertheless present. Once again, as with its two Main Streets, Highmore stands out as exceptional. Evidence that things could have occurred differently exists in the town lot platbook in the Hyde County Courthouse. Platbooks like this, available in every county, contain the original plats of the towns and all additions made to them over the years. There is an interesting entry on page five, dated July 3, 1882, just one month after Van Camp's arrival in town. It indicates that the survey was done "on or prior to June 30" by Thomas F. Nichol, whose work in Brookings, Lake Preston, De Smet, and other towns along the railroad had thoroughly familiarized him with the rules of laying out a town. Yet his plan for Highmore, while observing some of those conventions, projected a boldly different sort of pattern on the prairie landscape.

In Nichol's scheme, the central business street—Commercial Avenue—was the usual 100 feet in width, and the other streets had normal 80-foot widths. The business lots, fourteen to a block, were the usual 25 feet in width, although only 125 feet deep along Commercial Avenue. What made the plat so unusual were the streets that branched off at acute angles from the main business artery in a pattern resembling some sort of plant or tree. Had the proposed layout actually been implemented and had the town grown to large proportions, it might have eventually resembled a fan or a wheel. An appended note on the plat, however, indicates that it was vacated by order of the court on October 31, 1883, informing us that the imaginative scheme never got off the ground—or rather never got imprinted on the ground! Perhaps Van Camp realized that the scheme was too wild and different or that it would not be practical. Maybe it was simply that it impinged on Parker's land and would not have linked up with his plat.[23]

Rather than pursuing his imaginative vision, Van Camp fol-

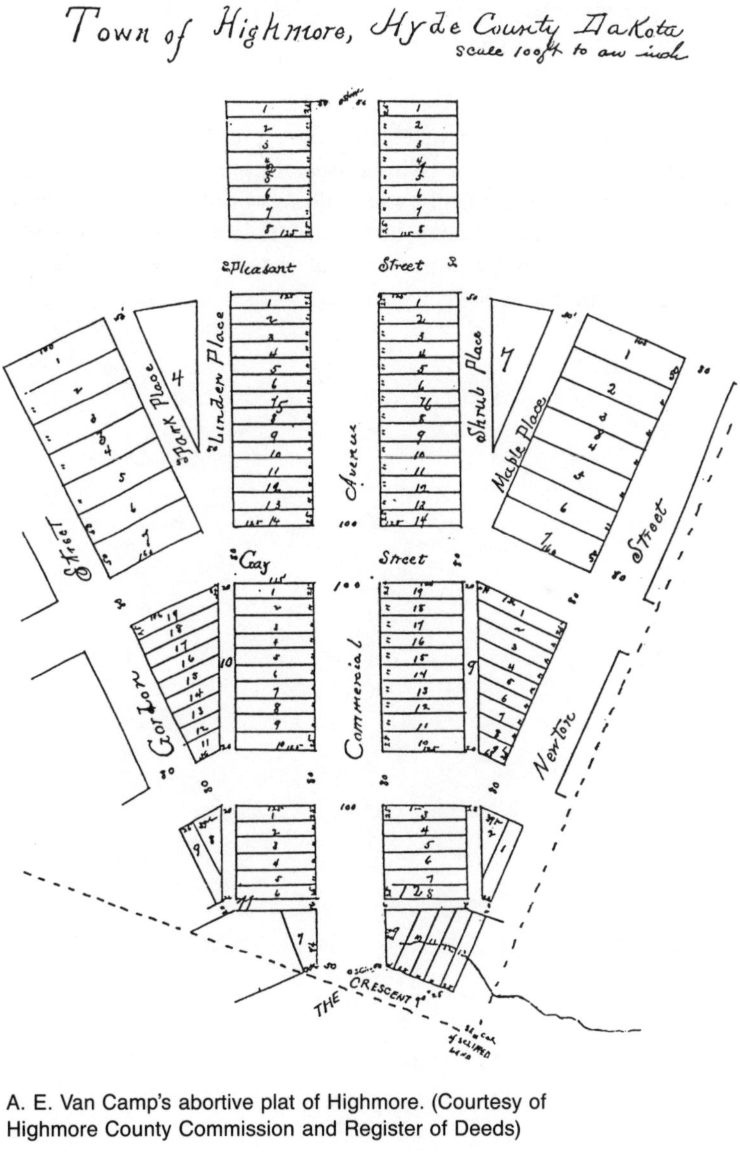

A. E. Van Camp's abortive plat of Highmore. (Courtesy of Highmore County Commission and Register of Deeds)

lowed the well-established mold of north-south and east-west streets—the perfect grid with origins in William Penn's Philadelphia. That way his plat fit neatly alongside that of Parker, and the casual observer would have had a hard time realizing that Highmore actually consisted of two different intermeshing town sites. E. C. Chilcott, the surveyor hired by Van Camp, also did Parker's survey. The only basic differences between the two were that Parker's lots were the usual 165 feet deep, while Van Camp's extended back only 125 feet, and Van Camp's alleys were 25 feet wide rather than 20 feet.[24]

There is more than meets the eye, therefore, in a county courthouse and the records it houses. Impressive as the courthouse may be architecturally, the building is only one of a succession of structures that have been used to conduct the county's business. The symbolic importance of a courthouse is as significant as the functions it performs.

HARROLD

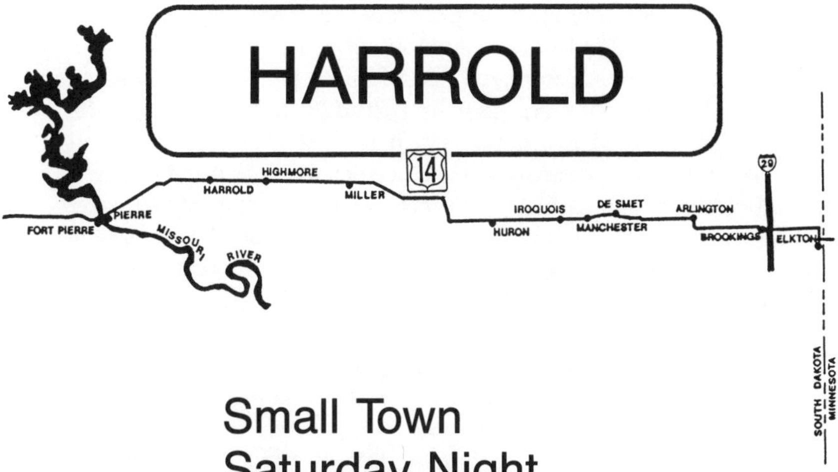

Small Town Saturday Night

For tourists who turn off Highway 14 and cut south across the tracks on Main Street (officially named Wyman Avenue), there is not much to see in Harrold, a town which once had 342 people but which now has below 200. Looking left, on the east side of the street, are the Bohning Grocery, the post office, the old First State Bank building, the Masonic Lodge, the "Bright Spot" building, the old Veterans of Foreign Wars building, and an old pool hall. Only the store, the post office, and the Masonic Lodge are still in use. Across the street on the west are the Centennial Cafe, the old Ford garage, and several other empty buildings. Another typical small town in trouble, squeezed by all the forces that are driving people out of rural America to shop, work, and live in larger towns and cities.

But look again. There is a story in those two buildings anchoring Main Street—Bohning Grocery on one side and the Centennial Cafe on the other. The long history of the former can tell us something about the quality of community that used to exist in the town, and the recent appearance of the latter reflects the continuing vitality of a community spirit that keeps small towns like Harrold going in the face of the long odds against them.

Nothing reflects more on the fabric of community in a small town than its eating spots.[1] Without a cafe or a coffee shop, people have to improvise, catching up on things down at the post office or at the filling station or on the phone. On my first visit to Harrold in 1985, I discovered a group of men drinking coffee at the dirt-strip airfield directly west of town. The restaurant was temporarily closed, because no one could make a go of it. Then, with the town's centennial approaching in 1986, folks rallied together and decided to do something about it.

A local moving company had acquired a building that it had no use for, but, at thirty-two by forty-two feet, it was just the right size for a cafe. Interest ran high at a community meeting called to discuss the matter, and the fact that the town's centennial celebration was just a few months away clinched the issue. No one was able or ready to invest the $25,000 that would be necessary for the project. So the Harrold Development Corporation was established with thirty-five investors kicking in $100 apiece to get it going. They arranged for the rest of the financing from the Dakota State Bank in the nearby town of Blunt, hired a manager to run the new venture, and came up with a name for it—the "Centennial Cafe."

Nearly everyone in the community got involved in the project in one way or another that winter. They installed paneling, laid carpet, put in new doors and windows, fixed up the restrooms, built cupboards and other furnishings for the kitchen, and cleaned and polished and fixed everything for opening day—Mother's Day—when more than a hundred smiling patrons enjoyed the new cafe. According to a story in the Highmore *Herald,* " 'A dream come true!' was the thought on everyone's minds, as they partook of manager Marie Lovell's bounteous feed."[2]

The story of the Centennial Cafe is instructive and inspiring. It shows what a community can accomplish when it perceives a need and decides to do something, and it demonstrates how local volunteers' efforts can compensate for deficiencies in population, market demand, and capital resources. The vitality and ultimately the survival of small towns have always depended upon intersecting vectors of community spirit and entrepreneurial initiative as well as economic and demographic realities. Historical circumstances establish conditions and limits upon a community's potential. Within those parameters, will and determination often determine the winners and the losers.

To learn the rest of the story, we have to cross the street and enter the Bohning Grocery. Here, written on the walls and the ceilings and evident in the floor and the aisles, exists another drama with less auspicious implications for towns like Harrold. Looking down, we can see the same wooden floors that thousands of patrons have trodden over the years as they bought supplies that would carry them over until their next visit. Three poles in the middle of the building support the roof and divide the store between the grocery section on the left and the general store section on the right, with dry goods, boots, gloves, paint, hard-

The Bohning store today.

Interior of the Bohning store in 1940. *Left to right:* Jim Scott, John Bohning, Gottlieb Winckler, Jack Bohning. (Courtesy of Sharon Winckler)

ware, and a variety of other items. The same furnace grate that can be seen in a picture taken in the store in 1940 still warms it today. Signs on the walls outside the store identify it as Bohning and Bohning Grocery—a store much like it was when it was established three-quarters of a century ago.

But there are differences, too, and ultimately these differences outweigh the similarities. The old decorative sheet metal was covered up when the ceiling was lowered and tile was installed to modernize the building's appearance. Windows along the side walls were covered up; now boxes and displays along the walls reach all the way up to the ceiling. Behind the counter hangs a pegboard, on which are displayed a variety of items, and over to the side are shelves with videocassettes of movies, fast-moving items and moneymakers since they were introduced several years ago. What is less obvious but more important is the change in role that stores like this have undergone. Once a vital part of the local economy, they have become, in effect, convenience stores. People now tend to use them to pick up a quart of milk or a pack of cigarettes and often drive to Pierre or Highmore or other larger towns to do the bulk of their shopping.

Paul and Sophia Bohning, who grew up near Hanover, Germany, emigrated to the United States in the mid-1800s and settled in north-central Iowa. The first Bohning to arrive in Harrold was Eilbert ("Al") Bohning, who arrived in 1911, when the town was still in the horse age. A few brave souls were beginning to purchase gas-driven chariots by then, but not until the 1920s did automobiles become commonplace, and the full implications of the automobile revolution would not become apparent until after World War II. Al Bohning's stay in Harrold lasted only about a year before he moved to Miller to operate a store with his brother Ed. Johann (he went by the name "John") Bohning moved his family from Clarksville, Iowa, to Harrold in 1914 and started a general merchandise store in a building that had been used for a time by Henry Huff and Fred Winckler. In 1918 he and his brother Bill entered into partnership, calling their operation the "Bohning and Bohning General Merchandise Store."[3]

John Bohning's son Claude (people call him "Jack"), who was eight years old when the family arrived in 1914, later wrote in the Harrold's centennial history book, "In those days Harrold was a thriving town, with two elevators, two general stores, one hotel, one barbershop, one saloon, one blacksmith shop, two hardware stores, two livery barns, one restaurant, two real estate offices, a print shop, a doctor, a picture show, a bank, a livestock buyer, a dairy, a butcher shop, a lumberyard and a post office."[4]

Jack Bohning played basketball, football, and baseball at Harrold High School. He told me that it was a little tricky playing in the new high school gym when it opened in 1921, since the players had to avoid hitting the overhanging balconies with their passes and shots.

After graduating in 1925, Jack Bohning went to work in the store with his father and his uncle, Bill Bohning. In those days, it took four or five, sometimes six, people to do all the work and take care of the customers. Until the 1920s, when truck traffic increased on the highways, all of the merchandise arrived by train. Dray teams hauled it over two blocks from the depot to the store. Commodities still were largely merchandised in bulk form—sugar, prunes and other dried fruit, and so forth. There were bulk cookies, bulk crackers, bulk pickles and sauerkraut. They had a pickle barrel and a cracker barrel and containers for dozens of other items. Vinegar came in fifty-five-gallon barrels. They would get twenty or twenty-five of them in the fall and roll them down into the basement, where it was cool. Wholesalers' representatives, or drummers, mostly from Sioux Falls and Sioux City, came through on the train to take their orders. Their main grocery supplier was Park-Grant, which had a representative in Huron.

Two passenger trains a day came through in each direction. Perishables like fresh fruit and bread were hauled in the baggage car. Ten-gallon cream cans would be sent back the other way. They would put wet sacks on them so the evaporation would keep them cool. In season, cattle trains loaded up at the stockyards, sometimes enough to fill forty or fifty cars to be sent to slaughterhouses at Sioux City and Chicago. Until the 1920s, the railroad served as the town's lifeline to the outside world, but during that decade the intrusion of trucks and automobiles began a profound transformation, the ultimate significance of which almost no one at the time could anticipate.

One thing that widespread car ownership did was to enshrine Saturday night as the most important community ritual in small towns like Harrold. During the early 1900s, and even earlier, Saturday was market day in many towns because so many farm families made it a habit to drive into towns to shop and transport goods to market. Then with the advent of automobiles and better roads, trips that previously had taken as long as several hours were reduced to fifteen or twenty minutes. Parents could pack the kids in the car and drive into town, stay to visit and while away time for several hours, and be home in time to sleep before church the next morning. Going to town on Saturday night became the most-looked-forward-to event of the week.[5]

A 1936 item in the Groton *Independent* captured the spirit of small town Saturday nights:

> Saturday nights in Dakota have ceased to be a period of the week. They have become an institution . . . a time when farmers forget their worries and work and gather at their chief trading points to mingle with their neighbors, exchange farm ideas . . . rub elbows with their urban brothers and enjoy themselves with the facilities their chief trading points afford.
>
> From miles around they gather, weather bronzed sons of the soil, with their wives and children. While the men folks talk politics, laugh and joke, the purchasing agents of the families run through the stores doing their weekly shopping. . . .
>
> What's going to become of the small town? That question is answered every Saturday night in hundreds of Dakota towns. Small towns are almost as important an item of rural life as the farm itself, not only because the farmer needs the small town and the small town needs the farmer, but because such places are the clearing houses of farm energy, thought, sociability, and requirements. "Saturday night" proves this beyond any shadow of doubt. It is an institution . . . a farmer's playtime and visiting time, giving him that close relationship with friends and neighbors not available in anything but a small town.[6]

Woodrow ("Woody") Heintz, who grew up in Harrold during the 1920s and 1930s and returned to barber there after serving in the army during World War II, well remembers Saturday night. When I spoke with him in November 1985, he told me about the 1940s: "Saturday nights you couldn't find a place to park your car. The side streets were full. A lot of times I would start barbering at eight in the morning and still be barbering at one or two the next morning. Stop a little for dinner and supper. And then Wednesday night was a big night here, too." Like many barber shops at the time, Heintz's had a shower bath, which was used by people without indoor plumbing. It cost a quarter. Customers and loiterers filled the chairs in his shop, thumbing through magazines, catching up on jokes and gossip, and listening to the radio. Leaving his place, they'd drift over to the pool hall, congregate under street lamps, or lean against cars discussing crops or the weather or the new tractors and automobiles they were thinking of buying.

Their wives, meanwhile, sat in cars chatting with friends or tramped from store to store to find a new dress or a pair of shoes for their children. The Bohning store had a bench running the length of the front window where fifteen or twenty people could sit and rest. According to Jack Bohning, sometimes they'd linger there for two or three hours on a Saturday night, swapping stories and trading recipes while the sun set. As people brought in their lists, store employees filled them, setting the boxes and bags off to the side until the customers returned to pick them up. Storekeepers often grew frustrated with people who waited until after midnight to get their stuff. They did most of their business on Saturday night and needed to keep their customers happy, but sometimes the thought crossed their minds that staying open till midnight or later was slightly ridiculous.

Meanwhile, while the parents made their rounds, children played games in the streets and alleys, took in a movie, or just walked around town. Small change—25 cents for the lucky ones—went a long, long way in those days. The building south of the Bohning store served as a movie theater. Band concerts were also popular.

Saturday nights in small towns like Harrold brought the whole community together—young and old, men and women, townspeople and country dwellers, poor and well-off. Folks put down their work and forgot their troubles for an evening and updated themselves on the week's happenings. Radio programs and newspapers could inform them about national and world events, market reports kept them up-to-date on business affairs, and farm journals and other publications educated them about scientific breakthroughs and new farming techniques. But before television, people's attentions generally remained focused on local affairs. Community ties remained strong. Most of their thoughts were geared to friends and neighbors, kinfolk, business associates, and others who lived nearby. The advent of the automobile expanded the area they were familiar with, but by and large, people's activities and concerns remained geared to the local area. Saturday night constituted the outstanding cultural expression of this fact, for once a week the community magically reconstituted itself in concrete form and in the process reinforced communal values and aspirations.

The foundations of the Saturday night ritual, however, were not cultural but economic. While people enjoyed the relaxation and camaraderie attending Saturday nights in town, economic factors brought them there in the first place. One was the need to do their shopping; the other was to market their cream and eggs. To a surprising degree, farmers depended upon the cream and egg economy for their well-being. Not much cash flowed through most families' hands until harvesttime, and the Great Depression only exacerbated the situation. What did provide a small but steady income was the return they received for their cream and eggs, most of which were shipped on the railroad to eastern markets. Every town contained produce buyers and cream stations, in some cases a half-dozen or more.

At stores like Bohning and Bohning General Merchandise in Harrold, people used the proceeds from their cream and eggs to purchase groceries. Each egg crate held thirty dozen eggs. Jack Bohning told me that on some Saturday nights they would fill fifty or sixty crates. The buyers had to candle the eggs (hold them up to a light) to check their freshness. There would always be a few rotton ones and some breakage. In the meantime, as many as thirty or forty ten-gallon cans of cream would be brought in. The Bohnings also bought poultry and shipped it out.

Gen Axmaker, who was born in 1900, told me in November 1985 that things were hopping in Harrold during the late 1940s. "Oh, golly, the town was booming. We'd come in every Wednesday and Saturday night." Her brother, Art Ingle, recalled dances that took place at the Skyrocket, a dance hall converted from a hotel that stood a block west of the Bohning store. Like people in other towns along the highway, he recalled Lawrence Welk's coming to play there. He remembered that during the 1940s things were starting to slow down in Harrold, which stimulated efforts to rev things back up again. Saturday night had been pretty lively previously. "Then after the war it seemed like Saturday and Wednesday lost out. The town—this was really a bustling town in the twenties and up until the drought hit there in the thirties—then things died out, and when the war came it was like almost deserted. The young guys were all gone. And when the war was over and the guys came back, we had a good civic organization—kind of brought that back to life—got a lumberyard started—and various things like that." Activity did accelerate for awhile, and Saturday nights resembled past times. But by the end of the 1950s in Harrold, the life had gone out of Saturday night.

There were too many other things to distract people. Television invaded their homes, its blue flickering glare enveloping watchers around its newfound hearth in the living room. Faster automobiles and better roads whisked people farther and farther away from home in less and less time. Running over to Pierre or Highmore, cruising past to Huron, Aberdeen, or Sioux Falls—this allowed people to drive to and from places in a day that they would not have thought of visiting previously. High school athletics grew ever more popular, displacing other forms of entertainment and sociability. With the rise of the record industry and a whole new youth culture centered around it, interest in local band concerts faltered. As the pace of life speeded up, the idea of everyone sitting down for hours on end just to talk while their children strolled around town came to seem rather quaint. Especially important in the demise of Saturday night were economic changes. The old cream and egg economy disappeared. Farmers now sold whole milk to local processors who often picked it up right at their farm. The egg business was taken over by huge producers who tended thousands of chickens in efficiently operated, scientifically designed facilities that dwarfed operations on small farms.

Sharon Winckler, a 1966 graduate of Harrold High School, grew up during the time when Saturday night was going out of style. Her family farmed five miles out of town, and they came into town on Saturday night with their cream and eggs just like everyone else. "In the wintertime, you came in in the afternoon," she told me in August 1988. "In the summertime we'd come in the evening, and everyone was in town. All the kids would walk. You'd just walk around the streets. It was weird. There was always someone out there for you to pair up with and just walk around." Until she was seven, they still had a movie in town for the children to go to. Sharon's mother would sit on the bench in the Bohning store to talk with her friends after doing her shopping. The men would stand outside, shoot some pool, or play cards.

By the early 1960s, when Sharon was in high school, people stopped coming into town on Saturday night. Today the ritual remains only as a memory of a kind of community togetherness that can never be recaptured. Now high school students drive over to Highmore or to Pierre, sometimes to Huron or other towns. People don't shop much for groceries in Harrold anymore. Sharon told me that they drive to larger towns, mainly Pierre. Lying thirty-three miles west on Highway 14, it boasts several large supermarkets and a new mall. "That road's too nice," she laughed. "They fixed up Highway 14, and it's too nice. People like to get in a car and go anymore." For her and her husband Marty (Harrold High School class of 1964), this is no academic matter. They bought out the Bohning store when Jack Bohning retired in 1975. Marty had worked there for fifteen years, beginning part-time while he was still in high school.

One thing that really hurt the Wincklers was when the Park-Grant warehouse stopped supplying them several years ago. It was simply a matter of economics; stores like those in Harrold don't generate enough revenue to interest the big wholesale firms. Having to pay more for their stock forced the Wincklers to raise the prices they charge their customers. It reduced their competitiveness even more. "We're just like a convenience store," Sharon sighed. When I visited the store in 1988, Marty was in Illinois dusting crops. He learned how to fly an airplane and now spends most of his time at that. There isn't much money to be made in the store anymore. During their first ten years of operation, business fell by two-thirds. Since then, with the loss of their wholesale supplier, things have gone further downhill. One thing that has made up for some of that is the brisk business they do in videotape rentals. Carrying those was Marty's idea, and it has been quite successful. But it is just one more reflection of the increasing privatization of people's lives and how much things have changed since everybody used to come to Harrold on Saturday nights.

One popular outlet for people's energies and something that continues to draw them together is softball. There is a picture of one of the local softball teams in the store. Once when Marty was in the store in November 1985, he pointed out to me that more than half of the players on the team were bachelors. "Not just young guys in their twenties either, guys in their thirties and some in their forties," he noted. This is a rural area where young men have fewer and fewer chances of finding a wife. Many young women graduate from high school, attend college, and never return. Or they go from high school to Pierre, Sioux Falls, or Minneapolis and get jobs. The marriage market is in a depression. Marty guessed there were thirty, maybe forty, bachelors around Harrold. And even when they do get married, they only have a couple of children. That's not many mouths to feed, even if people do their shopping in Harrold.

"Is there a future for stores like this in small towns?" I asked Sharon in August 1988.

"No," was her honest reply.

"Do you want to say that in a book?"

"Um-hmm. I sure do."

"You don't feel that would be bad advertising if I . . ."

"I think it's kind of sad, to be honest with you, because it's going to kill these small towns."

"And these people who depend on you—so many old folks. A high percentage of the population are elderly retired people."

"That's right."

"How will they get their groceries from Pierre?"

"I have no idea. Some of the ladies drive. . . . I know people that go clear to Aberdeen to shop. They have the Food Bonanza up there and I've heard a lot of them comment."

"Well, that's going a bit far afield, it seems."

"I'm *not joking!* Because the price is way lower, you know. But what are they going to do when they need a loaf of bread and milk? That'll be a *different* story."

And so it goes. The community rallies together, volunteers its time and effort, and invests some of its hard-earned dollars in resuscitating a local cafe. Meanwhile, inexorable social and economic forces are depleting the reservoirs of community interaction and cooperation and driving people in other directions for shopping, entertainment, and jobs. The outcome will be written in the history books of the future.

PIERRE

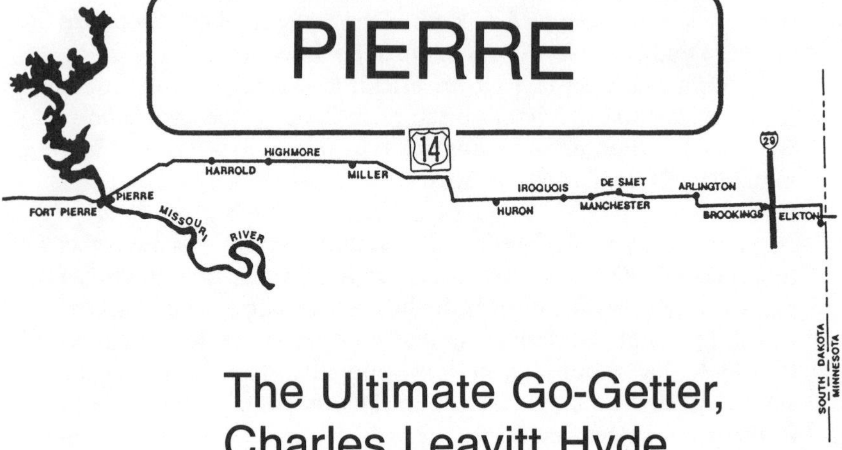

The Ultimate Go-Getter, Charles Leavitt Hyde

As you drive west on Highway 14 and approach the Missouri River, the landscape abruptly changes from gently rolling prairie to deeply crevassed hills and ravines for a mile or so and then glides into a rather steep descent down the bluffs toward the water. The capital city of Pierre (pronounced "peer," it rhymes with "deer"; the uninitiated who try to give it the French pronunciation are immediately identified as outsiders) extends east from the river for several blocks along the flat bottomlands and then rises on the hillside. Coming into the city from the northeast, Highway 14 follows Euclid Avenue. Several blocks from the Missouri, Euclid intersects Capitol Avenue, which is on a shelf of land a couple of hundred feet above the flat. The state capitol, the governor's mansion, several state office buildings, and the World War I Soldiers and Sailors' Memorial are located along Capitol Avenue to the left (southeast).

Anchoring one corner at Euclid and Capitol is the grand old St. Charles Hotel, which opened for business in January 1911, several months after the capitol itself was completed and just in time to accommodate lawmakers coming into town for the biennial legislative session. Five stories high and outfitted with the latest modern appointments, the St. Charles immediately became the best hotel not only in Pierre but along the entire line of the railroad in eastern South Dakota. Only the Marvin Hughitt Hotel, built in Huron a decade later, ever outshone it. For decades, the St. Charles catered to lawmakers and lobbyists, and many a story was told of whiskey drunk and deals made in the hospitality rooms that brought them together. Recently remodeled, the old hotel now houses offices and apartments.[1]

Kitty-corner across the street from the St. Charles is the old Carnegie Library, completed in 1904, the first one to be built in a town along the route (Huron got one in 1909 and Brookings in 1914). Now the building provides space for the Hughes County Shelter Care Facility and for the sheriff's office. Further up Capitol Avenue to the northwest, on the right side of the street, can be seen the Hughes County Courthouse, built in 1934, and beyond it the old federal courthouse and post office, finished in 1906. Across the street to the left (on the river side of the avenue) stand several brick office buildings—the Capitol Avenue Block (completed in 1908), the Pierre Street Block (1909), and the Hyde Block (1906). The latter two blocks straddle Pierre Street, which dead-ends at the courthouse and runs down the hill to the river, forming the major business street on the flat. Pierre Street is the town's Main Street.

Walking down Pierre Street from Capitol Avenue, one notices that the Hyde Block on the right actually consists of three different buildings. The three-story structure on the corner has stores on the first floor and offices on the upper two. Connecting it with another three-story structure farther down the hill is a one-story store. Passing through the arched doorway of the three-story building on the lower end of the Hyde Block, one will discover that this building was once the Hyde (or Grand) Opera House. Outside, in brickwork above the entrance, the word "Hyde" still announces it as such. While visiting Pierre in the summer of 1988, I stopped by the opera house for a visit because Bruce Grulke, a friend of mine who taught architecture at South Dakota State University, was acting as a consultant on a remodeling project and had invited me to drop by to see what they were doing.

When the Grand opened its doors in October 1906 (the first performance was a production of *Quincy Adams Sawyer* by a traveling theatrical troupe), the new opera house was labeled as "the finest as well as the most modern one in the northwest." With a seating capacity of eleven hundred (half on the lower level, the rest in two balconies), a thirty-by-thirty-two-foot stage, a twenty-two-by-thirty-two-foot proscenium arch, and ten dressing rooms, it was designed to be compared with the best theaters in the region.[2] Pierreites were grateful that its owner, Charles Leavitt Hyde, had added this architectural gem to their city's growing collection of attractions, but as was frequently the case with things that Hyde touched, this project also sparked considerable controversy.

The initial announcement that Hyde intended to build an opera house informed the public that he desired no special privileges or consideration for doing it. Later, however, he requested from the city a ten-year tax abatement on the structure, something a number of local businesspeople and other town leaders considered unjustified. In the Pierre *Capital Journal,* editor John Hipple, who frequently found fault with the go-getting businessperson, argued against a tax rebate, meanwhile criticizing the architect for designing too small an entryway and for failing to include an asbestos fire curtain in his plans. Hyde's labeling of his critics as "kickers" and "knockers" triggered a retort about his "notorious reputation" for "buying his goods outside his home town."[3] In small towns like Pierre, buying at home was virtually the first duty of every Main Street businessperson, so a more serious accusation could hardly be advanced.

When the tax rebate proposal was referred to the voters during city elections in April 1906, Pierre's citizenry approved it, though by a less-than-overwhelming margin (230 to 179).[4] After the building was completed, however, people had to admit that it presented an impressive appearance and that performances staged there provided a wonderful attraction for the up-and-coming city on the Missouri. Traveling theater companies from Minneapolis, Chicago, and elsewhere came through town regularly. Clint and Bessie Robbins and their entourage became special favorites, as they were everywhere else in the region, and the two of them established long-standing friendships with many people in town.[5] Often, however, the quality of the visiting road groups left something to be desired. One performance of *Romeo and Juliet,* which a few days earlier in Huron had caused a local editor to comment that if "the bard of Avon didn't turn in his grave last night, he never will," inspired the *Capital Journal* to observe that "the spielers who are at large in the state with these plays should be rounded up to amuse jack rabbits and snow birds instead of the confiding public."[6]

Vaudeville troupes, minstrel shows, and local amateur theatrical groups also staged performances; and high school graduations, Decoration Day ceremonies, union revival services, lyceum series, and band, orchestral, and choir concerts also drew people to the opera house. Shortly after it opened, Senator Robert M. La Follette of Wisconsin spoke on the subject of representative government. The house that evening was reported as nearly half full; since the speech lasted for three hours, one wonders if the count was taken at the beginning or at the end of the performance. La Follette's daughter Fola later spoke for woman's rights, Carry

Nation denounced demon rum, Richard O. Richards of Huron carried on his crusade for the direct primary, and many other well-known and not-so-well-known figures spoke on the stage of the opera house.[7]

A sign of what the future held in store appeared early on, several years after the opera house opened, when movies were shown on an irregular basis, but "not of the cheap, trashy Nickelodeon style so commonly seen," ads reassured the public.[8] Later on, after a fire partially gutted it during the 1930s, the opera house was fixed up and converted into the Grand Theatre, a movie palace. Eventually, after other movie theaters were built in town, it reverted to its original use, that of staging live theatrical performances, which are now put on by local amateur groups. That was why Bruce Grulke and his two friends were there in August 1988—to assist and advise the owners in remodeling the theater to make it more attractive for modern-day audiences. The place was not air-conditioned, and the stage needed fixing up, the walls redoing, the seats replacing, and the lights upgrading; in sum, the place was old and needed to be modernized.

Bruce introduced me to Don Gallimore, the manager of the Hyde Block, and his mother, Marjorie Gallimore. Don is a great-grandson of Hyde, she a granddaughter. So the building is now under the supervision of the fourth generation of the family. Marjorie's father, Charles Lee Hyde, ran it until 1980, when he suf-

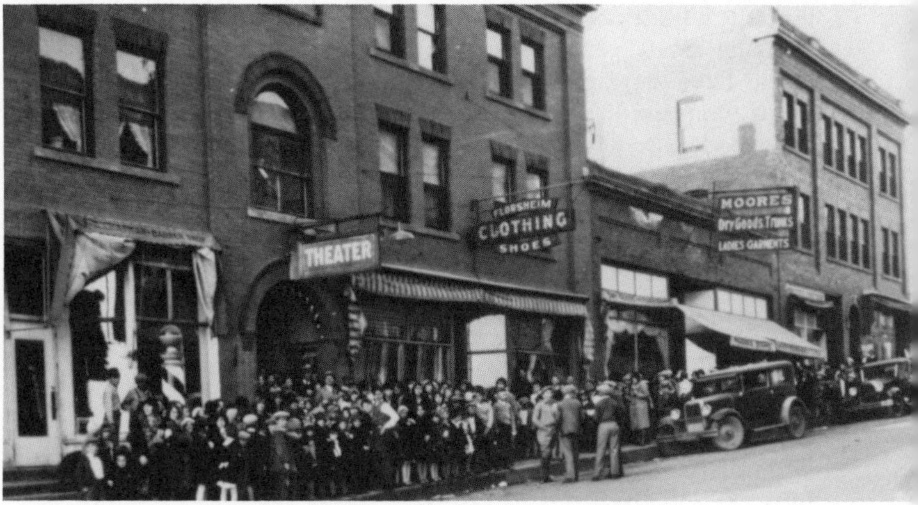

Pierreites gathered at the old Hyde Opera House in 1930.
(Courtesy of Henrietta Roberts)

fered a stroke. She took over for a time, and now Don takes care of the day-to-day operations. Marjorie pulled out a ledger dating back to the 1930s with records of attendance at the Grand Theatre. On certain days, besides listing the number of tickets sold, it also indicates the number of tires that were brought in. I asked her about this. It turned out that people were admitted free for bringing in tires on regularly scheduled days. The tires were burned in a furnace used to heat the building.

Don showed me the building's original blueprints, which he had run across in a cubbyhole under one of the stairways. He told me that the remodeling project they were working on had emerged originally out of the need to upgrade the theater in order to bring it into compliance with fire regulations. Taking the opportunity to deal with the air-conditioning problem and other deficiencies, they had contacted the Pierre Main Street Program, which is part of a nationwide network organized to improve the appearance of small town stores and buildings and to stimulate economic activity. The project snowballed from there. The Pierre Players, who regularly put on several of their summer performances in the opera house, wanted to continue using the old building if possible. It has a lot of atmosphere. Some people, I was told, drive a hundred miles or more to take in the plays, much of the attraction lying in the old opera house itself.

In building the Hyde Block and Opera House on upper Pierre Street in 1906, Don told me, his great-grandfather was anticipating an expansion in Pierre's population that would take it up the hillside, away from the flat, and eventuate in a town of as many as 100,000 people. The area down by the river then would likely have concentrated on facilities for riverboats and trains, while the direction of business development and residential construction would have been up the hillside. "Of course, times have changed," Don continued, "and we never followed that kind of expansion, and the mode of transportation changed and everything else changed, so we didn't see the river being used. The railroads are still being used, but not as many lines as maybe they had anticipated."

Pierre never grew the way Charles Leavitt Hyde hoped and expected it would, and he failed to profit from his real estate investments to the degree he had anticipated. But he didn't do so badly for himself, becoming one of South Dakota's richest and most successful businesspersons, perhaps *the* wealthiest at one time—not an inconsiderable achievement. If he didn't rank with the Carnegies and the Rockefellers, at least he ranked among the great western success stories during the late frontier period in the Upper Missouri Valley.[9]

Hyde reenacted the saga of the self-made man in America to perfection. His autobiography, like Benjamin Franklin's, recounts the story of a young man on the make, full of grit and determination, blessed with intelligence and physical stamina, and sure of his destiny.[10] On the frontier during the late nineteenth and early twentieth centuries, opportunities for men of daring and wit still existed, and Hyde was determined to take advantage of them.

His family background had prepared him well for the challenge. His father, James Franklin Hyde, traced his ancestry back to English immigrants in colonial Connecticut. Born in Pittsfield, Massachusetts, in 1813, he moved with his family to Ohio, and then as a young man he went to Pike County, Illinois, later moving to the town of Lincoln. He taught school for many years, became a county superintendent, and also served as county treasurer, a member of the Lincoln city council, city comptroller, and city treasurer, not retiring from the last position until May 1911, when he was ninety-seven years old. Active in the Masonic order, the elder Hyde was known as a kind and gentle man who worked hard, was conscientious and upright, and remained loyal to his friends.[11]Harriet Blake Hyde was twenty years old and nineteen years younger than James Franklin Hyde when she married him after his first wife died. They had three children—Clara, who died young; Franklin, who moved to Winnipeg; and Charles, the youngest, born on June 23, 1860. Harriet Blake Hyde, Irish by background, was a serious-minded woman and a diligent reader, who introduced her younger son to Darwin's *On the Origin of Species by Means of Natural Selection* and *The Descent of Man*. Later, the reading of books like Thomas Paine's *The Age of Reason* and *Rights of Man* further schooled the youth in unorthodox ways of thought, a defining characteristic of his all through life.[12]

Charles Levitt Hyde always marked out his own pathway in life. In his autobiography he admitted to having been a naughty child. As a youth he loved the outdoors and physical activity, became a champion wrestler, and excelled in gymnastics. Swimming, fishing, and skating took up much of his time. Buying his first shotgun at the age of fifteen turned him into a hunter for life, and he spent a lot of his time as an adult traipsing around South Dakota, Canada, and the Upper Midwest in pursuit of birds and game. Never very large (weighing 130 to 140 pounds as an adult), Hyde took great pride in his ability to lift heavy weights and defeat opponents larger than himself. When he was around sixty, he bested a young man from a nearby town who stood six feet two inches tall and weighed 212 pounds in a contest to see who could lift a car and hold it in the air the longest. Not once but dozens of times Hyde demonstrated his ability to lift a Model T Ford in the air by grabbing the wooden spokes of its wheels. In his autobiography there is a picture of him at the age of sixty-five, stripped to a pair of shorts to reveal his muscular build.[13]

Not surprisingly, Hyde, from youth to adulthood, was a scrappy fellow. He loved to engage in fights and contests that pitted himself against others. While gregarious and possessed of many friends (among them: state historian Doane Robinson, Congressman Charles H. Burke, and businessman John E. Mallery), he also attracted more than his share of enemies. Life for him was always a battle—against the elements and other challenges standing in his way, against other men, against himself. The secret of success, Hyde said in looking back upon his life, is constant struggle, self-control, and self-denial. Tobacco, liquor, and other indulgences were to him anathema. Perseverance, steady judgment, frugality—these were essential. His struggles taught him that the "first or most important characteristic for achievement is energy; one must work and work, and, when tired, rest and then work again."[14]

That rule motivated Hyde from the very beginning. He was only sixteen when he left his home in Lincoln, Illinois, to seek adventure and fortune in the West. A two and a half year stint as a cowboy in Colorado and Wyoming, he later wrote, made him grow "from a boy into a man." After working for a year as a reporter for the Chicago *Inter-Ocean,* he spent his early twenties, from 1880 until 1886, traveling around the West selling hardware specialties for an Eastern manufacturing firm. By day he sold hardware; by night he often performed as a championship roller skater, often under an assumed name, usually winning the purse or the bet. Checking his baggage through to a town down the line, he often walked five or ten miles to the next town carrying his sample case rather than wait several hours for the next train to arrive. Always on the go, Hyde was a man on the make. The $200 to $300 a month he was earning was extremely good pay for the time. Most of it he saved, and as time went by, he began to invest some of it in property. By the time he was twenty-six, he claimed to have visited practically every county in twenty different states as well as most of the larger cities in the United States. All of this was a good education for him. "Sometimes I was lonesome and homesick," he later wrote, "but I was laying the foundation for a fortune and building character as well."[15]

During the spring of 1884, while placing an advertisement in the Warren, Ohio, *Tribune,* the ambitious young salesman spied a nineteen-year-old farmer's daughter who was working in the office. Her name was Kittie Robinson, and after observing her from several different angles as she moved about her work, Hyde concluded that she was "a girl the nearest to perfection that I had yet seen." Her carriage was "magnificent," and the shape of her head "indicated a very high grade of intelligence, integrity or conscientiousness, energy or ambition, agilty or physical competence, and at the same time a serene complacency that indicated courage and a fearless, firm will." Hyde did what one might have expected him to do under such circumstances. He took a few weeks' layoff from the firm he was working for, obtained exclusive rights from a book company to sell its books in the area, and rented a room in the boarding house where Kittie Robinson was staying.[16]

The two soon became acquainted, but it took more than a year, by which time Hyde was back on the road with his regular job, before he persuaded his object of affection to marry him. They settled down in July 1886 in their new home in Lima, Ohio, where they bought a wallpaper and carpet store. One wonders how the Hyde story might have turned out had they remained in Lima, but eighteen months later, after selling the store for about twice as much as they had paid for it, they were on their way to Pierre, Dakota Territory, which, Hyde calculated, possessed the best potential for growth and development and for building a personal fortune for him and his family (eventually there were five children: three sons and two daughters).[17]

Hyde had surveyed the situation carefully, concluding that Pierre offered the greatest opportunity for advancement and would eventually become a city in league with Omaha, Denver,

Charles Leavitt Hyde in 1905. (Courtesy of Don Gallimore)

and Minneapolis—the greatest metropolis in the Upper Missouri Valley. A year later, in 1889 (the year of South Dakota statehood), Pierre would win the great prize of being selected as the capital, but other than that the prospects of the town remained decidedly gloomy for several years. The rejoicing over the capital lost much of its edge as the decade of the 1890s proceeded. South Dakota was caught up in a terrible drought and agricultural depression that began just about the time the Hydes arrived and that turned many South Dakota farmers to populism, enabling the new protest party to capture political control over the state during the 1896 election.

Hyde, however, was not discouraged. He took his opportunities where he found them. He bought land in Hughes County (Pierre was the county seat) and built up a herd of cattle that soon numbered over one thousand head. He often accompanied carloads of cattle from Pierre to the stockyards in Chicago. In the meantime, he also started buying up properties for speculation. He later estimated that he made over two thousand land transactions between 1886 and 1930, most of them between 1888 and 1912. He bought and sold over one hundred thousand acres of prairie land, making $1 to $10 profit per acre, and he also bought and sold about one thousand lots in and around Pierre.[18]

To boost Pierre and also to advertise his own real estate business, Hyde started publishing a four-page monthly newspaper called the Pierre *Rustler* in January 1892. It reprinted items from other newspapers about business prospects, railroad building, weather conditions, agricultural and mineral resources, building improvements, and anything that made the Northwest, South Dakota, and Pierre look like a progressive, prosperous area. As editor and publisher of the newspaper, Hyde himself probably wrote many of the longer, more fulsome articles about the wonderful natural gas resources around Pierre, the prospects for railroad connections to the city, and the surefire land profits to be made by wise investors. His own ad, which ran regularly in the *Rustler,* asked readers, "WHY NOT BE RICH? A few hundred dollars invested in Pierre today will amount to a fortune a few years from now. Write to me for special quotations, maps and circulars. Chas. L. Hyde. The Real Estate Dealer. Pierre, S.D." In the initial issue of the *Rustler* he wrote, "If you do not fully comprehend the full significance of our name look it up in your International Unabridged."[19]

Maintaining one's optimism in Pierre during the 1890s must have been difficult. Its population slipped from 3,235 in 1890 to 2,306 in 1900, dipping lower than that before 1897, when the depression of the 1890s began to recede and make way for better times. Signs heralding the return of prosperity began to appear by 1898, but not until after 1900 did it take hold in earnest. The February 1901 *Rustler* confidently predicted,

> About every 20 years, in the history of this nation, there has come a period in the newer portion of the country where literal fortunes are made in a few years time from the advance of real estate. Such a period of time is now not only due, but has actually commenced in the west, and certainly no place is so sure to be in the center of the field of rapid advancement and development as Pierre, and it must be that here is one of the golden points, where a few hundred dollars invested now will grow to many thousands during the next five years. The time of depression is passed. The time of advancement and expansion is at hand.

Hyde mentioned a friend of his who had bought a fifty-foot lot in Seattle for $400 in 1878 and had sold it without any improvements twelve years later for $50,000. Another acquaintance of his had bought four lots in Denver in 1877 for $100 each and had sold the bunch six years later for $60,000. Hyde looked for Pierre to show the same kind of advancement.[20]

Besides the return of prosperity, three other developments contributed to Pierre's prospects after 1900. First, it emerged victorious over Mitchell in a capital removal vote on the general ballot in 1904, which was the last effort by other cities to take the capital away from Pierre. The vote was 58,617 to 41,155, and immediately afterwards, during the legislative session of 1905, lawmakers proceeded to authorize the building of a magnificent new capitol to replace the rickety, old, two-story wooden structure that had served until then.[21] Second, homesteaders began moving across the Missouri River onto land that until 1890 had been part of the Great Sioux Reservation. Though open for settlement for a decade, few farmers or ranchers had ventured out into the region because of drought and depression. By 1902 and 1903, however, Pierreites began to witness a steady stream of agriculturalists taking up land across the river, and businesses in town stood to gain by supplying them.[22]

Third, the Chicago and North Western Railway announced in September 1905 that it would bridge the Missouri River and extend its line west to Rapid City. For years, speculation had abounded about when the tracks would be laid, but always officials in Chicago had postponed construction. They might have laid the rails as soon as the early 1880s had not the Indian reservation stood in the way. During 1906 and 1907 railroad construction crews worked busily in Pierre raising tracks, putting in a viaduct, building new shops, and, most importantly, building the bridge across the river. There was considerable speculation that company officials might decide to shift the division headquarters from Huron to Pierre or at least upgrade the status of Pierre as a passenger depot and freight transfer point. Every time company president Marvin Hughitt and his entourage visited Pierre to observe personally the progress being made, newspaper editors and businesspeople in town tried hard to learn more about what was being planned, but he and everyone else connected with the railroad maintained their customary reticence, never divulging more than was absolutely necessary.[23]

During the spring of 1907 construction began on a large, modern passenger depot, just west of Pierre Street and north of the old freight depot. Built of brick, 337 feet long and two stories high along part of its length, when it opened in February 1908, it made the impressive appearance that Pierre's residents desired and inspired even greater hopes among Hyde and his fellow boosters that Pierre was on its way to becoming another Minneapolis, Omaha, or Denver. Hyde noted that Pierre's natural market region extended throughout central South Dakota and that it had no competition for dominance for a hundred miles or more in every direction.[24]

Hyde's decision in late 1905 to build an office block and opera house was preceded by the construction of several other buildings along Capitol Avenue. A new state capitol was approved by action taken during the 1905 legislative session; it was under construction from August 1907 to June 1910. The first major construction project along the avenue, however, had been the new post office and federal court building, which was initiated in May 1902, with a congressional appropriation of $5,000 to purchase a site for it. The lot chosen was situated one block west of the courthouse on the corner of Capitol and Huron avenues and was sold to the government by Hyde, who owned many properties along Capitol Avenue, which he enthusiastically promoted as the heart of future development in the hill district. The following year Congress appropriated $175,000 for actual construction, which was completed in October 1906. Built of the same kind of Bedford stone used in the capitol and designed along the same classical lines as many public buildings of the period, the new post office presented an imposing appearance and stimulated great pride among Pierre's citizens, who enthusiastically noted that the $175,000 appropriation for the building exceeded all but 13 of the 173 subsidies approved by Congress during the session and put Pierre above such towns as Montgomery, Alabama; Colorado Springs, Colorado; and Atlanta, Georgia. Meanwhile, with a $10,000 gift from the steel baron Andrew Carnegie, a new granite block library building went up a block east of the courthouse during 1903 and 1904.[25]

Thus, Hyde's announcement in September 1905 that he would build a large brick office building on the corner lot south of the courthouse and that he would follow that up with several other brick buildings on Capitol Avenue during the next several years was just one additional piece of good news for Pierre's boosters, who already were seeing their dreams being fulfilled.[26] The Hyde Block and Grand Opera House opened in the fall of 1906. The Capitol Avenue Block, located to the east of the Hyde Block, opened in 1908, and the Pierre Street Block, situated on the corner of Pierre Street and Capitol Avenue directly west of the Capitol Avenue Block, opened in 1909. Two years later, the St. Charles Hotel opened for business. Hyde, who never believed in borrowing money, advertised his buildings on Capitol Avenue as "a street without a mortgage."[27]

Things seemed to be proceeding nicely for Hyde, and the city was growing and prospering, too (even if the 3,656 people counted in the 1910 census didn't quite match the 4,000 that Hyde and others advertised it as). Then disaster struck. One setback was ecological, as drought set in, especially in the area west of the river, in 1911, which started overeager settlers packing and on the way back home.[28] Much more personally distressing was Hyde's indictment in federal district court in October 1910 for mail fraud in the sale of land.

By then he had accumulated a personal wealth estimated at $2 million to $3 million, which made him a target for people who resented his rapid rise to wealth and for those who doubted that he could have become so successful using strictly legitimate means.[29] The real estate business was peculiarly susceptible to the exaggerated statement, the inflated claim, and downright fraud, and in the eyes of some people at least, Hyde was guilty of such practices. "The king of the land jugglers," they called him.[30] Also, there were those with businesses on the flat who resented Hyde's continual efforts to promote development in the hill district, which they feared would reduce their own position down by the river. Hyde himself blamed his woes, in part, on disgruntled businesspeople who hoped to stop, or at least retard, his push for new building up on the second level. The original complaints against him apparently were initiated by a bank clerk in Hyde's employ who had been discharged for dishonesty.[31]

The case took a year to come to trial, and it split Pierreites into two camps—those who stood by Hyde and those who didn't. It was hardly possible to remain neutral in the matter. For his part, Hyde denied any wrongdoing, rallied his friends and supporters behind him, and tried to carry on his activities as best he could.[32] On a wall in his office he hung a copy of Rudyard Kipling's poem "If," which begins:

Charles Hyde's Capitol Avenue Block, Pierre Block, and Hyde Block (with Drugs canopy) changed the appearance of Capitol Avenue during the early 1900s. The three-story Hyde Opera House is visible beyond the Hyde Block. (Miller Studio photo; courtesy of South Dakota State Historical Society, Pierre)

If you can keep your head, when all about you
Are losing theirs, and blaming it on you;
If you can trust yourself when men doubt you,
And make allowance for their doubting too;
If you can wait and not be tired waiting,
Or being lied about, don't deal in lies,
Or being hated, don't give way to hating,
And yet don't look too good nor talk too wise.

He included these lines in a statement he gave out to explain his innocence of the allegations raised against him. "I have never sold any Pierre real estate to anyone that I did not confidently believe would make the purchaser a very profitable investment," he assured people. "That I have been too optimistic in my judgment of the immediate advantages and near future prospects of Pierre

may be self evident to some. It is for the future to show whether or not I was so unwarranted in my optimism. I have believed all statements I have made to be truthful and warranted."[33]

For someone like Hyde, the charges preferred against him were nothing short of ridiculous and could only have been motivated by ignorance or spite. At the trial in Sioux Falls in December 1911, he was accused of selling worthless lots far from town to out-of-town buyers, eighteen in all, the highest price being $57.50. They were all on the hill where Hyde expected the town's development to proceed and on which he had staked his own financial future. He argued that the lots would be worth ten times as much as he had sold them for once Pierre reached a population of 25,000, and several witnesses testified in his favor that the lots were, in fact, valuable. The properties were only a mile or a mile and a quarter from the post office. Other witnesses, however, asserted just the opposite, the government relying largely on testimony from residents and businesspeople on the flat who opposed and refused to believe in development up the hill.[34]

The government further charged that Hyde had widely distributed maps of Pierre showing two street railways in operation, when none in fact existed at the time, that he sent out maps picturing several railroads entering Pierre, and that he used stationery indicating that resources in the Pierre area included petroleum, coal, cattle, sheep, and a gas plant, as well as other things. In all of this, Hyde was guilty of the same kinds of exaggeration and overstatement that were commonplace in the editorials and stories of almost every small town newspaper, in the advertising issued by every local commercial club, and in the booster talk of every Main Street businessperson in Dakota. In fact, there *had been* a street railway operating in Pierre and another one was being considered when Hyde's map was originally printed. The first was soon discontinued and the second was never built, but he continued to use the map anyway. It would be only a slight exaggeration to say that no town worth its salt did *not* believe that four or five new railroads would build to it in the foreseeable future. Hyde did not go out of his way to create false impressions and usually, but not always, stuck to the literal truth in making his claims. Though coal and oil may not have been present immediately around Pierre, they *were* present (in limited quantities) elsewhere in the state, and his stationery depicted state resources, not local ones, if one inspected it closely.[35]

Hyde enlisted a galaxy of prominent friends and well-wishers to testify to his good character and intentions. John E. Mallery, the mayor of Pierre and a storekeeper in the Hyde Block, indicated that in all of his many business dealings with Hyde he had found him "reliable and trustworthy, doing as he promised he would do." South Dakota Attorney General Samuel W. Clark said that Hyde had "acted with the utmost fairness and frankness in any business dealings that I have had with him, and in all business dealings that have been called to my attention."[36]

Comments like those of Hyde's fellow go-getting businessman, P. F. McClure, however, could cut both ways: "His optimism is something remarkable and beyond the ken of us common mortals." In selling his lots and expecting their value to increase, Hyde was anticipating no more for the buyers than he did for himself. He would not have become the rich man that he was had he not been a risk taker. U.S. Senator Coe I. Crawford, who had known Hyde in Pierre before moving to Huron, wrote, "Mr. Hyde is above all things an optimist. He looks into the future, and with a splendid enthusiasm and optimism coupled with another trait—which is a valuable one when not too lively—imagination, he looks beyond the present environment of community and sees possibilities in growth and expansion which others cannot see, but which to him are verities."[37]

Some government officials were intent, however, upon making an example out of Hyde in order to serve notice to other aggressive real estate operators that they would have to keep their claims totally honest and aboveboard. Hyde's conviction and sentencing in December 1911 to a $1,500 fine and a fifteen-month jail term caused "real astonishment and consternation in the community," according to his friend Doane Robinson, the state historian.[38] Robinson stood by him as did many other friends who urged President Taft to pardon the real estate king. A petition for Hyde's pardon was endorsed by the state's governor, secretary of state, and attorney general, as well as many other state officers, two judges of the state supreme court, the two U.S. congressmen and two senators, and the pastors of every church in Pierre. The Pierre *Capital-Journal,* on the other hand, spoke for those who considered Hyde to be "the unfortunate victim of his own greed for what we believe to be a disease for acquiring money."[39]

To carry his case to the president for a pardon, Hyde retained the services of Wade Ellis, a former schoolmate of Taft's who had served for a time as assistant to the attorney general in charge of trust prosecutions. Edward E. Wagner, U.S. attorney for South Dakota, was convinced of Hyde's guilt and resigned from his position when he was contradicted by Attorney General George W. Wickersham and then was ordered to come to Washington to discuss the case with his superior.[40]

The decision was not an easy one for the president to make. The evidence against Hyde was contradictory and the charges themselves less than earthshaking. Yet to pardon a wealthy, prominent defendant like Hyde might create the appearance of a double standard of justice for the rich and the poor. Wickersham himself felt compelled to refute rumors that certain Justice Department officials had pushed the case against Hyde just to put to rest rumors that they had been soft on influential criminal suspects. President Taft, interestingly enough, had visited Pierre in October 1911, shortly before the case went to trial. The president's first glimpse of town had been from the new Chicago and North Western Railway depot, and he had been driven along Capitol Avenue past Hyde's properties on "the street without a mortgage." His entourage had stayed at Hyde's brand-new St. Charles Hotel, and he had been entertained at a luncheon there on Sunday after attending services at the recently completed Methodist Church, which was just a couple of blocks away from Hyde's buildings in the hill district. Sunday evening the president had stayed overnight at the home of Congressman Charles H. Burke, the man responsible for obtaining the appropriation for the new federal building built on one of Hyde's lots on Capitol Avenue.[41]

The fact that Taft had recently visited the hill district in the capital, however, was merely coincidental. The question at hand was whether or not there was justification for pardoning the Pierre entrepreneur. It was not an easy issue to decide and was not finally made until virtually the last moment, the announcement coming on the evening of March 3, just hours before Woodrow Wilson was sworn in as the new president on the following day. Taft relied upon the report of Attorney General Wickersham, which concluded that Hyde's only serious offense had been to keep using the maps with the nonexistent streetcar lines on it, which was hardly a major crime. Hyde spent the day of his pardon working in his office, telling reporters and friends who stopped by to see him that he was confident that everything would work out all right and that he would be exonerated.[42]

By this time, however, Hyde was already cutting back on his real estate operations. The March 1913 issue marked the last appearance of the Pierre *Rustler*. "While the past 3 years have had some disappointments for we who were expecting great developments here, there is no good reason why anyone should alter their optimistic opinion of the future of this young city," he wrote.[43] Hyde continued to boost the hill district and to manage his buildings and properties, but his vision of a large, bustling city on the banks of the Missouri never came to fruition. In his autobiography, published posthumously by G. P. Putnam's Sons in 1939, he resignedly noted, "One of the great disappointments of my life has been that Pierre failed to grow as quickly and extensively as we anticipated." While making no mention of his trial in the book, Hyde readily admitted that he had been overoptimistic in his sale of outlying lots at the time but justified his actions and continued to hold out the hope that his faith might ultimately be vindicated. "The land [where the lots were sold] is high and reasonably smooth," he observed, "and a city of 20,000 or less at Pierre would make every lot I sold worth 10 or in some instances 20 times the price I received for it."[44]

By the time of his death on September 10, 1938, however, Pierre retained its quiet, villagelike atmosphere and had grown to a population of only a little more than 4,000 people. Hyde had become a legendary figure in the area. Among the pallbearers at his funeral was Governor Leslie Jensen, and honorary pallbearers included Doane Robinson and former congressman Charles H. Burke. Stores and business houses closed during the funeral out of respect for Pierre's greatest booster—a throwback to an era when the pioneer spirit ruled and anything seemed possible.[45]

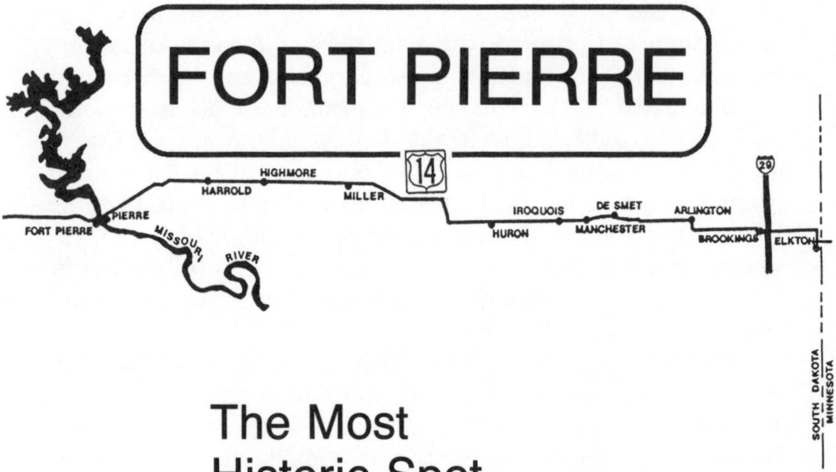

The Most Historic Spot in South Dakota

To the unsuspecting traveler, the town of Fort Pierre, located on the west bank of the Missouri River directly opposite Pierre, would appear to be a poor relation to the capital—its satellite, sister city, suburb, call it what you will. What Camden, New Jersey, is to Philadelphia, what East St. Louis is to St. Louis, what Windsor is to Detroit—that, it would seem, is Fort Pierre's relationship to Pierre. With a population of 1,789 in the 1980 census, few businesses on Main Street, and a general lack of pretense, this tidy little town might not appear to be the most interesting of places.

Yet appearances deceive. Although nothing obviously indicates it, this is the most historic spot in South Dakota. Long before the settlers arrived, American Indian peoples frequented the place, setting up camp here and holding council with each other during their wanderings through the surrounding country in search of buffalo.[1] Here the Bad River, so named by the Sioux (or Dakotas), who had witnessed its frequent spring rampages when its usually tranquil waters turn ferocious, empties into the wide Missouri. Pierre lawyer and amateur historian Charles E. DeLand, writing in 1902, called the location "the most important commercial point in the entire northwest within the limits of the Louisiana Purchase." Trails from several directions converged here, connecting with points on the James, Big Sioux, Minnesota, and Mississippi rivers, as well as with places to the west. The Bad River route was a natural one to take to the west and southwest.[2]

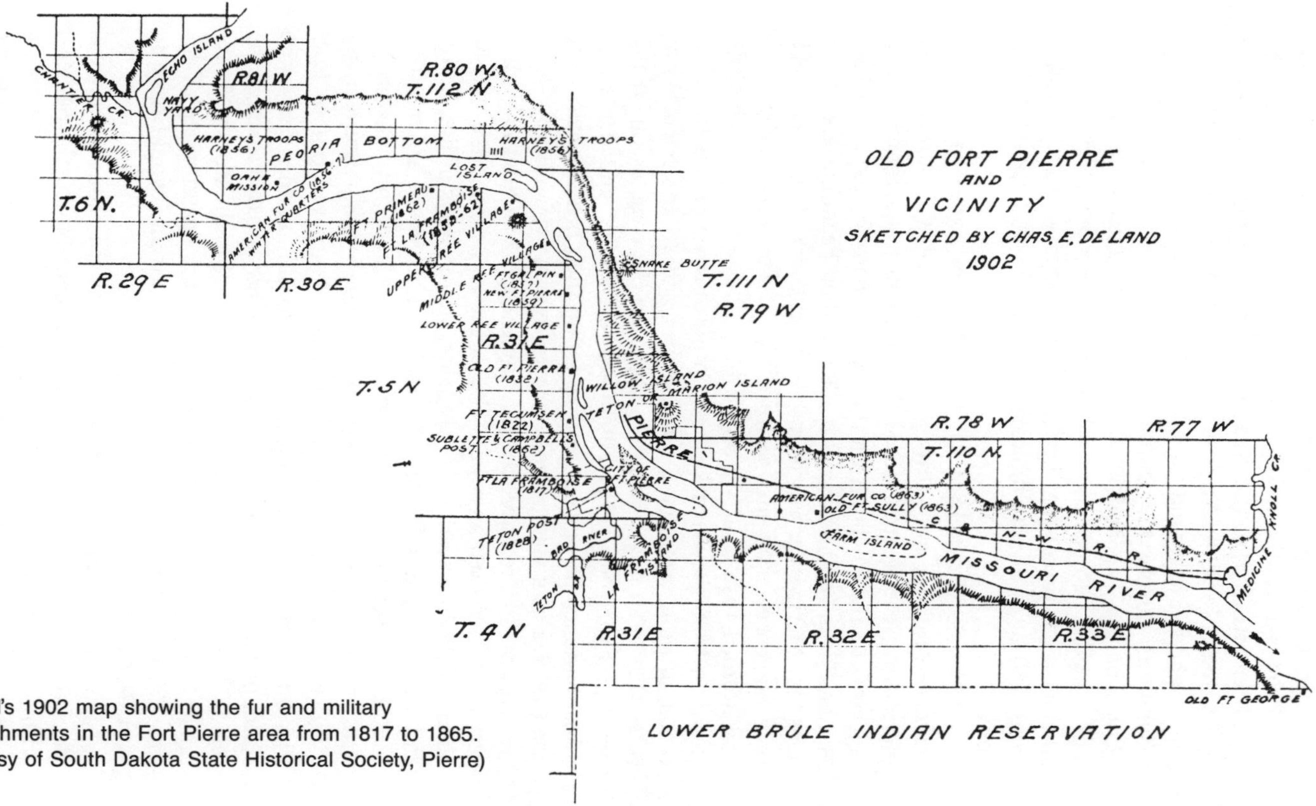

DeLand's 1902 map showing the fur and military establishments in the Fort Pierre area from 1817 to 1865. (Courtesy of South Dakota State Historical Society, Pierre)

Even before the Sioux arrived on the scene around the middle of the eighteenth century, other Native American groups had long been attracted to the area. Village sites strung out for about eighty miles along the Missouri from near present-day Chamberlain to above Pierre and may have contained as many as 10,000 inhabitants during the Initial Coalescent period around A.D. 1250. The area around Pierre contained numerous villages of seminomadic peoples over a long period of time. Pottery and other artifacts discovered in the area and fortifications enclosing about 130 acres of land indicate that this was an important location.[3]

In his 1902 article, Charles E. DeLand, who spent many years researching and writing about the early history of the Pierre–Fort Pierre area, noted the continuing geographic importance of the flat lowlands on the western bank of the river. Various American Indian peoples made this their headquarters. It was here that Meriwether Lewis and William Clark experienced their first dangerous encounter with the Sioux. The Astorians of 1811 and Manuel Lisa's party stopped here on their way up the Missouri. In 1832 the artist George Catlin discovered this to be the center of Sioux country. John Frémont and Joseph Nicollet, on their 1839 mapping expedition, came up the river as far as this point and then headed overland. Here Catholic and Protestant missionaries came in later years to set up their headquarters or to use the area as a staging point for forays into the West.[4]

At Fort Pierre, more so than anywhere else in South Dakota, perhaps better than anywhere else in the entire region, could be observed the intersection of two contradictory ways of life, native and European, usually defined by the more recent arrivals as a contrast between civilization and savagery: modern versus primitive, progress versus retrogression, Christian versus heathen. By 1840, when Rev. Stephen Return Riggs journeyed out to Fort Pierre to survey the prospects for Protestant missions there, the Jesuit priest Pierre-Jean De Smet had already crossed through the region on his way to evangelize the Flatheads in the Rocky Mountains. In later years the Belgian priest would spend much of his time with the Teton Sioux and other groups and would pass by Fort Pierre often.[5]

Riggs had heard much about the western Sioux (who lived west of the Missouri River) from the eastern Sioux (the Santees) with whom he had been working in Minnesota. Setting out in September 1840 with fellow missionary Alexander Huggins, he journeyed from Lac-qui-Parle, near Lake Traverse, to Fort Pierre in order to determine the feasibility of setting up a mission. It took them fifteen days to cover the 245 miles with a horse-drawn cart, eleven days to return (including days of rest on the Sabbath). Their four days at Fort Pierre, including a service held inside the fort to which all the nearby Native Americans were invited, convinced Riggs of the untapped potential of the mission field there, but it would be another thirty-two years before a mission was established on the Missouri, and when it came, it was Riggs's son Thomas who carried on the mission work, while his son Alfred got into educational work.

Based upon his observations and inquiries in 1840, the elder Riggs estimated that there were approximately thirteen thousand Teton Sioux living west of the Missouri River and sixty-four hundred Yankton and Yanktonnais to the east of it in present-day South Dakota in addition to approximately fifty-five hundred Santee Sioux in Minnesota. He was encouraged by the Tetons' receptivity to his message, considering them more favorably disposed toward Christianity than were most of their relatives in the vicinity of Lac-qui-Parle. "As yet," he observed, "they have not formed a prejudice against it." Nevertheless, he did not push immediately to establish a mission at the location because of the mobility of the groups in the area. "Like the buffalo they follow they are ever roving," he noted. But hopeful that they could be induced to change their life-style, he speculated, "Still it seems probable that a mission-station on the banks of the Missouri or some of its tributaries would gather around it families as fast as would be desirable. They are all fond of corn and, I think, would be easily induced to plant if they could have some assistance in the commencement."[6]

The missionary's optimism about changing the Native American way of life would be echoed over and over again as settlers pushed into the region and sought to establish their own values and ways of doing things there. The notion that the American Indians themselves had established some sort of workable accommodation with their environment and that they adhered to values and traditions worth preserving scarcely occurred to most of the invading settlers. The clash of cultures, relatively benign in nature for several decades, turned ugly and tragic after 1855, the year the U.S. Army arrived at Fort Pierre, converting it into the first military fort in the region. The expansion of European cultural styles in South Dakota in later years occurred at the expense of the Native American cultures that had first occupied the area, and the effort to reconcile the two ways of life still goes on today.

The missionary and educational effort of the Riggses

stamped their influence on the area during the late 1800s. It was fitting and appropriate, therefore, that the first automobile bridge to be built across the Missouri River there (part of Highway 14) should be dedicated to the memory of Rev. Stephen Return Riggs. At the dedicatory ceremonies in the state capitol on June 28, 1926, Rev. Jesse P. Williamson, a grandson of Thomas S. Williamson, who had been Riggs's missionary partner in Minnesota nine decades earlier, was chosen as speaker of the day. He recounted the 1840 cross-country journey and other historic events that had centered there, exhorting his audience to "appreciate that we are on historic ground, that we stand not only at the geographical center of South Dakota, but at the place which is now recognized as the historic center of our great State. This big winding valley of the Missouri and these surrounding hills have been the scene of more first significant historic events than any other spot within the borders of our commonwealth."[7]

Not surprisingly, considering the importance that the location possessed for Native Americans over several centuries, the first confirmed European visitors to set foot in the state left their biggest impression on the Fort Pierre area. The visit of the La Verendrye brothers, Francois and Louis-Joseph, in 1743 was part of a larger project of expanding the French fur trade and searching for an outlet to the Pacific Ocean. Their father, Pierre Gaultier de Verennes, Sieur de La Verendrye, like other visionaries of his type, was driven by several motives: adventure, profit, nationalism, and curiosity.[8] Of noble background and experienced as a soldier, he demonstrated considerable acumen in the fur trade in French Canada after obtaining a license from the French government in 1715. In 1726, at the age of forty-one, he was placed in charge of a trading post on the Nipigon River, north of Lake Superior, at the western edge of French settlement at the time. Soon he determined to explore the lands to the west and to search for a route to the western sea, a goal that had eluded scores of intrepid adventurers from many countries for more than two centuries. In 1738, venturing south and west from his current base of operations at Lake Winnipeg, he led a party of twenty-two persons, including sons Francois and Louis-Joseph, as far as the Mandan villages on the Missouri River in present-day North Dakota.

The next journey, in 1742 and 1743, was undertaken by the sons, as the elder La Verendrye was forced to stay behind to take care of business and perhaps his health, too. Accompanied by two French coureurs de bois, they spent time with various Native American peoples in the western Dakota region, then joined a group of Bows going out to make war on their enemies. The hills the sons visited and described in their journals were once thought to be the Big Horn Mountains or perhaps even the Rockies, but judging from the distances involved and their normal rate of travel, it appears that they skirted the Black Hills before angling back toward the Missouri River, where they arrived at the mouth of the Bad River on March 19, 1743. They remained for two weeks there at the fort of the Bows, having heard about a French-speaking trapper who lived about three days' journey away and in hopes that they might be able to meet him. "I would have gone to find him if our horses had been in condition," Francois La Venendrye (who was known as "the Chevalier") wrote in his journal. Desirous of returning to home base and sensing that further delay would be fruitless, the brothers set out on their northward journey on April 2, but not before leaving evidence of their presence at the place.[9]

On March 30 Francois La Venendrye buried a lead plate—eight and a half inches long, six and a half inches wide, and about an eighth of an inch thick—on the tallest hillside overlooking the river. Scratched on it was an inscription identifying them as being present there on that date and establishing the French claim to the region. The Chevalier recorded in his journal, "I placed on an eminence near the fort a tablet of lead with the arms and inscription of the King and a pyramid of stones for Monsieur le General; I said to the savages, who did not know of the tablet of lead that I had placed in the earth, that I was placing these stones as a memorial to those who had come to their country."[10]

The plate remained undiscovered on the hillside for 170 years until it was unearthed on February 16, 1913, by a group of schoolchildren who were hiking around the area.[11] By then the stones had been removed and wind and rain had begun to erode the hillside, exposing one edge of the plate, which was stumbled upon by the children. One of the boys suggested they sell it to the local print shop to be melted down for type, but when a couple of state legislators caught wind of their find, they had the plate inspected by state historian Doane Robinson. He quickly established its identity, and the children were paid a hefty financial reward for their find, which was put on display by the South Dakota State Historical Society. Robinson and others had long anticipated the discovery. Just a few years earlier he had written, "This leaden plate if ever discovered would be of inestimable value." Considering that he thought it had been buried on a hill overlooking the mouth of the White River, eighty miles southeast of Fort Pierre, he was certainly right on that point![12] Francis

Parkman, the great nineteenth-century romantic chronicler of western history, thought the plate would be found near the mouth of the Niobrara River.[13]

Twenty years later, when the Verendrye Monument was dedicated on the hill, speaker of the day George Philip remarked, "It can be asserted with justice that we now stand on the most historically romantic and romantically historic spot in South Dakota."[14] The governor and the French consul general from Chicago were present at the ceremonies along with Doane Robinson, Mount Rushmore sculptor Gutzon Borglum, Charles E. DeLand of Pierre, the first European child to be born in the Dakotas (at Fort Pierre on March 20, 1857), and others.[15]

But the access road to Verendrye Hill remained poorly marked and hard to find, and little was done to maintain the grounds around the monument. Doane Robinson's son Will, who became secretary of the State Historical Society, wrote the mayor of Fort Pierre in April 1951, complaining that while escorting a group of schoolchildren over to see the monument he wanted to turn around immediately and go back home. "The landscape was literally covered with blown paper and the roadside was actually covered with debris," he wrote. "This offended me but my offense was trivial beside the reaction of a couple of out-of-town school children who simply could not see how such a condition could occur within 100 yards of the most important historical land mark in the great Northwest."[16]

Several years later the Fort Pierre *Times* reprinted an editorial from the Canova weekly paper expressing similar sentiments. The visiting editor had taken a couple of grandsons, who had learned about the historic spot in school, over to see it. They had found it necessary to ask a gas station attendant how to find the monument. Then, since the road was not marked, they had gotten lost and wound up on the wrong hill before finally figuring how to get there. In addition, according to the editor, "the road up the hill, once blacktopped, is in terrible condition with large holes in it and absolutely dangerous to travel on. The Verendrye site is one of the most important historical spots in the state and most tourists would certainly want to visit it but we doubt if very many do under the circumstances. We think the road to the site should be improved and markers placed along the highway telling people how to get there."[17]

For such a historic site, the hill attracted relatively little attention, though the three flagpoles standing near the monument with its bronze plaque were easily visible from the highway that ran below it. Recently a local committee started a drive to have the U.S. Park Service take over management of the site, something members hope to achieve by 1993, which will be the 250th anniversary of the Verendrye visit. On August 30, 1989, to commemorate the centennial of South Dakota statehood, a rededication ceremony was held, attended by Governor George Mickelson, French Consul General Richard Narick, Senator Tom Daschle, and ninety-year-old Ethel Roberts—one of the three schoolchildren who had discovered the plate in 1913.[18]

Adding to the significance of the occasion was the simultaneous celebration of the bicentennial of the French Revolution in 1989. John Moisan, one of the ceremony's organizers, noted, "Because France and South Dakota are uniquely tied, we thought it was a good opportunity to do this." The hillside, he noted, is probably the state's most historic site. "It's the most significant site in five states," he told a reporter. "It's the first recorded site of Anglo-Saxon people visiting the state. It's the site where Frenchmen claimed the site for France."[19]

The Verendrye Monument.

Although Native Americans were in the majority when the Verendryes camped at the mouth of the Bad River in 1743, none were evident in the story of the 1989 rededication or in the accompanying picture. It is well to remember that when the Chevalier buried the plate on the hillside, he was also hiding it from the American Indians gathered there. He covered the location with stones, saying that the stones were put there as a memorial for those who had come into the country. Calling this the most historic spot in South Dakota is, in effect, celebrating the late arrival of Europeans here and indirectly endorsing the process whereby they eventually established control over the land, dispossessing its original inhabitants.

Little was made during the state centennial celebration of another centennial occurring in 1989: the year marked one hundred years since Congress passed legislation opening up for settlement nine million acres on the Great Sioux Reservation west of the Missouri River.[20] Under terms of the Treaty of Fort Laramie of 1868, which set aside all of what later would become West River South Dakota as a reservation for the Sioux, three-fourths of the adult males would have to agree before any part of it was relinquished. In 1877, after the Battle of the Little Big Horn, Congress illegally punished the Sioux for their victory over General George Custer by taking back all of the Black Hills and the areas along the western boundary of Dakota Territory without obtaining the required permission. After decades of litigation in the federal courts, the U.S. Supreme Court ruled in 1980 that this action had been one of the most flagrant violations of law in American history and that the Sioux were entitled to compensation.

The land cession of 1889 was not easy to accomplish. A three-man treaty commission had to use every bit of persuasive power it possessed to convince the Sioux to agree to trade their land for some rather miserly financial considerations. In the end it was threats more than reason that did the trick. Judge Gideon Moody, soon to be elected as one of South Dakota's first two U.S. senators, stated the mood of much of the populace succinctly:

> The extinguishment of the Indian title to so large an area of our state must be insisted upon and that speedily. If the red man refuses to accept the terms so considerately tendered him, the right of self-preservation manifestly requires that congress must legislate in the interests of the white man. . . . Those lands must be opened to settlement, and the plausible but foundationless obsta-

> cles of the visionary claim of the Indian to the progress of civilization must be removed and speedily.[21]

But unlike in Oklahoma, where the Sooner land rush became fabled in story and song, there was no great rush to settle West River South Dakota in 1890. Drought conditions were beginning to set in and soon would get much worse. Depressed farm prices and a nationwide economic depression further discouraged settlement, which did not pick up significantly until around the turn of the century. Then when the Chicago and North Western Railway bridged the river in 1907 and extended its track to the Black Hills, there was a rush of settlement into the area until another drought in 1910 and 1911 sent many of the settlers scurrying back home.

Here at the Missouri River, therefore, where the Bad River joins the "Big Muddy," can be found the intersection of several important historical realities and forces. First, and most obvious, the rivers meet here: the great Missouri and what on some maps was called the "Little Missouri" but which Lewis and Clark called the "Teton," in honor of the American Indians who lived there, and which the Tetons themselves called the "Bad," based on their own experience with its turbulent unpredictability. Beyond that, topography dramatically shifts around the Missouri River, with gently rolling hills east of it and much more pronounced hills and ravines west of it. The 100th meridian, generally considered to be the significant dividing line between prairie and plain, between tallgrass and shortgrass country, between traditional and dryland farming—in fact, between wholly different ways of life—runs less than twenty miles east of here. South Dakotans tend to place less importance on the meridian itself, which after all is only an abstraction, than they do on the river, which is nothing if not concrete and formidable.[22]

The Missouri River over several centuries played a dual role—both as highway or conduit and as barrier or roadblock.[23] The lifeways of the early American Indian groups who established their villages at sites along the river were heavily influenced, it is apparent, by the practices of peoples located farther downstream, especially by the Mound Builders at Cahokia, near present-day East St. Louis. For the Native Americans, therefore, the river established connections with neighbors, near and far, but it also constituted something of a barrier. The river could be crossed in canoes, and it could be swum, to be sure, and when the water was low almost waded at points, but it also established a dividing line between groups. The Teton Sioux pushed west from Minnesota during the early 1700s, warred with the Arikaras and pushed them up the river toward North Dakota, and by about midcentury crossed over to the west, where they followed the buffalo, while the Yankton and Yanktonnais Sioux followed a less nomadic life-style east of the river.

If the Missouri was something like a semipermeable membrane for Native Americans, settlers moving into the area beginning in 1880 found it to be a veritable wall. The railroad stopped at the water's edge at Pierre. Under terms of the Fort Laramie treaty, whites were forbidden to settle in the region west of the river and with few exceptions were able only to pass through to get to the Black Hills. The Chicago and North Western Railway undoubtedly would have liked to extend its line through the reservation to Rapid City and was able to obtain rights to a square mile of land on the west side of the river (this "Mile Square" later was located in the heart of the town of Fort Pierre) to use for railroad facilities. But there would be no tracks laid west of the river until 1906 and 1907 when this railroad and its great rival, the Chicago, Milwaukee, and St. Paul, both extended their tracks west from the Missouri River at Fort Pierre and Chamberlain. The opening of reservation lands to settlement in 1890 failed to provide the needed impetus, what with drought and depressed economic conditions at the time. Thus, for a quarter of a century after the railroad arrived at the Missouri River, it formed more of a roadblock than an entry into the West River region.

Nevertheless, if divisions persisted, the point still served as an intersection between East and West. The Black Hills gold rush after 1874 stimulated tremendous movement into the area. Congress authorized three wagon trails across the reservation to move people and goods to the goldfields, the most important of which was the Fort Pierre–Deadwood Trail, which opened in 1876. Passengers and freight came up the Missouri on steamboats and then crossed over by bull train—huge caravans of wagons pulled by oxen and mules. When a Chicago and North Western branch line was extended northward to the Black Hills from Chadron, Nebraska, in 1886, providing the Black Hills with direct rail connections to the East, traffic on the Fort Pierre–Deadwood Trail soon fell to a trickle. But for a decade the spectacle of bullwhips and the roar of the bullwhackers on the gumbo trail provided a colorful chapter of frontier history.[24]

Besides standing at the intersection of the two rivers, the railroad and the Missouri River, the wagon trail and the river, East and West, and prairie and plain, Fort Pierre also stood at the intersection of past and present. New technologies—first the steamboat and then the railroad—clashed with traditional ways practiced by the Native American cultures, whether nomadic or settled. The culture that people of European backgrounds carried with them—including books, newspapers, pianos, plows, windmills, baseball, lodge halls, and chicken pie suppers—clashed strongly with the buffalo-centered culture of the Sioux and the corn-centered culture of the Arikara, who had preceded them. European settlers were surprised when Native Americans failed to appreciate their ways of doing things, while the Native Americans themselves experienced difficulty in deciding what in the settlers' culture they were willing to adopt and what they should reject.

This cultural conflict had occurred across the continent ever since the first Europeans arrived with their beads, trinkets, guns, and liquor. In Dakota it was here at the confluence of the Bad and the Missouri that the intersection of European and American Indian cultures was most dramatically played out. The spot acted like a magnet, drawing the two sides together. Sometime after 1795 Registre Loisel of St. Louis built a fur trading post on Cedar Island, a few miles down the Missouri from the mouth of the Bad River. A Sioux winter count (an annual graphic depiction of the year's major events painted on a hide) from that period indicates that "Little Beaver"—the Sioux name for the trader—built the post in 1801–2. He died in 1804, and the post was later taken over by Manuel Lisa.[25]

Lisa, a St. Louis trader of Spanish extraction, became the biggest operator on the river. Shortly after the return of Lewis and Clark in 1806, Lisa organized a keelboat expedition that went up the Missouri all the way to the Big Horn River in Montana, and during the winter of 1808–9 he took the lead in organizing the St. Louis Missouri Fur Company (later the Missouri Fur Company), which dominated the trade on the Upper Missouri until his death in 1820.[26] The encounter of Lewis and Clark with the American Indian peoples along the river had been instructive. One of the expedition's primary goals en route had been to inform the Native Americans of U.S. control over the region and to obtain facts about the groups living there. President Thomas Jefferson was especially interested in the Sioux because of their power and importance in the region. It was at the Bad River where Lewis and Clark ran into their first serious trouble with the Teton Sioux, after having experienced generally friendly encounters with other American Indian peoples along the way. The Tetons had been in the habit of stopping whites going up the river (the few who had already done so), demanding tobacco and other items, and releasing them only when they were ready. On the second of their four days at the Bad River, Captain Clark had been forced to draw his sword when the Tetons grew threatening. The keelboat's cannon was trained on the Tetons to intimidate them, and not until the boat pulled away from shore was the altercation ended. Partly the problem was misunderstanding because of a poor interpreter. Partly it was happenstance, partly a clash of interests between the two groups. Here, in September 1804, at the very beginning of significant interaction between Europeans and Native Americans in the Upper Missouri region, things had almost gotten out of hand, and shots had almost been exchanged. Had such a tragedy occurred, the Lewis and Clark expedition would have aborted; the survivors no doubt would have had to return to their home base in St. Louis.[27] Thus, unless the clash of interests between the two cultures could be narrowed and unless their ability to communicate with each other could be greatly increased, tragedy lay in store for them. Unfortunately, that tragedy would be played out eighty-six years later at Wounded Knee Creek, 150 miles to the southwest, where once again guns would be drawn and this time, unfortunately, fired. Afterwards, 31 U.S. soldiers lay dead in the snow and more than 250 Native American men, women, and children would be buried in common graves.

The clash of cultures was observable when Lewis and Clark came through in 1804, but its eventual outcome could not yet be predicted. During the next several decades, as the fur trade developed, the site where Lewis and Clark had their major confrontation with the Sioux would become the central intersection for American Indians and whites in the area. Manuel Lisa located several posts along the Upper Missouri after 1809, including ones at the mouth of the Big Horn River and at Council Bluffs. In 1812 he built one just south of the future North Dakota–South Dakota border and in 1813 established one near the Big Bend, south of Pierre. All of them eventually were abandoned for one reason or another.

The first fur trading post that managed to survive for decade after decade, and therefore the site that goes down as the oldest point of continuous European settlement in South Dakota, was located at Fort Pierre. The original post erected there, however, was called Fort La Framboise after Joseph La Framboise, a French trader who had come overland with two partners from Prairie du Chien on the Mississippi with goods to trade. They built a post out of driftwood on an island in the river. The trading post was rebuilt on the mainland in 1822 and renamed Fort Tecumseh. A third fort began to be contemplated as early as 1828 or 1829 but was not actually completed until 1832.[28]

By that time the steamboat had arrived on the Upper Missouri, the first one coming up the river and going all the way to Fort Union at the mouth of the Yellowstone River in 1831. The following year the same vessel, which was named the *Yellowstone* and which had been specially constructed with a small draft in order to navigate the frequently shallow channel of the treacherous Missouri, came up just to Fort Tecumseh, where it took on a load of buffalo hides, furs, peltries, and ten thousand pounds of buffalo tongues for its return to St. Louis. Pierre Chouteau, Jr., who was in charge of the Upper Missouri branch of the American Fur Company and Lisa's successor as the king of the fur trade in the region, came along on both trips and in 1832 had the new fort named after himself—Fort Pierre Chouteau, Jr. Soon it became popularly known as "Fort Pierre," and over time the French pronunciation gave way to a monosyllable rhyming with "deer."[29]

On the second journey of the *Yellowstone* in 1832, George Catlin, a Philadelphia artist, came on board to pursue his dream of becoming the historian and limner of the American Indians of the West before their cultures disappeared in the wake of settlement of the region.[30] He was able to stay almost two weeks at Fort Pierre and eventually spent eight years in the West chronicling the Native American experience. His are the first representations we have of the area around Fort Pierre. He showed an encampment of about six hundred tipis surrounding the palisaded fort. From the bluff he was standing on a mile or so away, the fort (which was 325 by 340 feet) looked rather small.

Catlin's first portrait, *One Horn,* was of the head chief of the Minneconjou Sioux visiting the fort at the time. None of the assembled American Indians had ever seen such a lifelike portrait. After some of the other chiefs and medicine men were allowed to see it and word of its excellence got around, the rest wanted to take a peek at it too. "Nothing short of hanging it out of doors on the side of my wigwam would in any way answer them," Catlin wrote, "and here I had the peculiar satisfaction of beholding, through a small hole I had made in my wigwam, the high admiration and respect they all felt for their chief, as well as the very great estimation in which they held me as a painter and a magician, conferring upon me at once the very distinguished appelation of Ee-cha-zoo-kah-ga-wa-kon (the Medicine Painter)."[31]

Catlin found himself caught between the people and their leaders. The medicine men, feeling threatened by his "medicine," generally took "a decided and noisy stand against the operations of my brush; haranguing the populace, and predicting bad luck, and premature death, to all who submitted to so strange and unaccountable operation!" For several days Catlin had no sitters, but then one of the chiefs stepped forward and told the rest that Catlin meant no harm and that there was nothing to fear. Soon Catlin was busy at work, turning out portraits for posterity.[32]

Other artists and scientists would pass through the area during succeeding years, taking notes and registering their impressions, interested in the flora and fauna, the topography of the area, and the native inhabitants. Some, like Karl Bodmer, the Swiss artist who came up the river with his patron, Prince Maximilian of Wied-Neuwied in 1833 and 1834, would observe the American Indians sympathetically and admiringly; others, like the ornithologist John James Audubon, who traveled through in 1843 when he was fifty-eight years old, took much more negative views. The second mapping expedition of Joseph Nicollet and John Frémont brought them up the river in a steamboat in 1839 to Fort Pierre, from whence they proceeded in a northeasterly direction toward Devil's Lake and then back down the Minnesota River. Frémont and Nicollet's maps did more to establish the geography of the Dakota region than anything else done up until that time.[33]

Most fraught with implications for the future, however, was the arrival at Fort Pierre of the Harney expedition in 1855. For some time U.S. Army officials had been considering establishing a military fort in the region for the protection of settlers and as a way of establishing governmental authority there. The fur trade was about played out by this time, and movement along the Oregon and Mormon trails through Nebraska had speeded up during the 1840s, stimulating conflict with the Teton Sioux and other Native American groups. In 1848 a military post was established at Fort Kearny. The following year Fort Laramie had a garrison. In 1853 Fort Riley was established.

The so-called Mormon cow incident in August 1854 was the event that precipitated the establishment of a military fort at Fort Pierre. A Minneconjou Sioux was accused of killing a stray cow belonging to a Mormon emigrant traveling through western Nebraska. A small punitive force under the command of an impetuous young lieutenant, J. G. Grattan, was annihilated by the Sioux after the soldiers treacherously shot the head man of the group they were to take the alleged criminal from. General William S. Harney was dispatched with a thousand men the following year to teach the Sioux a lesson. He did so at Ash Hollow, killing eighty-six, including women and children (Harney's losses were four dead and several wounded). After proceeding to Fort Laramie, he pushed northeastward into the heart of Teton country along the White River and then moved up along the Bad River, stopping at Fort Pierre to set up winter headquarters.

Although the army had paid the Chouteau fur company $45,000 for the fort, it was so dilapidated that Harney judged it completely unusable. In addition, the landing by the river was in poor condition and there was little timber nearby for fuel or forage for horses. Harney was forced to string his troops up and down the river for eighteen miles over the winter. Not surprisingly, he decided to abandon Fort Pierre the following year, and in 1857 a new military fort farther down the river near the Nebraska border was established at Fort Randall.[34]

In these events can be detected another sort of intersection at Fort Pierre—one between hope and reality. The hope that Fort Pierre would offer a suitable location for a military fort was blasted by what Harney discovered once he got there. Years of occupation at the site had virtually denuded the riverbanks of timber for miles in either direction. In another sense, the hope that a show of force would establish peaceful relations with and

Catlin's 1832 painting, *Fort Pierre, Mouth of the Teton River, 1200 Miles above St. Louis.* (Courtesy of the National Museum of American Art, Smithsonian Institution; gift of Mrs. Joseph Harrison, Jr.)

compliance from the American Indians proved a chimera. The intersection between hope and reality manifested itself frequently at the location. The relatively quick playing out of the fur trade lowered the curtain on one hope. The drastic decline in traffic on the Fort Pierre–Deadwood Trail after 1886 had the same effect for another. High hopes and expectations for economic growth and development west of the river after the Great Sioux Reservation was opened to settlement in 1890 were frustrated first in the 1890s, then after the drought of 1910–11, again during the 1930s, and more than once since then. The flush economic times experienced during the 1950s, when the great Oahe Dam was built just a few miles north of Fort Pierre, raising hopes that the prosperity injected by the building boom might permanently raise the town to a new economic plateau, gave way to more realistic expectations once the earth-moving equipment went on to other projects and the people working on the dam were laid off.

Today you can read about the history of Fort Pierre on historical markers along Highway 83 through town (it branches off from Highway 14 where the road swings north of town a mile or so). Piercing the horizon up on the gumbo hill overlooking the town are the three flagpoles and the Verendrye Monument, paying homage to the French explorers. On Deadwood Street, which is the main street, is the Verendrye Museum, occupying an old auditorium. There visitors can view a large painting of the old fur post, stories about the railroad's Mile Square, a 1951 *Life* magazine cover featuring local rodeo star Casey Tibbs, a Ku Klux Klan display with robe and headdress, and a hundred other artifacts and exhibits. Here one can see on display evidence of the intersection of cultures at Fort Pierre: Native American blankets, war clubs, and other artifacts; a hundred kinds of barbed wire and twenty kinds of stirrups; cowboy hats (ringing the entire room), saddles, buffalo heads, and a stuffed pheasant; horse-drawn buggies and scores of automobile hood ornaments and nameplates; electric razors, horse blankets, and pocket knives; sewing machines, pianos, and typewriters. There is plenty relating to American Indians, but it is heavily outweighed by the kinds of things that settlers brought along with them.

As you enter the museum, near the old ticket booth where you used to pay to get into the auditorium, there hangs a picture of James "Scotty" Philip and his wife Sarah.[35] Scotty Philip is one of South Dakota's great folklore heroes; he's known as the "Buffalo King" because in 1901 he purchased a herd of approximately ninety buffalo from Pete Dupree and kept them in a corral he had specially built for them on his ranch just north of Fort Pierre.

Just a few years earlier, millions of them had roamed the region; by the early 1880s just a few hundred were left. Philip had emigrated to the United States from Scotland at the age of fifteen in 1873. Sarah Larabee was the fourth daughter of a fur company employee and his Cheyenne wife. Two of her sisters also married white men, while the oldest married Crazy Horse, the famed Sioux warrior.

Under federal law Philip was entitled to operate a ranch on the Great Sioux Reservation because his wife was a Native American. They had a ranch along the Bad River a few miles south of the old Fort Pierre–Deadwood Trail. (The town of Philip, located near the site of his early cattle operation, was named after him.) The business was quite successful, and later he moved to the ranch just north of Fort Pierre. He served as a county commissioner and state senator and was sometimes mentioned as a possible candidate for governor. That never materialized, but in his life and career one can discern, in dim outline, the ambiguous legacy of Native American–white relations in South Dakota. In his marriage to a Native American woman can be found another intersection: on one level an amicable relationship that promised hope and reconciliation between the two cultures; on the other hand, in

This painting of the fort hangs in the Verendrye Museum.

this case as in most others, it was the male who benefited most from the relationship—just as it was the settlers who dominated relationships with American Indians and benefited most from them. It was at the intersection of these two cultures that South Dakota's early history revolved, and it is at the intersection of these two cultures that much of South Dakota's future will be played out.

MIDLAND

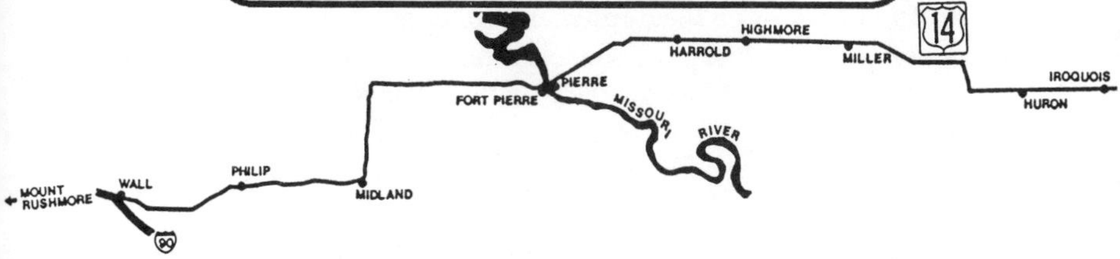

Railroad Depots in Towns on the Black and Yellow Trail

Midland's Main Street runs parallel to the railroad tracks, a fact that sets it apart from all of its East River counterparts on Highway 14. East of the Missouri River, every town was laid out in the form of the letter T, with its Main Street running perpendicular to the tracks. But when the Chicago and North Western bridged the river and connected Fort Pierre with Rapid City in 1906 and 1907, the pattern prevailing east of the river was abandoned. At Fort Pierre, whose origins antedated the railroad by ninety years, the tracklayers swung south around the business section, which was situated close to the Missouri River. Fifty miles to the west was Midland, which had arisen in 1890 as a stagecoach station and provisioning point for people moving onto reservation lands opened for settlement by the Sioux Treaty of 1889. The town had taken its name from its location approximately midway between Fort Pierre and the forks of the Cheyenne River. When the railroad arrived in 1906, surveyors laid out Main Street a block north of the tracks and parallel to them. Farther west, at Wall, Main Street was laid out at an acute angle to the tracks. People have often observed that West River psychology differs from its East River counterpart, so it is interesting to note that even the shapes of the towns in this region vary from those east of the river.

Today the first thing that catches the eye of tourists driving down Midland's Main Street is the well-preserved two-story railroad depot that has been moved a couple of hundred yards from its original location right up to the street. A sign identifies it as the Midland Pioneer Museum. Outside, in a fenced-in area, are an old claim shanty, some farm machinery, a couple of baggage carts, and other historical artifacts. The museum is open three days a week during the summer months, but even in the off-season Janice Bierle, a local rancher who grew up in the area and who now serves as the museum curator, will drive into town to open it up for you if she is available. She is one of many people in the area who take an active interest in local history and who realize that if they don't work to preserve old artifacts and landmarks, no one else will.

In July 1988 Janice told me that the idea for establishing a museum gathered momentum when the community celebrated its seventy-fifth anniversary in 1965. A formal proposal gained approval the following year at the annual meeting of the West River Pioneer Club, one of several local history groups in the area. The Midland Pioneer Museum Association was organized and by 1972 had collected $2,100. The next year, when the Chicago and North Western Railway decided to dispose of the depot, the association was able to purchase the building for $500. Since the company wanted it moved off railroad property, the association purchased three lots at a nominal price from the Oakton State Bank, built a foundation with volunteer labor, and in May 1975 moved the two-story structure six hundred feet west and over to Main Street, rotated it ninety degrees, and converted it into a museum. It opened officially in June 1977.[1]

The museum now contains almost five hundred artifacts and exhibits, displayed in crowded profusion, in the same fashion as other town and county museums like it. The items were donated or loaned by local residents who wanted others to know how people used to live, Janice told me. The first-floor waiting room has a coal-burning stove, coffee cans, photo albums, tools, a player piano, a vacuum cleaner, a typewriter, gas lamps, shotguns, a Remington rifle, jars, bottles, and other items. To the rear, in the freight room, are displayed saws, cream cans, saddles, shovels, bedpans, ceramic soap holders, scoops, potato mashers, food whips, egg slicers, spatulas, cake boxes, footstools, a barber's chair, a bank safe, a baby buggy, paint signs, about a hundred different types of barbed wire, a cash register, a wooden icebox and a wooden washing machine, a shirt iron, teakettles, telephones, mailboxes, horse nose protectors, gas stoves, a wooden wheel soaker, a neck yoke, and a variety of other things. Upstairs, in the depot agent's living quarters, there are more exhibits, filling the old kitchen, living room, and two bedrooms.

There never was indoor plumbing, so the agents and their families, as well as train passengers, had to use an outhouse.

Photographs on display in the museum depict activities in and around the depot and indicate just how central a place the railroad depot occupied in towns like Midland. A panoramic view of the town taken by a photographer during the early 1900s shows houses, barns, churches, stores, and livery stables sprawled in the Bad River valley, looking new and rather fragile. In the center of the photograph, connecting the town to the railroad and to the rest of the country, stood the two-story depot. The depot in a town like Midland was an integral part of the local economy, the place from which people departed and to which they returned when traveling by rail, and one of the busiest locations in town. It was, without question, a local hot spot—one of those places that acted like a magnet, drawing in people and providing a stage for communal activity.[2]

Stepping into the Midland depot was like entering every other depot along the Chicago and North Western line, since they were all built according to standard plans issued from company headquarters in Chicago.[3] West of the Missouri River, as towns

The old Midland depot, constructed in 1907, is now a museum.

sprang up there in 1906 and 1907, the railroad built two-story depots to accomodate the depot agents and their families, who often had trouble finding adequate living quarters in the towns. A generation earlier, when the tracks had been laid through eastern Dakota Territory, some of the original depots had been single story structures, and later on many of the two-story buildings were replaced by one-story ones. Though standard plans were used, sizes varied somewhat, depending on the amount of business the company expected to generate at a site.

Unlike some depots that sported two waiting rooms (one for men, the other for women and children), Midland's had a single one for everybody. In the middle of the building, situated between the waiting room and the freight room, was the depot office, where tickets were sold, records kept, and messages received and sent by telegraph. Protruding from it was a bay window allowing the agent to peer in either direction down the tracks. People coming in to ship or pick up freight would walk in the door and turn left to talk to the agent at the counter and then turn to their right and go through another door to enter the freight room. Stairs from the ticket office led up to the living quarters on the second floor.

On a wall of the depot office hangs a large framed map showing the routes of the Chicago and North Western system in 1917. Near it hangs an old bamboo hoop used by depot agents to transmit dispatches and messages to the engineers when their trains weren't scheduled to stop at Midland. The agent would stand by the tracks and hold out the hoop so the engineer could

In this panoramic view of Midland taken about 1910, the railroad depot stands out as the link between the local community and the outside world. (Courtesy of Midland Pioneer Museum)

extend his arm while he was speeding by and snare it. He would then quickly remove the message and drop the hoop so the depot agent could retrieve it and use it for the next train. Nat Stimson, longtime depot agent at De Smet, told me in January 1987 that sometimes an engineer would hold on to the hoop for several extra seconds as a joke or just to be mean. That meant trudging down the tracks another fifty or hundred yards to retrieve it. In addition, the engines often kicked gravel up from the roadbed, bouncing it off his shins and leaving them black-and-blue. Frustrated by those annoyances, Nat rigged up a device on a pole that he could set in the ground beside the tracks and attach messages to with string. This allowed engineers to reach out and snatch them along with the string while he sat comfortably in his office or stood a safe distance away. The contraption violated company regulations, but it improved his comfort and the appearance of his shins, and, as he put it, what company officials didn't know couldn't hurt them.

Nat was a second-generation depot agent. His father Henry before him had taken the job at De Smet in 1905, after stints at Crandon and Canistota and in two towns along Highway 14—Cavour and Iroquois. On Easter Sunday, just weeks after the family occupied their second-floor accommodations, the depot burned to the ground after a baggage handler accidentally dropped a lantern he was lighting, the flames quickly spreading through the oil-saturated floors of the building. For several months, until a new one-story replacement structure could be built, a boxcar was pressed into service as a temporary depot.[4]

Nat's brother H. A. ("Al") also became a depot agent and wrote a book about his experiences in De Smet and several other towns. He recalled that as children, sitting in their second-floor lookout, he and his brothers could watch trains approaching from either direction, and through the side windows they could spot farmers driving into town in their wagons and buggies. As youngsters, the boys' playground was

> the cool black loam beneath the depot. On stormy days we played upstairs or in the freight house. Our view was elevators, lumber yards and the action around a depot. Often we ran downstairs to see the trains come in. If there seemed to be no action downstairs we watched the morning freight or afternoon passenger roar into town just beneath our window. One day we saw Levi Cross' cow hit by the passenger train and thrown over the railroad ditch. We almost grew up at that window waiting for something else to happen.[5]

Train depots in towns like Midland and De Smet served a variety of functions—some obvious, some more subtle. Besides catering to the needs of passengers, farmers, storekeepers, mail-order catalog customers, and shippers, they also served as information centers for the community. Telegraphic messages were sent and received there; mail sacks arrived and departed on trains running in both directions. The post office was usually located nearby; a local drayman or somebody else was contracted to carry mail sacks and freight back and forth between the post office and the depot. Before the arrival of the automobile, the railroad did more than anything else to break down the isolation of the small town, and the depot was where it all happened.

More than that, the depot was a community gathering place. Many of the activities that occurred in and around it were unrelated to its ostensible functions. The depot agents were some of the most visible and well-acquainted personages in the towns, this despite the frequent moves that many of them made. Seniority applied when vacancies arose, so agents who wanted to move to a place put in their "bids" for it. When the successful bidder moved, it opened up another place for bidding, and the process continued like a game of musical chairs. As more senior agents took over the choicer locations, those further down the ladder scrambled their way up behind them.[6]

In their book *The Country Railroad Station in America,* H. Roger Grant and Charles W. Bohi called the depot a "community hub."[7] That characterization certainly applied in towns along the Dakota Central, where depots were magnets for people with or without business to do there. Loitering around the depot just to watch the train come in was common. People enjoyed identifying the locomotives and new equipment that was added over time. In the early days, before many buildings had appeared in a town, depots often doubled as meeting places for groups and organizations. The Aurora depot, for instance, hosted religious services every Sunday morning and evening until a church could be built in town. Cornet bands practiced there, and dances were held there.[8]

Local newspapers reported the comings and goings of both prominent and ordinary people. During the governorship of Arthur Mellette, residents of Brookings always knew when he passed through town on the train from his home in Watertown, because the local newspaper had a paragraph on it. Theodore Roosevelt, William Howard Taft, Eugene Debs, Calvin Coolidge, Franklin Roosevelt, and Carry Nation were some of the famous personages who traveled the line. Politicians, businesspeople, traveling salesmen and women, and entertainers sometimes stopped by the newspaper office to inform the editor about their whereabouts. In Huron, reporters met trains at the depot to gather information for local paragraphs.

While trains stopped at Brookings, Huron, and Pierre, passengers could detrain and get a bite to eat in the depot lunchroom or restaurant. Built in 1883, the Depot Hotel at Huron—also known, after its proprietor, as the Kent House—was quite distinctive architecturally and served high-class meals in its restaurant. The large brick depot that replaced it after it burned down in 1913 also had a commodious dining room.[9] Pierreites today can still recall the elegant fixtures and white tablecloths at the restaurant in their depot.[10] When the new brick depot opened in Brookings in 1905, it was also fitted out with a lunchroom that served both passengers and a local clientele. In these towns, when people tired of the fare offered at the other eating establishments, they could get a change of pace by going to the depot.

Towns lacking the size to obtain a large brick depot like the ones at Brookings, Huron, and Pierre had to make do with the standard wooden structures. But even in these towns, residents fretted about appearances and pressured railroad officials to keep the depots fixed up and looking neat. Paint and repair crews came through periodically, to the welcome of the townspeople. In 1919, for example, the depot at De Smet was redone in two tones of green, a startling departure from the usual red or maroon. The following year in Brookings, the *Register* reported, "The annual spring 'clean-up and paint-up' campaign hit the Northwestern

Railway Station last Saturday. The windows were cleaned and the sashes given a fresh coat of paint."[11]

Some towns sported a small railroad park near the depot. Usually, it seems, they were put in at the initiative of the townspeople rather than that of railroad officials. Local residents considered the depot and its grounds to be reflections upon themselves and wanted their village to project as attractive an image as possible to outsiders. The first and frequently the only impression that passengers obtained of a place occurred as they peered out the windows of their coaches when the train pulled into the station. Their view of Main Street was like an entryway into the town, and people formed quick impressions of it. If local residents were unable to persuade company officials to build them a larger or handsomer depot, at least they expected the grounds around it to be in tip-top shape. Among communities that installed walks, benches, shrubs, trees, and flowers to create little railroad parks near their depots were Brookings, De Smet, and Miller.

Usually activities around the depot remained low-key—people waiting for a train to arrive, folks sitting and chatting about the weather, cream cans being lined up for loading onto the train, children cavorting and playing games. During the 1920s, town leaders in De Smet granted dispensation from the usual 9:00 curfew to allow youngsters to watch the 9:15 passenger train come through.[12] Occasionally the action around the depot was considerably livelier. At Miller one night in 1919, after the last evening train had departed, it was after midnight when the night man on duty left to carry some mail over to the post office. By the time he returned, $30 had been stolen from the depot office. Suspicion pointed to two strangers who had been sleeping in the waiting room, part of an expanding "floating element" that people observed in the area about that time.[13] More excitement erupted at Midland when a man who became enraged during a quarrel with the depot agent withdrew to get a gun and returned to kill his antagonist.[14]

More frequent than robberies or assaults around the train yard were injuries and accidents. Railroading was one of the most dangerous occupations in America, and the newspaper paragraphs of the time illustrate why this was so.[15] In 1904, a board being used in the construction of a new depot at Brookings clipped a young brakeman who was riding past on a through freight. It knocked him down, throwing him off the train, after which a wheel severed one of his legs below the knee.[16] Other train workers fared even worse. In 1887, according to an item in the Brookings County *Press,*

> A young man in the employ of the C. & N.W. railway at Lake Benton [east of Elkton] was on a shaft above the water tank oiling the wheel of the wind mill Tuesday morning when he lost his hold, falling first to the roof of the tank, then to the flat car and off to the ground landing on the ice. Dr. Mattice was immediately summoned, being sent from Brookings on a special, but the unfortunate man was dead when the doctor arrived. One of his legs was broken, both of his arms were broken, and his skull was crushed. He had been married but about ten days, and Dr. Mattice says the grief of the young widow would almost melt a heart of stone. He says the corpse was the most mangled one he ever saw.[17]

People's images of railroad depots, therefore, were not always positive ones. For some they remained ambiguous. At the depot arrived the remains of dead loved ones for burial in the family plot. There young men departed for training camps during both world wars, often with hundreds of people crowded on the platform to wish them well. Similar crowds welcomed those who returned. Sometimes there was rowdyism, sometimes violence. "There is a gang of young loafers in the city, who throughout the day can at most any time be seen on the street smoking their pipes and evenings persist in congregating at the depot and making themselves more or less obnoxious," complained an observer in Brookings around the turn of the century.[18]

Mostly, however, people remember these depots nostalgically as places where they mingled and talked, came and went, hoped and dreamed. So long as passenger trains remained in service, people could commute to other towns to shop or visit or even to take in a movie. Platforms were often crowded with freight from Chicago and Minneapolis: farm machinery, furniture, shoes, clothing, musical instruments, bicycles, and so forth. Stopping to chat with the depot agent, lighting a pipe or a cigarette, lingering for a moment with fellow townspeople—in these ways local residents made the depot an important gathering place in a community. Here was a good example of perceptual geographer Yi-Fu Tuan's observation that places are centers of meaning known "not only through the eyes and the mind but also through the more passive and direct modes of experience."[19]

Today the Chicago and North Western depots are mostly gone, either torn down for lumber or moved to new locations to serve other uses. When passenger service ceased during the early

1960s, few people seemed to care much about what happened to them. The Miller depot was taken to a farm twelve miles south of town, where it was used for storing antiques. The one at Volga was moved fifteen miles east onto a farm to become a storage shed. Similar fates awaited depots at Ree Heights, which was used for a time as an artist's studio before being moved to a farm two miles south of town, and at Harrold, which found a new home on a farm a mile north of town.

The St. Lawrence depot was used to store sacks of feed until it was torn down in 1989. On a lot several blocks away is the old Vayland depot, which was transported eight miles up the road into St. Lawrence, where is it used today as a residence. For a time, the old Philip depot also performed that role, but today it stands empty, sadly falling apart on a lot north of town where it was relocated in 1957. Its replacement was a small, nondescript one-story prefabricated steel unit, functional enough, to be sure, but totally lacking the charm of the older building.[20] After the Blunt depot was sawed in half, part of it was used for a time as a residence on a farm five miles southeast of town. The other part continues to decay on a lot in Blunt. The Brookings depot houses a radio station. The Huron depot is used as a furniture and tire warehouse. The Pierre depot was torn down and replaced by a Holiday Inn motel, which subsequently has gone through several owners and name changes. The rest of the depots along the line apparently were all torn down and used for lumber.

If most people seemed to attach little sentiment to the depot buildings as they were being torn down, boarded up, or carted away during the early 1960s, that attitude appears to be changing somewhat. Several years ago, the boards were removed from the windows of the De Smet depot, and today it houses an attractive city museum. The Volga depot, after sitting for years on a farm south of Brookings, was recently moved to Walnut Grove, Minnesota, to become part of the Laura Ingalls Wilder museum complex there. Thanks to the generous contribution of one of its members, the Hand County Historical Society recently purchased the old Miller depot and moved it back into town to become a museum alongside the society's historical house. During the summer of 1988, with the state centennial approaching, a group of local women in Miller painted a huge mural depicting their town's history on the side of a store building. In the middle of it is the depot, representing the centrality of the railroad and of the depot in the life of the community. The mural served as a backdrop for the picnic celebration of the local community club at the end of the summer.[21]

In considering objects that might best symbolize the small town past, railroad depots stand out. They grace the covers and title pages of centennial history books published in Aurora, Harrold, and Midland and were featured in centennial logos for Ree Heights, Highmore, and Brookings.[22] Besides Main Street itself, which contains a collection of frequently changing stores, the depot stands out as the single most significant historical place in a community—a spot that possesses great significance, meaning, and emotional references for people. The continuing presence of or the memories that people retain of homes, churches, schools, city halls, county courthouses, opera houses, pool halls, cafes, restaurants, banks, stores, post offices, ball fields, and other places also bind people to the past. But more than any other single structure, the railroad depot symbolizes what these towns were all about.

Historian Daniel J. Boorstin observed how the American

Townspeople gathered at the Brookings depot in 1916 to welcome soldiers home from service along the Mexican border. (Courtesy of Historic Preservation Commission, Brookings)

style in historical monuments differs from the European. "Aristocratic cultures recapture the glories of their history in the crumbling monuments of ancient castles, forts, and palaces," he wrote. "The ruins of the past must be left unrepaired because past magnificence (even in ruins) is more awe-inspiring than the glossy neatness of pigmy moderns." By contrast, Americans, he noted, generally take a different tack, not enamored of ruins and antiquity. Unlike their European counterparts, Americans, in their quest to cross the continent, built only what would suffice until they could afford to build something better.[23]

Boorstin's observation applies directly to midwestern railroad depots, which often get converted into historical monuments. Officials of the Chicago and North Western Railway in Chicago, who were primarily interested in economy and efficiency, constructed standardized depots that could be, and sometimes were, moved from place to place with relative ease. Aesthetic considerations seldom counted, the exceptions being in the three largest towns along the line that obtained larger, more ornate brick buildings, which were constructed between 1904 and 1913. But if the wooden depots in towns like Midland did not inspire choirs of praise for their architectural charms, they played, nevertheless, central roles in the lives of their communities. They were centers of community activity and linked the community to the outside world. More than that, they symbolized what the community was all about, first, as a product of the railroad but, more importantly, as a group of people welded together by common purposes and values and similar aspirations and dreams.

PHILIP

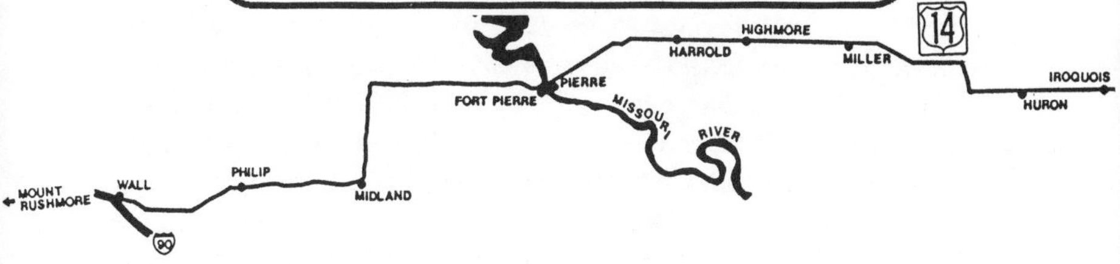

Memories at the Local Hardware Store

Few South Dakota towns of any size were without a photographer during the towns' early days. Making a living at the trade, however, was seldom easy, so photography studios tended to come and go as people entered and left the business and moved from place to place in the hope of drumming up more customers. Gustav ("Gus") Johnson of Philip was unusual in that he was on hand as soon as the town was established and continued to pursue his work there for nearly half a century. The several thousand photographs that he left behind—most of them taken before 1930—constitute an unusual photographic record of the growth and development of a single town in South Dakota and of the people who lived there.[1]

Johnson joined the flood of homesteaders who streamed into the region along the Bad River when the Chicago and North Western Railway bridged the Missouri and built west from Fort Pierre in 1906 and 1907 to link up with Rapid City at the eastern edge of the Black Hills. He was in his late twenties in 1906 when he arrived with his wife and three small children to claim a homestead near the Bad River. Three of his sisters and two brothers located a little to the northwest along Grindstone Creek, which flows into the Bad River.[2]

Johnson had become interested in photography as a hobby back in Elk Point, where he had grown up, and decided that there was money to be made in it that could supplement the family income. Once he fulfilled the residency requirements for his homestead, he moved his family into Philip and took a job in E.

M. Larson's general store and began taking pictures on the side. During 1906 early arrivals like the Johnsons prepared for the coming of the railroad, whose crews were pushing west from Fort Pierre and east from Rapid City, eventually linking up several miles west of Philip. By September 20, when the town site of Philip was platted, several stores had already sprung up there in anticipation of the settlers who would soon be arriving.[3]

The tracklayers arrived on May 11, 1907. The first train chugged into town three weeks later. When regular passenger service started between Fort Pierre and Rapid City on August 15, Johnson was on hand to record the scene with his camera. When the first baby was born in town, he got a shot of it. When the first fire broke out, he lugged his equipment to the scene. During the next several years, his photographs documented the first, second, third, fourth, fifth, sixth, and seventh fires that broke out in town. Exactly how people determined which conflagrations were large enough to count is not known, but fires were certainly important landmarks in a town's collective memory. Celebrations constituted another kind of historic occasion. Johnson was there to capture the moment in black and white at Fourth of July festivities and at political speeches, American Indian encampments, and circuses, as well as at fires, train wrecks, and funerals. When Carry Nation came to town to denounce the liquor trade, he met her at the depot to take her picture. One of his saddest assignments was to photograph a young child in a coffin so the family could have that one image for a memory.

For several years Johnson maintained a small studio in his home. But he never contented himself to wait for customers to come to him. More than most in his profession, he carried his camera all over the countryside looking for opportunities. Farm families would interrupt their chores to put on their Sunday-go-to-meeting outfits for the photographer. For him, taking pictures was basically a job—a way to make some extra money for his family. He greatly enjoyed taking pictures, but he was not interested in them as art—or as history, for that matter. His entrepreneurial approach made him a sort of photographic speculator, shooting scenes that he then printed on postcard stock and offered for sale to anyone who wanted to buy them. He'd send his children to the depot when trains came through to offer his postcard photographs to the passengers: Main Street scenes, banks and stores, Native Americans, schoolchildren, floods and fires, celebrations, parades, homes in town and claim shacks in the country. There wasn't much unusual scenery to sell; for the most

Gustav Johnson in his photo lab.
(Courtesy of Evelyn Haberly)

part, his pictures depicted the simple, everyday activities of local residents.

Evelyn Johnson Haberly told me that she remembered she and her brother getting a penny apiece for these postcards when they peddled them at the depot. She disliked being dragged around town and countryside by her father to help lug his bulky and cumbersome equipment. She usually would rather have been playing, but her father reminded her that she was the oldest and that without her help he couldn't do his work. She was just five years old when the family arrived in 1906, but she was a great help to her father during the next several years. Looking back at it, she wouldn't have traded that experience for anything. Perusing the photographs her father had taken, she recalled many of the scenes because she had been there when they were taken. Studying the pictures dredged up memories and stories of the way things had been in Philip during the early days. Her younger brother and sisters (eventually there were five children) later urged her to keep the pictures so that they would all be in one place. From time to time she would pull them out to take another look at them.

For Philip's fiftieth anniversary celebration in 1957 she mounted most of them on large pieces of tagboard, 30 or 40 to a sheet, and put them on display downtown for people to look at. She stood by them and answered questions and reminisced about the circumstances surrounding their taking. On several occasions after that she displayed all or part of the collection. The history of Haakon County, published in 1982, contains a twenty-four-page section with approximately 150 of her father's pictures, and in 1988 she had a company in Texas print a one-hundred-page book containing about 600 of the pictures. When I visited with her at her home, she pulled the tagboard sheets out from under her bed, and we spent an enjoyable afternoon perusing the 3,000 or so photographs and talking about them.

A quarter to a third of them had been neatly captioned by her father. Only a small number were dated. Most of the captions are vague ("Pine Street Looking East, Philip S.D.") rather than specific ("Harvesting on F. E. Morison Farm, Philip S.D., July 23 1915"). Some of the photographs had been taken from a distance or from the height of a hill, a water tower, or a grain elevator in order to obtain a bird's-eye effect. Those pictures generally have few or no people in them, or the people remained unaware of the photographer's presence. Most of the time, however, the photographer had been within a few feet or yards of his subject—an intrusive presence—and people had struck poses for him. Certain formulas seemed to be followed for taking these kinds of photographs, as people stood by doorways and behind counters, perched on horseback or on swings, eyes gazing intently at the camera, waiting for the shutter to click or the flash to go off when indoors.

From these photographs we can learn much about building styles, interior decoration, clothing, tools, machinery, and other items of material culture. When dates are attached to the pictures, change over time can be monitored. Sometimes we find it easy to imagine ourselves in the settings, conversing with the people, yelling "Hi-eigh!" at the horses, or pulling the throttle on train engines. But the problem with this activity is just what the statement suggests: we must *imagine* these things. We cannot confirm or understand the experience from the pictures alone. Photographs are wonderful windows into history, but they do not allow easy entry into the past itself, for that cannot be known directly. We apprehend it only though traces that actors leave behind. These photographs, useful as they are, are therefore limited in what they can tell us.[4]

Susan Sontag reminded us that "the camera's rendering of reality must always hide more than it discloses."[5] The camera does not penetrate the minds of its subjects, does not even tell us what they are saying, let alone thinking. Beyond the conscious lies the subconscious, a realm unknown to the camera. We look at faces and imagine that we can apprehend what lies behind them, but facial expressions are notoriously deceptive, and these are posed, not candid, expressions. What photographs like these largely lack is a notion of human relationships, of human feelings, of tragedy and triumph, cares and joy. The intricate web of power, the spell of love and dreams, and the drama of intense desire are mostly absent. The poetics of domestic and community politics requires words to explicate. It is safe to say that photographs like these can seldom do more than intimate at such realities hidden under surface appearances. Halftone prints do a wonderful job of limning what is transparent, providing us with a much fuller pictures of people's daily transactions than word portraits are usually capable of. But to go further we need other tools.

To aid our understanding, we need to have captions that explain the context within which the photographs were taken. We need to be able to locate photographs in time and place, and we need to begin asking questions about who, what, where, when, and why. "The caption is the missing voice," observed Susan Sontag, "and it is expected to speak the truth. But even an entirely accurate caption is only one interpretation, necessarily a limiting one, of the photograph to which it is attached."[6] One of Johnson's photographs shows a crowd of onlookers at a fire, as firefighters battle the blaze. The photographer's caption informs us that this is the fourth fire in Philip, taking place on January 28, 1911. A large sign on the building's false front identifies it as Linn's Store, and it is easily recognizable as such from other photographs that have been preserved. The hill in the background of the picture (a house is visible atop it to the left) confirms what we know from other sources: the store was located on Pine Street, a half-block west of Main Street. Today it is the site of the First National Bank. Until Highway 14 was rerouted north of town, it used to run through town on Pine Street.

The photograph of the fire pricks our curiosity, transporting us back in time. As Alan Trachtenberg noted, "Photographs give immediate access to the past. Thus they make vivid and near-at-hand what written history is all about. At the same time," he warned, "the immediacy is always qualified in some way, in some manner often hidden from us. We can usually tell at a glance what a photograph is about. But the image does not always tell us everything we want to know about it."[7] An understatement, if there ever was one! Further investigation informs us that this was a fire quickly doused, that the building—one of the oldest business places in town—survived there for many decades. The building was a seed store, and the owner at the time was actually Frank Rood, who in August 1908 had bought it from J. M. Linn, who had built it and operated a grocery store in it. In September 1913, Rood, who had been Philip's first mayor, sold the store to F. E. Pohle and moved to Pierre, later serving two terms as secretary of state.[8]

Pohle operated his feed and seed store there for more than four decades. When Philip celebrated its fiftieth anniversary in 1957, he took out a half-page advertisement in the history that was published about the town that year and reminded people, "Since 1913 I have been located in the same spot—Selling and buying seeds used and raised in this country."[9] Old-timers in Philip today remember the building well, but not as the feed and seed store and, for a time, cream-buying station that it was. Rather, they fondly recall Pohle's Hall, on the second floor, which "Pop" Pohle rented out (or allowed the free use of) for basketball games, roller-skating, dances, boxing matches, and other activities. Before a new courthouse was built in 1930, it even doubled as a courtroom for several sessions.

Evelyn Johnson Haberly remembered that its low ceilings caused problems for the basketball players. Some recall, however, that at each end of the court a hole, or a raised place, in the ceiling around the basket made it possible for players to put a little more arc on their shots. By 1935 people were ready to modernize. Midland, to the east, had built a new brick gym and auditorium in 1929. Wall, to the west, also enjoyed a good facility. With New Deal relief programs in operation, town officials hoped to take advantage of federal dollars to help subsidize the construction of a new auditorium that would house the best basketball court in the area. A couple of years earlier, the local American Legion post had given the city two lots a block east of Pohle's Hall for the purpose.[10]

In February 1935, Philip's citizens went to the polls and voted 238 to 48 to issue $10,000 in bonds to finance an auditorium. In May, relief workers and volunteers—mostly high school boys and several men in town—excavated the basement and poured the foundation. After Congress established the Works Progress Administration that summer, city officials succeeded in getting the building designated as a WPA project in November, and the federal government wound up paying about one-quarter of the cost of construction. It was a large building, 60 by 120 feet with a 20-foot ceiling. A large stage, raised 3 feet above the surface of the hardwood playing court, occupied the south end of the building. Below the stage were the dressing rooms and heating plant. On the north end were double doors leading out onto Pine Street (Highway 14). After construction had begun, it was decided to add balconies on the east and west sides. They were 7 feet wide and held three rows of seats. Below them, on the first floor, were five rows of bleachers on each side. Altogether, the seating capacity was approximately one thousand. The final touches were completed during the second week of July, fifteen months after construction began.

The first basketball game, against Midland, had already been played in the Philip Auditorium on February 20. Immediately it became the basketball showcase of the region—the best gymnasium, according to local opinion, between Pierre and Rapid City. People remember the many district tournaments that were held there during the 1940s and 1950s.[11] Ray Baker, a Main Street Clothier who moved to town in 1941, recalled that people "just jammed in like sardines" at the tournaments. "And the crowds, of course, were just wild, and it seemed even more so by them being crowded in there so much." Midland, Wall, and Kadoka were some of Philip's biggest rivals. Baker remembered one ball game where he wound up sitting with a group of Kadoka fans who were so full of energy and excitement that he took a pounding from all the backslapping and shouting that was going on. Rival coaches would sit in the stands when their teams weren't playing and judge the moves of their counterparts, recalled Gary Brooks, a 1962 Philip High School graduate who was the fifth of a string of basketball-playing brothers at the school, beginning in 1944. He remembered several times after a lay-up when he kept right on

A postcard view by Johnson of a 1911 fire in Philip. (Courtesy of Evelyn Haberly)

going out the double doors at the north end of the court and onto the sidewalk.

During the 1920s and 1930s in South Dakota, high school athletics came into their own as a rallying point for community pride and loyalty. Before that, school sports were just feeling their way. From the earliest days, town baseball teams, sometimes fortified by salaried players, had drawn out crowds of spectators and sparked rivalries—usually friendly, sometimes bitter—between neighboring communities. With the building of high school gymnasiums or city auditoriums, like the one in Philip, basketball moved out of the old opera houses and makeshift playing courts into more modern facilities, which, in turn, began to be replaced by new gymnasiums in the 1960s and 1970s in many places.

For a quarter of a century Philip Auditorium was the scene of many exciting games and district tournaments. Beyond that, community bake sales, high school plays, concerts, dances, and even funerals took place there. Even after the auditorium was built, Pohle's Hall was still used occasionally for community events, but most things now were held in the auditorium. Bernard O'Connell, who currently runs a funeral monument business in the old Bank of Philip building, recalled when an average of two dances a month were held in the auditorium. They drew out large crowds; it was a slow night when less than a hundred tickets were sold. Baker remembered when Leon Wheeler used to manage the dances. He'd bring in name bands, from Lawrence Welk to Tommy Dorsey. The latter, it appeared, was not particularly thrilled to be in Philip, South Dakota, and more or less went through the motions the night he came to town. On the other hand, Welk, a North Dakota native, had made a name for himself on Yankton radio station WNAX and felt at home in the small town South Dakota setting. Baker remembered Welk wore a tie at Christmastime and he brought his orchestra back two or three times. Most of the bands, of course, were smaller traveling outfits from the Midwest, out of Omaha and places like that, or local groups whose rates were more affordable.

In 1962, with the construction on the hill of a new high school and a combination gymnasium–National Guard armory, basketball games moved out of what soon came to be called the "old auditorium." The new gym, to save costs, had a tile floor rather than a wooden one. Its seating capacity was about twice that of the old facility's. High school dances moved up the hill into the new building. Elvis and Fabian had already captured the attention of the younger generation by this time, and a new teen culture was on the ascendant. The Beatles came along two years later. The days when community dances could draw out large crowds of people of all ages were over. Welk had gone on to television, providing nostalgia trips for the older set. The city auditorium continued to cater to roller-skating and occasional community activities, but it was difficult to heat and in need of major repairs. City government officials began to think about how they might unload it, and some even talked of tearing it down.

Resolution of the dilemma came with an offer from Jim Ingram to take the building off the city's hands and convert it into a hardware store. Baker, who was serving as mayor at the time, recalled that because of vandalism problems, the high cost of maintaining the building, and the need for making some major expenditures to repair it, city officials took advantage of the opportunity to have it converted into a tax-paying property. Some people wished the city would hold on to it, but the financial burdens seemed too great. Ingram paid $1 for the structure in 1974 and put perhaps $100,000 into remodeling it. He lowered the stage to the same level as the rest of the floor, removed the balcony on the east side, enclosed the other one for a storage area, and covered the hardwood floor with tile and carpet (he sounds apologetic even now about having to do it).

Ingram's hardware store.

Today a visitor walking through the store's new glass doors may notice nothing about it that distinguishes it from scores of similiar stores around the country. But a closer inspection, and information from people who know its story, reveals that there is a lot of history in this building. The cornerstone indicates that construction started in 1935. A plaque near the entrance carries the following information: "Philip Auditorium. Built By City of Philip and Works Progress Administration. Project No. 331, 1936." The windows on the east and west side are now covered. The hooks in the ceiling from which the east balcony was suspended remain; a perceptive observer might inquire about them. A walk around the new balcony that Ingram added to the back of the store for further display space reveals the top of the proscenium arch that used to open onto the stage. Downstairs the arch is hidden behind the wall of a storeroom that was put in to hold extra inventory and supplies. The reason he didn't remove the arch during remodeling was the heavy expense of doing so and the furnace ducts inside it that were converted to cold air returns. Here in the storeroom the original hardwood floor can be seen, and clearly visible at places where they aren't covered up are the red and black out-of-bounds lines and other markings for the basketball court.

The day I searched for Philip Auditorium in the hardware store, Ingram remarked with a wistful smile, "This old place holds a lot of memories."

WALL

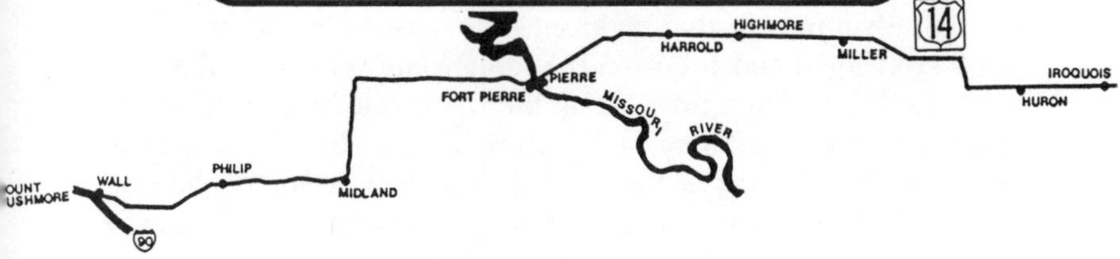

History in a Tourist Trap

At Wall, 116 miles west of the Missouri River and 323 miles from the Minnesota border, Highway 14 connects with Interstate 90, following it all the way to a point just beyond Sheridan, Wyoming, where it cuts west toward its terminus at Yellowstone National Park. The town of Wall owes its name to the sharp drop-off above which it is located—a two-hundred-foot-high geological formation skirting the northern edge of South Dakota's Badlands. It owes its location to the railroad, which arrived in 1907.[1] Its current prosperity and worldwide fame it owes to a bit of luck and the persistence of Ted and Dorothy Hustead, who bet their future on this little town on the windswept western Dakota prairies and persevered to make a modest fortune in the process.

The towns of Cottonwood and Quinn, to the east of town on Highway 14, have almost entirely dried up; a dozen or two residents hold on amidst abandoned buildings and vacant lots. West of Wall, on Interstate 90/Highway 14, the towns of Wasta, New Underwood, and Box Elder are doing scarcely any better, victims of technological and economic changes that have put the squeeze on so many small towns like themselves. Cars speed by on the interstate, hurrying to reach Rapid City or Sioux Falls and points beyond; the days when rivalries for traffic between Highway 14 (the Black and Yellow Trail) and Highway 16 (the Custer Battlefield Trail) are now only a dim memory.

Trail associations for both claimed their routes to be the best and fastest ways from eastern points to the Black Hills and to

Yellowstone National Park. During the Dirty Thirties they competed for scarce state and federal funds so they could hard-surface their roadways and create the kind of dustless highways that people hoped would attract tourists and business, with Highway 16 usually slightly in the lead. The town of Wall possessed a special advantage in that eighteen miles east of it the two highways converged and followed the same route west toward Rapid City, cutting through town along the north side, above the single block of stores straddling Main Street. Later, when the Interstate Highway System was inaugurated during the Eisenhower administration, Wall was fortunate to have the new four-lane highway skirt the south edge of town (after an alternate route several miles north of Wall was rejected) and to have successfully lobbied for two exits when normally a town of its size would have received only one.[2] With a north-south road funneling sightseers up from the Badlands, about a dozen miles to the south, tourist attractions and motels proliferated in Wall alongside the drugstore.

Cars approaching the town from either east or west today can't miss the signs advertising the Husteads' "world-famous" Wall Drug. Lady Bird Johnson's highway beautification program eliminated most of the signs, which span from coast to coast and even grace some foreign countries. A few remain, however, with messages like "Wall Drug or Bust"; "Have You Dug Wall Drug?"; "As Written about in the Wall Street Journal"; and, most memorable, "Free Ice Water—Wall Drug." The story of Wall Drug has been told and retold so often that it has taken on the quality of legend. Now world-famous, it was once merely another struggling little business in a South Dakota town doomed to typicality. As dry year succeeded dry year during the Great Depression years of the 1930s, it almost did not survive. All over western South Dakota, indeed, all over the region, people abandoned the struggle against the elements and moved away, large numbers of them joining the trek westward to seek salvation on the Pacific coast. "Blown out, baked out, and broke"—that's how the predicament on the Great Plains was characterized in the acclaimed documentary movie, *The Plow That Broke the Plains,* produced by the Farm Security Administration in 1936.[3]

That summer in Wall, a town of about 300 people, Ted Hustead lay awake nights trying to think of a way to make a go of it with his little drugstore on Main Street. He and his wife Dorothy had bought the store five years earlier with a $3,000 legacy from Ted's father. They had given themselves five years to make a go of it. Now the time was almost up, and business was moribund. Dorothy's father had warned them when they had ventured out that "Wall is just about as Godforsaken as you can get."[4] Had they not received emotional support from friends and neighbors and especially from their priest, Father John Connally, the young couple might have despaired.

Then, as the story has often been told, one hot Sunday afternoon in July, Dorothy Hustead received an inspiration. Why not entice weary travelers in off the highway by offering them free ice water? People would surely welcome a respite from the deadening heat and the swirling dust of the road. She even had an idea for a sign: "Get a soda. Get a beer. Turn next corner. Just as near. To Highway 16 and 14. Free ice water. Wall Drug." Ted and a local high school boy went to work the next several days painting signs on the order of the popular Burma Shave signs. The rest, as they say, is history.[5]

People did pull off the highway to get their free ice water, and most of them stayed to purchase other items. Ted and Dorothy hired eight girls to help them serve their customers. Hundreds, and eventually thousands, of signs sprouted up along the highways, dotting the country from coast to coast. During World War II, soldiers overseas sent requests for signs, which they posted from Europe to Asia. One, written in Chinese and English, indicated, "Shanghai to Wall Drug Store, 9,066 miles." According to a 1973 *Wall Street Journal* article, the advertising paid off. One survey indicated that 45 percent of all westbound autos

Signs like this help to lure visitors into Wall Drug.

and a slightly smaller proportion of those going the other way turned off to visit the store.[6]

What people see today when they turn off the interstate and drive up Main Street to park in front of Husteads' Wall Drug (or, more likely on a busy day, along a side street or in one of the store's several parking lots) are the typical tourist come-ons. Beyond the motels, which flank several streets, are the Black Hills Gold Emporium, the Rushmore Mountain Taffy Shop, the Badlands Bar and Lounge, the Cactus Cafe, the Wild West Historical Wax Museum, the Buffalo Gift Shop, and other shops and stores. The entire town is geared now to catering to tourists—as many as twenty thousand a day during the summer.[7]

The drugstore itself deserves the reputation it has acquired as one of America's unique tourist attractions, earning it feature stories in publications from the *Wall Street Journal* to *Playboy* and *USA Today.* Covering two-thirds of a city block on the east side of Main Street, it did $5.5 million worth of business in 1985. Four dining rooms, an apothecary, an art gallery, a western clothing shop, a jewelry emporium, a shoe store, a chapel, a pottery and iron shed, and numerous other shops, displays, and nooks and crannies provide attractions enough to occupy visitors for hours if they want to take the time. During the busy summer months an endless stream of visitors passes through the aisles. They can view dozens of western paintings covering the walls of several rooms, laugh at the six-foot "jackalope" (combination jackrabbit and antelope) in the rear annex, enjoy the mechanical banjo pickers and other displays throughout the store, select postcards to send home, and even stop to reflect for a moment in a sixty-seat chapel. For most, it is a move-on-in, take-a-look, and let's-be-on-our-way experience. Afterwards, they can tell people that they've "done" Wall Drug. A fascinating experience, all in all, but then, compared to Disney World or Independence Hall, small potatoes.

What people ought to do is stay a little longer and look a little closer. Wall Drug, more than being simply another (especially fascinating, to be sure) tourist attraction, reeks of history. Hundreds of old photographs decorate the walls in several rooms and hallways. The history of the town of Wall can be traced in one group of them. In the "Back Yard" annex are close to twelve hundred historical photos which Ted purchased from Leonard Jennewein, a history professor at Dakota Wesleyan University, who financed a trip to Europe by selling copies from his collection at the Friends of the Middle Border Museum in Mitchell.[8] The pictures provide a panoramic history of the early decades of

Dakota history: claim shanties, log cabins, sod houses, Native American reservations, cowboys, the 1874 Custer expedition into the Black Hills, railroads, gold miners, threshing crews, the massacre at Wounded Knee, and hundreds of other scenes.

In the corner behind the hand-carved walnut bar in the Western Art Gallery Dining Room hangs a Harvey Dunn painting. Most of the paintings in the room may not qualify as great art, but they do have stories to tell. They portray western scenes—on the range, in rodeos, in mountain canyons, under hot orange suns, and in the dead of winter. Humor is a major theme in many of them, but heroism outranks it. There are lots of horses here; almost every picture, it seems, is full of them. American Indians are here too, for they owned this territory before the settlers came. A few women are portrayed now and then. Mostly the paintings depict life on the range, not on Main Street. Here one can see graphically displayed the popular history of the Dakota cattle frontier.[9]

Ted Hustead, flanked by waitresses, waits for customers at Wall Drug's soda fountain in the late 1930s.

An apothecary museum anchors the "Western Mall," an annex that was added to the drugstore during the 1960s. Ted and Dorothy's son Bill was primarily responsible for planning the addition, and it was he who insisted on including several attractions related to history. "He knew just what he wanted to do with the mall, down to the last detail," Ted told me when I visited the drugstore in July 1988. More useful for history than the apothecary museum, which recreates the ambience of an old drugstore, is the Hole-in-the-Wall Bookstore, bulging with local history. Besides carrying the usual kinds of state and local history books, it contains a large inventory of regional and Native American history, not just a copy or two of each, but often a dozen or more. There are several hundred titles on American Indian history alone. Next to them, neatly arranged in racks, are books on the history of railroads, the fur trade, the Missouri and Mississippi rivers, settlement, ethnic groups, women, agriculture, military forts, the environment, and other subjects. Probably no other bookstore in the state offers a better assortment of history books.

Bill also installed a family picture gallery, a long, narrow room about four feet wide plastered with pictures of Ted, Dorothy, Bill, and the rest of the family, posing with employees, friends, acquaintances, the great, the near-great, and people on the street. There are pictures of Ted and Dorothy when they were young, wedding photos, shots of their children as they were growing up—then their weddings, and their children. Among the hundreds of framed photographs are shots of Bill Bradley and his wife visiting the drugstore, Ronald Reagan and Marjorie Hustead, Karl Mundt and Bill Hustead, Lyndon Johnson and Mrs. Leonel Jensen (a close family friend), and basketball star Patrick Ewing in Senator James Abdnor's office with a Wall Drug sign. The family's history is also traced on a family tree that goes back to Robert Husted, who emigrated to America in 1635. It was a sixth-generation family member, Moses Hustead, who changed the spelling of the family name. Ted (b. 1902) is the eleventh generation of Husteads in this country.

Ted admitted to me that he never had any particular interest in history as a student or as a young man, but in the last twenty years or so that has changed. Visitors who shared the same last name or suspected that he might be related to them piqued his interest in family history. A cousin from Bakersfield, California, who was passing through described some research he had been doing at the Mormon archives in Salt Lake City. From archivists there Hustead discovered some facts about his ancestors he had never known, especially about his mother, whose maiden name was Bell. It struck him just how little he really knew about her. She had been a teacher, but where had she obtained her education? How did she meet Ted's father? How did he happen to decide to become a doctor? Ted knew where his father had gone to school, but why did he attend there?

Besides working on his own family's history, Ted grew increasingly interested in the history of the region. Many drugstore patrons visited the area to see the Badlands, which begin a few miles south of the town. One of Ted's friends, Leonel Jensen, a rancher of pioneer stock who lived near Wall, promoted the concept of organizing automobile caravans to track down local history and trace old cattle and wagon trails crisscrossing the area. While working on his own ranch and others in the area, Jensen had frequently come across evidence of American Indian camps and outlaw hideouts in the Badlands, campsites of fur traders and trappers, and tracks left by military expeditions, stagecoaches, and freight wagons. Enlisting the help of state historian Will Robinson, the Wall Chamber of Commerce, and Ted Hustead, he organized the first "Vanishing Trails Expedition" in 1960.[10] It traced part of General William S. Harney's 1855 route from Fort Laramie to Fort Pierre, where his soldiers occupied the first military fort in what later became South Dakota. In 1964, more than

Ted Hustead, with a glass of his famous ice water, and his son Bill. (Couresty of Ted E. Hustead)

two hundred cars carrying a thousand people followed the trail that Big Foot and his band of Sioux took through the Badlands on their way to Wounded Knee in 1890. Fifteen more expeditions were conducted, the last one in 1975. The story is told in the book entitled *The Vanishing Trails Expedition,* which can be purchased in the bookshop.

For the Husteads, history links them to family saga, places them firmly within their geographical region, overlaps with artistic renderings of their cultural milieu, visibly recreates the development of the town of Wall, offers an attraction drawing paying customers in through their doors, and provides a dramatic context for their drugstore. It is not so much a drugstore (although it does sell drugs) as a fantastic self-created cultural-historical artifact with a life of its own. Other tourist attractions successfully exploit history for commercial purposes, but here at Wall Drug, one gets the impression that the history would not be necessary to draw in the tourists and that the history that, in fact, is present in such profusion is there because the Husteads think it belongs there. It does seem right and appropriate.

With luck, the visitor can discover even more history at Wall Drug. Most days Al Strandell can be found sitting at a table, sipping coffee and talking to his friends. None of them remembers stories the way Al does, but none of them are ninety-five years old either. These days, Al lives in an apartment house several blocks from the drugstore. He usually gets a ride over in the morning from the postman and then hitches a ride home with a friend. He has lots of friends, the Husteads among them.

When Ted and Dorothy visited Wall in 1931 to determine whether or not they wanted to move there, Al urged them to stay. He was still ranching at the time, and he and his wife would eat dinner at the Miller Hotel when they came to Wall to trade. Mrs. Miller introduced them to the Husteads, and over the years they became good friends. Al served the town as mayor for sixteen years and often worked together with Ted on the town council. He recalls the day they led a delegation of townspeople to a hearing at the state capital to protest the discontinuance of railroad passenger service on the Chicago and North Western line. The first question posed to them was, "How did you gentlemen get here?" Having to admit they had traveled in cars, not by rail, their balloon was deflated before they even started.

Al was only two years old when his family moved from Jackson, Minnesota, to western South Dakota in 1895, after having made a couple of earlier forays into the area. They began ranching ten miles south of the little town of Pedro, near the Cheyenne

Al Strandell.
(Courtesy of Don Strandell)

River. Al was fourteen by the time the Chicago and North Western Railway laid its tracks across the prairie from Fort Pierre to Rapid City, and the town of Wall was established about forty miles south of their place in 1907. He recalled for me the days when stagecoaches still raised dust on the old Fort Pierre–Deadwood Trail. Pedro was a little off the main trail, but drivers would sometimes detour over to it to pick up a passenger. One of Al's jobs as a child was to ride into town twice a week to pick up the mail that came in on the stage. "But that stagecoach never came in and left like it shows in the movies," he laughed. "It started slow, and it left slow. In the movies they're always running. It wasn't that way."[11]

They drove cattle to Hermosa, south of Rapid City, and shipped them by rail to Chadron, Nebraska, and from there east. With the Chicago and North Western's arrival in 1906–7, every little town along the tracks had a stockyard for shipping out stock. If a rancher had a carload, he often rode along to Sioux City or Chicago. The railroad allowed them to ride free in the caboose. Drought hit the area hard in 1910 and 1911, devastating crops and decimating herds, but most families hung on and refused to quit.[12] They gave 1911 the nickname "Next Year." Not enough rain fell to make the seeds grow, Al recalled, but during the fall they did get a little moisture. The quitters left. The ones who stayed behind possessed a stick-to-itiveness—a blend of fatalism and optimism—that saw them through the hard times that came along periodically. For old-timers, the Dirty Thirties turned out to be just one of a long series of hardships and challenges.[13]

For Ted and Dorothy Hustead, the Great Depression decade was punctuated by the ice water episode. In a single moment, they metamorphosed from just another hopeful couple minding a none-too-successful store on Main Street to one that took an idea and converted it into fortune and fame. Al and his wife Bonnie in the meantime started a grocery store on Wall's Main Street in 1939 after twenty years of ranching and a brief stint with a used clothing store in Rapid City. They did well with their grocery, but well in the way that any Main Street storekeeper might have done in a town like Wall. After his wife suffered a stroke, Al sold the store and took up house painting, also investing money in houses and renting them out. Now the spot where their store once stood occupies a small corner of Wall Drug. As the Husteads expanded their operation, they bought out the stores surrounding them on the east side of the street, including the one that Al and Bonnie had owned.

The saga of the Husteads is the quintessential success story—faith, dedication, and hard work eventually yielding their reward. It is the type of fable that Norman Vincent Peale liked to use to illustrate the power of positive thinking. In fact, after meeting the Husteads, the popular exponent of the self-made man published an article written by Ted about the ice water drugstore in his publication, *Guideposts.* It is reprinted in brochures that are handed out free to customers at the drugstore. Ted's philosophy can be gleaned from the sayings he has hanging on a wall of his second-floor office in the drugstore. One of them, from St. Benedict, admonishes, "Idleness is the enemy of the soul." Idleness was never one of Ted's vices.

Al Strandell also preaches the power of positive thinking. After engaging in ranching, storekeeping, and a variety of other occupations ("You know I did everything but steal horses," he tells people), he spends his later years dispensing cheer and practical wisdom to folks. Every day he rides to the drugstore and strikes up conversations with people, recounting the history of the area and passing out copies of clippings from newspapers and magazines—stories, poems, and wise sayings. Some of them are things he has written himself, including a regular local newspaper column he contributed for a decade or so, entitled "Al Says." As I talked to him, he pulled out several envelopes, extracting an item from each one, courtesy of a photocopy machine.

Nine decades of history found expression in Al's words and gestures, in the work-weathered hands and the wide smile that came easily. He represented a type of personality—shaped by years of living in the area, molded by the challenges, the struggles, the triumphs and failures he had experienced—that one frequently encounters in Wall. Like Huck Finn, he is wont to say, "I've been there before." Here is what Al wrote in a column he entitled "Old Timer":

> An old timer tells his friends: I survived World War One. One auto accident. Went through the dry 30's. Went broke. Got stuck in the gumbo. Had to haul water three miles for the hog house. Chopped wood and burned cow chips to cook rabbit and wild onion soup. Raised my family on almost nothing. Went through three of the worst blizzards on record. Went through two depressions. Had a run-in with a skunk. Prayed for rain. Got hail and dust storms and saw transportation go from the ox cart to the moon. And some young whippersnapper comes along and tells me I don't know what life is all about.

As Al approaches the century mark, he looks back at life satisfied that he has lived it to the fullest. He understands that a home is more than a house and a town is more than its buildings. History consists of more than wars and depressions, railroads and automobiles, run-ins with skunks, and Fourth of July celebrations. History is what you make of it, how you respond to the events that reel off minute by minute, day by day, year by year, decade by decade. History is the human spirit made concrete. In these small towns along Highway 14 history can be found in many places—unexpected places only if one lacks the imagination to look for it there. History finds embodiment in dreams, hopes, frustrations, striving, resignation, anger, joy, hatred, and love. The last clipping Al handed me, from "Al Strandell's Collection of Poems," was called "Roses for Mother's Day":

> I cut a bunch of roses,
> So my mother could have a share.
>
> Then when I turned and looked again,
> I found new roses there.
>
> I think that they are saying
> Now don't you see it's true,
>
> When you give Joy to someone else,
> Much more comes back to you.

MOUNT RUSHMORE

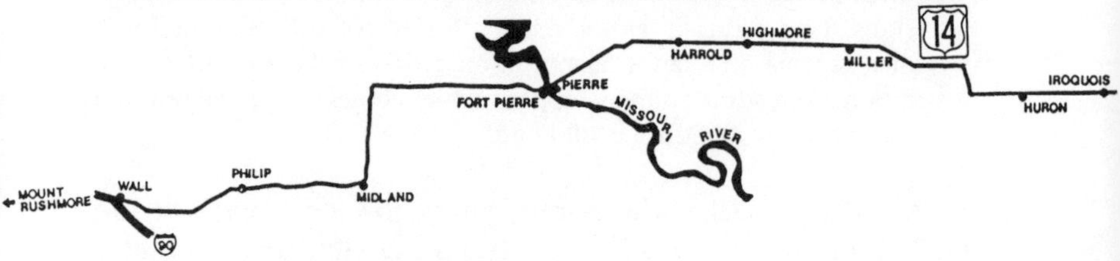

History Carved on a Rock

At Wall, Highway 14 merges with Interstate 90 and proceeds west toward Yellowstone National Park. Cars cruising along the divided four-lane concrete speed by the towns of Wasta, New Underwood, and Box Elder on their way to Rapid City. Once, these were stops along the Black and Yellow Trail. People who imagine that being located along an interstate highway confers economic benefits on a town should observe these hamlets, which hardly rate a glance from travelers gliding past them in their air-conditioned chariots.

Back in the 1950s, when Congress inaugurated the Interstate Highway System, there were some who hoped that Highway 14 might become part of it. Such a prospect never stood much of a chance, however, even though it meant that Pierre would be one of only five state capitals not linked by an interstate. The politicians and highway officials planning the stretch between Sioux Falls and the Black Hills could have chosen to divert traffic far enough north to go through Pierre, but following Highway 16 (the old Custer Battlefield Trail) shortened the distance considerably. It was the most direct route.[1]

By the 1920s promoters of the Black and Yellow Trail and the Custer Battlefield Trail were already competing vigorously for tourist traffic heading toward the Black Hills. After the dedication of Mount Rushmore in 1927 tourist traffic picked up, although the Great Depression had a dampening effect on it until the end of the 1930s. The number of visitors recorded at Mount Rushmore increased from 108,000 in 1932 to 197,000 in 1935 and to over 300,000 in 1939.[2] Businesspeople and trail boosters in towns along both routes stepped up their campaigns for dustless highways during the middle of the 1930s, and by 1937 both roads were almost completely hard-surfaced.

At Cottonwood, Highways 14 and 16 once joined each other and proceeded west together toward Rapid City. There, Highway 14 still swings north toward Sturgis and Spearfish, skirting the eastern and northern edges of the Black Hills, while Highway 16 pierces directly into the mountains, taking tourists within several miles of Gutzon Borglum's mountain-carving project. In 1925, when the tempestuous sculptor had chosen Mount Rushmore for his patriotic work, some observers had urged against the location because of its remoteness. There were no roads leading to it; the only way to reach it was by walking and climbing through rugged terrain.[3] Two years later, when President Calvin Coolidge arrived to dedicate the monument, he had to ride the last two miles over rough trails by mountain burro.

As part of the bargain for obtaining a congressional subsidy to begin work on the monument, the South Dakota legislature agreed to finance the building of a road to Mount Rushmore from Rapid City as well as to develop other access roads in the mountainous area. It was difficult to obtain more than a few thousand dollars from South Dakotans for the construction of the monument itself. Building three hard-surfaced roads leading to the mountain cost the state's citizenry more than $1 million by 1937. Approximately $2 million more was spent during the following decade on roads within a fifteen-mile radius.[4] A close connection existed between building the monument itself and building roads in South Dakota. Good hard-surfaced roads were a prerequisite for substantial tourist traffic. The completion of the monument guaranteed continually increasing numbers on those roads. Writing in the early 1950s, Gilbert C. Fite, in his excellent book about Mount Rushmore, noted its economic value to South Dakota, calling it "one of the state's most valuable assets." Officials at the time credited it with generating 75 percent of the state's tourist trade.[5]

That would have gratified Doane Robinson, the man who conceived the idea of mountain carving in the Black Hills. Robinson, who served as the first state historian, beginning in 1901, was a widely published poet and author and a popular lecturer. Moreover, he was the state's foremost booster. One reason he came up with the idea was his desire to commemorate the region's history, but equally important in his thinking were the economic benefits to be derived from luring tourists to South Dakota to view the massive granite figures he hoped to have carved on pinnacles in the Black Hills. The year 1923 saw route numbers assigned to state highways. Meanwhile, graveling crews succeeded in covering most of the main routes through the state that year. It was at that significant juncture in highway history when Robinson wrote sculptor Lorado Taft in December 1923 about his idea for carving historical figures in the Needles, granite outcroppings in the Black Hills. "I am thinking of some notable Sioux, as Redcloud, who lived and died in the shadow of those peaks," he wrote. "If one was found practicable, perhaps others would ultimately follow." "In my imagination," he later told the well-known artist, "I can see all the old heroes of the west peering out from them [the mountains]: Lewis and Clark, Fremont, Jed Smith, Bridger, Sakaka-wea, Redcloud, and, in an equestrian statue, Cody and the overland mail."[6]

Ill health prevented Taft from leaving Chicago, so Robinson took his idea to Senator Peter Norbeck, who had served two terms as South Dakota's governor before going to Washington in 1921. Norbeck had been preaching the gospel of park and game development in the Black Hills for twenty years. He was also an automobile enthusiast, and in 1905 he and a friend had been the first to drive a car from the Missouri River to the Black Hills. While governor, he had joined the good roads advocates, utilizing the historic 1916 Federal Highway Act to accelerate the drive for road building. During his term in Pierre, the South Dakota Transportation Department had been established. Norbeck viewed tourism as a major factor in the future development of the state. During the late 1920s, he would personally lay out the route of Iron Mountain Road, choosing breathtakingly scenic approaches to Mount Rushmore and planning tunnels that framed the sculpture for automobile travelers as they drove through them. Nevertheless, when first approached by Robinson in early 1924 about carving historic figures in the mountains, Norbeck reacted cautiously at first, but soon he grew enthusiastic about the idea and turned into one of its staunchest advocates. His support was essential for getting the idea off the ground.[7]

Having won Norbeck's tentative approval, Robinson was ready to relate his brainstorm to the people of South Dakota. The forum he used was the annual meeting of the Black and Yellow Trail Association at Huron on January 22, 1924. In a talk entitled "The Pull of the Historic Place," he suggested that mountain carvings could be a way to focus people's attention on and to educate them about the past. Hitched to that goal was the commercial motive of attracting tourist traffic, a subject that was much more interesting to the convention delegates. Robinson emphasized that improving the state's scenic attractions would draw more tourists into the region, and he asserted that every community should have something that they could utilize for this purpose.[8]

Tourists' cars parked below Mount Rushmore around 1939 while the monument was still being sculpted. (Courtesy of South Dakota State Archives, Pierre)

Several days later an Associated Press story datelined from Pierre described Robinson's proposal for massive and spectacular sculptures in the Needles of the Black Hills that would depict the history of the state. "Hundreds of visitors would be drawn into the state to view such a landmark," Robinson contended. His major emphasis from the very beginning, therefore, was on the commercial value of the project. Perhaps as the state historian, he realized from past experience that this would be the best way to sell his idea to the public.[9]

Not everyone was immediately convinced, however. Although Robinson estimated that the total cost would not exceed $100,000, some people wondered where the money was going to come from. "He seems to think that by making this radical alteration on nature's handiwork it will please tourists and will add to the tourist traffic through the Black Hills country," editorialized the *Queen City Mail.* Characterizing the Needles region as "one of the greatest specimens of nature's handiwork on the American continent," the paper noted that it might be feasible "to change them into monstrous monuments expressive of historical incidents of the Black Hills country" but that it should not be done. "To set the hand of man at work to improve on that of nature is a desecration which should not be permitted." The Yankton *Press and Dakotan* dryly noted, "The idea is not likely to meet with unanimous favor." It went on to observe, "We who live out on the plains are quite satisfied with the beauties of our great Black Hills as bequeathed to us by nature."[10]

Although South Dakotans were less than unanimously enthusiastic about the mountain-carving project, Robinson's concept immediately appealed to sculptor Gutzon Borglum when it was broached to him. Borglum—flamboyant, controversial, unpredictable—instinctively grasped the historical ramifications of the proposal. If state historian Robinson had more than history on his mind in conceiving his project, sculptor Borglum, who was enlisted to work on it, had more than art on his mind in accepting the challenge. While Borglum certainly considered his work on Mount Rushmore to be artistically significant, he considered its historical and symbolic implications to be even more important. Fifty-seven years old when Robinson contacted him in August 1924, Borglum was fiercely patriotic and nationalistic and an apostle of a distinctly American art. "Art in America should be American, drawn from American sources, memorializing American achievement," he wrote.[11]

Instantly attracted to Robinson's proposal, Borglum immediately made plans to visit the Black Hills to look over the situation. When he came into view of the Needles and other granite outcroppings, he exclaimed, "There's the place to carve a great national memorial!" And a bit later, "American history shall march along that skyline!"[12] The following year, when he returned to choose a particular location for executing his grand work, he asserted that "the whole world will speak of South Dakota." Senator Norbeck was able to join the party for a while as it surveyed the mountains for a location with the proper rock formation and the correct lighting. Borglum placed great importance on obtaining the right angle so that the sun would light up the sculpture to best advantage.[13]

When Borglum glimpsed a six-thousand-foot granite-topped mountain remotely situated away from any roads and several miles northeast of Harney Peak (the tallest point in America east of the Rocky Mountains), he quickly surmised that he had discovered exactly what he was looking for. The face of the mountain was ideally situated for lighting; the sun shone on it much of the day. Though the peak had never been officially named, it was widely known around the area as Mount Rushmore. According to one story, during the 1880s Charles E. Rushmore, a New York attorney who was in the Black Hills checking the titles of potential mining properties, had been tramping through the area when he spied it. With him at the time were William Challis, a local prospector and guide, and David Swanzey, a resident of the nearby mining village of Keystone. (The latter later married Carrie Ingalls, a younger sister of Laura Ingalls Wilder.) When the New Yorker inquired about the name of the mountain looming before them, Challis quickly replied, "Never had any, but it has now—we'll call the damn thing Rushmore."[14]

Borglum's vision of his mountain sculpture underwent revision during succeeding years, but always it was grandiose. He was fascinated with the notion of massive sculpture and believed in doing things on a grand scale. America itself was huge, and its art should be equivalent to it, Borglum contended. He had been advocating gigantic American art for almost a quarter of a century. "We are living in an age of the colossal," he liked to say. "My big mission in life is to get the American people to look at art in a big way and to get away from this petty stuff," he told Senator Norbeck.[15] "A monument's dimensions should be determined by the importance to civilization of the events commemorated," Borglum insisted.

> We are not here trying to carve an epic, portray a moonlight scene, or write a sonnet; neither are we dealing with mystery or tragedy,

> but rather with the constructive and the dramatic moments or crises in our amazing history. We are coolheadedly, clearmindedly, setting down a few crucial, epochal facts regarding the accomplishments of the old world radicals who shook the shackles of oppression from their light feet and fled despotism to people a continent; who built an empire and rewrote the philosophy of freedom and compelled the world to accept its wiser, happier forms of government.
>
> We believe the dimensions of national heartbeats are greater than village impulses, greater than city demands, greater than state dreams or ambitions. Therefore we believe a nation's memorial should, like Washington, Jefferson, Lincoln, and Roosevelt, have a serenity, a nobility, a power that reflects the gods who inspired them. . . .
>
> I want somewhere in America . . . a few feet of stone that bears witness . . . of the great things we accomplished as a nation, placed so high it won't pay to pull it down for lesser purposes . . . carved high, as close to heaven as we can. . . . Then breathe a prayer that these records will endure until the wind and the rain alone shall wash them away.[16]

Borglum's vision of history was a more expansive one than Doane Robinson's. The state historian had wanted to memorialize some of the famous frontier characters and Native Americans identified with the region and in the process to promote tourism and economic growth. Borglum, while recognizing the usefulness of commercial and tourist possibilities for promoting and raising money for the sculpture, envisioned a gigantic artwork that would stand long after contemporary civilization had passed away and provide information for future visitors about the people who had once lived there. His sights were as much on the future as upon the past. He would be carving out immortality for American civilization as well as for himself (although he insisted upon not having his name impressed on the mountainside).

Talking to a group of Boy Scouts in 1937, Borglum recalled a speech he had made when President Coolidge had come to dedicate the monument a decade earlier. Explaining that "it's a little hard trying to get on a platform and talk to the President of the United States," Borglum told the boys gathered around him that

> I had forgotten what I had to say, except that I remembered that I was to carve on this cliff a monument to our people and our government. I managed to say that and I added, "a monument that will outlast our civilization." The President was shocked, and I was shocked, because I realized that they thought in a sense of our little day while I thought in terms of history and of what nature is

> always doing, changing, and growing, rubbing out today and preparing for tomorrow. And I hastily added, "That's an awful thing to say, Mr. President, but that's the course of life."[17]

At first, South Dakotans remained skeptical about Borglum's project. Raising money for it, even among South Dakotans who stood to benefit from it, proved extremely difficult, and only toward the very end, when federal money flowed more freely, were Borglum and the project planners able to forget for even a little while their money worries. As the years ticked off and the faces of Washington, Jefferson, Lincoln, and Theodore Roosevelt emerged from the stone, the general public gradually became convinced of the importance and grandeur of the undertaking. Almost everyone who actually came to see the mountain was impressed by it. One member of Congress, who had been skeptical of its worth before viewing it in 1937, later confessed, "I went there with a definite prejudice against it and came away feeling very favorable to it."[18] Each pilgrim to the "Shrine of Democracy" interjected his or her own feelings into the work of art, investing it with meaning and significance. There were a few who refused to be impressed or who rejected it outright, but they were in the minority.

Yet Borglum believed that purely emotional responses to the four faces on the mountain were not, in the end, sufficient. He believed in the historical importance of his monumental artwork, but he did not think that it alone would establish what needed to be conveyed. A future visitor doing an archaeological study of the area would need more than the visages alone to understand what they signified. Therefore, Borglum proposed an inscription that would record significant events in the history of America for ages to come and stand alongside the faces on the mountain. Later he decided that the inscription should be placed on the reverse edge, behind the faces. In the artist's view, according to historian Gilbert C. Fite, "If it were to last 500,000 years, as some geologists said, the four faces without explanative text might someday be meaningless."[19]

What makes the faces so impressive, in addition to their size, is the knowledge we bring with us about U.S. history. We view them through the lenses of our own values, beliefs, and ideas. But if we did not carry this information and cultural baggage, they might be the faces of priests, soldiers, businessmen, or thieves. Just like unlabeled photographs in a museum or buildings of which we have no knowledge, just like words in a language that we do not understand or the gestures of a person whose culture

Proposed historical inscription on Mount Rushmo
(Courtesy of Mount Rushmore National Memorial)

IN THE YEAR OF OUR LORD
1776
THE PEOPLE DECLARED THE ETERNAL RIGHT TO SEEK HAPPINESS, SELF-GOVERNMENT AND THE DIVINE DUTY TO DEFEND THAT RIGHT AT ANY SACRIFICE
1787
ASSEMBLED IN CONVENTION THEY MADE A CHARTER OF PERPETUAL UNION FOR FREE PEOPLE OF SOVEREIGN STATES ESTABLISHING A GOVERNMENT OF LIMITED POWERS UNDER AN INDEPENDENT PRESIDENT, CONGRESS AND COURT CHARGED TO PROVIDE SECURITY FOR ALL CITIZENS IN THEIR ENJOYMENT OF LIBERTY, EQUALITY AND JUSTICE
1803
1819
1846
1848
1850
1867
1906

we are unacquainted with, the four faces on Mount Rushmore would be a great curiosity to us but meaningless nevertheless.

The inscription idea, however, turned out to be something of a fiasco. Borglum, on a typical impulse, had invited Coolidge to write the inscription when the president had dedicated the monument in 1927, and in the federal law passed two years later authorizing $250,000 for doing the carving, he had been specifically named to write the inscription. When Coolidge finally got around to the task several years later, however, Borglum, without telling anyone what he was doing, slightly revised his wording. When news of this leaked out, it caused an uproar and the former president quickly made it clear that he would have nothing further to do with the project. Borglum had simply assumed that slight editorial changes of the type he had rendered were not only harmless but necessary, even if the words he was amending were those of a former president.[20]

The basic problem, beyond Coolidge's lack of literary grace, was the impossibility of saying much about history in the brief compass allowed. With the letters having to be three feet high to make them visible to distant viewers, only about five hundred words would fit into the space on the mountain set aside for the inscription. Borglum's instincts in wanting to use words to convey history, rather than relying entirely upon the visual effects of the sculpture, were sound. But he did not reckon with the difficulty of trying to compress history into so few words.

Borglum's conception of the important historical facts worth remembering was, in fact, quite a limited one. For him, the history of the United States was to be found in the story of the westward movement—the expansion of a nation across the continent from ocean to ocean. Before Coolidge ever began writing his essay, Borglum revealed the eight events that he considered epochal in U.S. development: the Declaration of Independence, the Constitution, the Louisiana Purchase, the admission of Texas to the Union, the settlement of the Oregon boundary dispute, the admission of California, the ending of the Civil War, and the construction of the Panama Canal.[21] The space these facts were to be inscribed on would be in the shape of the Louisiana Purchase. Such a reading of U.S. history could be justified, but it certainly would not appeal to everyone. Just as Laura Ingalls Wilder's childhood conception of U.S. history was that it consisted of the memorization of a certain limited number of facts, names, and dates (albeit more than eight), Borglum's idea of encompassing U.S. history in eight episodes indicates he failed to acknowledge both the complexity of that history and the fact that historical interpretation depends heavily upon the historian's outlook, values, and preconceptions. In proposing these events, Borglum revealed his own preconceptions and ideological tendencies.

In the end, the idea of a historical inscription on the mountain faded away because there was no time, no money, and no space to complete it. However, this did not happen before Borglum started carving the year "1776" in the area where Lincoln's face would later take shape. The sculptor further developed his idea for a hall of records before having to give it up. He planned for a large room, eighty by one hundred feet, to be located in the area behind the faces. In it glass-walled cabinets would house

> the records of the West World accomplishments, the political effect of its philosophy of government, its adventure in science, art, literature, invention, medicine, harmony—typed upon aluminum sheets rolled and protected in tubes. . . . On the wall above them, extending around the entire hall will be a bas-relief showing the adventure of humanity discovering and occupying the West World; it will be bronze, gold plated. There will be 25 large busts of great . . . men and women, together with one panel reserved for our own day—why and by whom the great Federal Memorial was conceived and built and the records of that work.

All of this would constitute the most complete archives in the world; the steps leading up to it would be like nothing ever done in history outside of the steps leading to the Parthenon in Athens.[22]

Borglum's vision was nothing if not grandiose. His historic vision was truly romantic, and his own place in history, he expected, would thus be memorialized. Along with busts of Benjamin Franklin, John Hancock, Patrick Henry, and others in the hall of records, "I will give Susan B. Anthony a place with the gods in the Great Hall," he said. "Her friends should be happy."[23] All of these plans, however, came to naught. The members of Congress who were subsidizing the work only wanted to see the faces appear out of the rock. Historians, learning of Borglum's version of the past, thought that as a historian he made a good artist. The general public had little conception of his plans, and if they did, they showed little interest in them. After blasting out a tunnel fourteen by twenty feet and about seventy-five feet deep into the mountain, Borglum was forced to concentrate his attention on finishing the faces and never lived to pursue his dream of a historic archive.[24]

Borglum's ironic reference to Susan B. Anthony's bust among the demigods in the Great Hall was aimed at proposals made during the 1930s that her likeness be added to those already on the mountain. Earlier, Democrats and admirers of Woodrow Wilson had been miffed when he was left off and Theodore Roosevelt included. Many Democrats refused to support the project because of this. Bernard Baruch, who could have afforded to contribute a large sum, was a Wilson fan and rejected fund solicitors. By the 1940s, and especially after his death in 1945, Franklin Roosevelt was often proposed as an addition to the memorial. Before his own death in 1941, Borglum always rejected such proposals, saying there was no more room left to carve on the mountain. Even if there had been, he had no intention of doing another face.[25]

Almost half a century later, another president, who liked to identify himself with the image of Franklin Roosevelt, had his name bandied about as a possible fifth face on the mountain. R. Emmett Tyrrell, Jr., a conservative journalist who promoted the movement, reported that Ronald Reagan smiled when shown an artist's sketch of him on Mount Rushmore, but most observers considered the boomlet more of a gag than a serious proposal.

"The simple fact is there is no more suitable rock to carve anyone at Mount Rushmore," announced Tom Griffith, executive secretary of the Mount Rushmore Society.

"Small-minded people, typical small-minded people," Tyrrell responded.

Letters to the editor reflected people's concerns about possible changes in the monument. "I feel we must do whatever we can to stop this," a former South Dakotan wrote the Huron *Daily Plainsman*. "It seems to me it would almost be blasphemy to allow them to desecrate our beautiful, wonderful national monument in the beautiful Black Hills of South Dakota."[26]

Words like "blasphemy" and "desecrate" reflect a great deal about how we Americans view these kinds of ritual spaces. They are more than physical places. They are even more than historical monuments. In truth, they are secular shrines, engendering feelings of awe and reverence not unlike religion. They remind us that history is more than the mere recitation of fact; it binds us together as a people, and it undergirds the values and beliefs we cherish. History is contested ground, yet it poses as fact—well established and authoritative. The faces Borglum carved in the mountain were, for the most part, noncontroversial—the heroic fathers of our country—Washington, Jefferson, and Lincoln. (Although Jefferson and Lincoln certainly had their detractors in their own time.) But one, Theodore Roosevelt, was only recently departed (he died in 1919). His inclusion was considered inappropriate by many people; he seemed too controversial.[27]

More significant than who is on the mountain is who was left off. It included no woman, no black, no Native American; no poor person, no radical, no apolitical person; no doctor, no truck driver, no police officer. During the 1920s and 1930s there was more agreement than there is today about what history consists of and about what is important in history. If such a monument were to be proposed today, it is hard to believe that any consensus would emerge on whose faces to include, and it is questionable that Congress would approve funds for it. Our view of history

One of Borglum's early working models for Mount Rushmore. Note the Chicago and North Western Railway map in the background. (Courtesy of Mount Rushmore National Memorial)

has become more complex. It includes many more groups and individuals than it used to. In that sense, it is truer to reality, but it is also more difficult to grasp and more difficult to convince others of its validity.[28]

When Borglum was carving his mountain, he took great delight in telling people that the faces had always resided inside the granite; all he was doing was to blast away the unnecessary rock from around them.[29] Yet he would have been the first to admit that the artistic touch meant everything to the finished product. Jefferson's face, once to the left of Washington's, was moved to the right. The model Borglum worked from in his studio was constantly modified over the years. His conceptualization of what the project would finally bring forth continually changed, although he held firm ideas about the character of the men that he was trying to bring out.

As the work progressed, Borglum viewed the faces through powerful field glasses from points miles away, watching the light reflect on his artwork as the sun passed overhead. He continued to refine his work—removing inches here and half-inches there—until he got it the way he wanted.[30] It was this final finishing work that distinguished a work of art (though some continued to deny it that status) from an engineering marvel.

Like written history itself, which depends upon the artistry of the historian, who selects materials, too, and fits them together to form a finished narrative, a sculpture is the product of the interaction between the natural environment and the human interpreter. Many people view history as nothing more than names, facts, and dates. They naively consider it to be a given, waiting to be discovered, and grant the historian or historical observer no interpretive role. But just as no one will take seriously Borglum's assertion that the sculpture was already in the rock waiting for him to bring it out (astute as that insight was in some ways), we need to recognize that historical understanding depends upon our insight, our ability to ask the right questions, our perceptiveness, our powers of interpretation, and our creativity. We will be as true to the past as we can be, but we will also keep in mind that history has many mansions and that the house we occupy is only one of them.

NOTES

INTRODUCTION

1. Alexis de Tocqueville, *Democracy in America,* ed. J. P. Mayer and Max Lerner (New York: Harper and Row, 1966); James Bryce, *The American Commonwealth,* 2 vols. (New York: Macmillan, 1888). See also Marc Pachter and Frances Wein, eds., *Abroad in America: Visitors to the New Nation, 1776–1914* (Reading, Mass.: Addison-Wesley Publishing Co., 1976); John Graham Brooks, *As Others See Us: A Study of Progress in the United States* (New York: Macmillan, 1910); Jane L. Mesick, *The English Traveller in America, 1785–1835* (New York: Columbia Univ. Press, 1922); Max Berger, *The British Traveller in America, 1836–1860* (New York: Columbia Univ. Press, 1943).

2. Harrison E. Salisbury, *Travels around America* (New York: Walker and Co., 1976); John Gunther, *Inside U.S.A.* (New York: Harper and Brothers, 1947); Neal R. Peirce and Jerry Hagstrom, *The Book of America: Inside Fifty States Today* (New York: Warner Books, 1984).

3. Richard Reeves, *American Journey: Traveling with Tocqueville in Search of "Democracy in America"* (New York: Simon and Schuster, 1982); Eugene J. McCarthy, *America Revisited: 150 Years after Tocqueville* (Garden City, N.Y.: Doubleday and Co., 1978); Ian Frazier, *Great Plains* (New York: Farrar Straus Giroux, 1989), p. 81.

4. Berton Roueché, *Special Places: In Search of Small Town America* (Boston: Little, Brown, 1982); Geoffrey O'Gara, *A Long Road Home: Journeys through America's Present in Search of America's Past* (New York: W. W. Norton, 1989); Bill Moyers, *Listening to America: A Traveler Rediscovers His Country* (New York: Dell Publishing Co., 1971); Ernie Pyle, *Home Country* (New York: William Sloane Associates, 1947); Charles Kuralt, *On the Road with Charles Kuralt* (New York: Ballantine Books, 1985); Charles Kuralt, *Dateline America* (New York: G. P. Putnam's Sons, 1979); Erskine Caldwell, *Around about America* (New York: Farrar, Straus and Co., 1963); John Steinbeck, *Travels with Charley: In Search of America* (New York: Viking Press, 1961).

5. Steinbeck, *Travels with Charley,* pp. 5, 7, 28.

6. Roueché, *Special Places;* Bill Bryson, *The Lost Continent: Travels in Small-Town America* (New York: Harper and Row, 1989).

7. William Least Heat Moon, *Blue Highways: A Journey into America* (Boston: Little, Brown, 1982); Angus Kress Gillespie and Michael Aaron Rock-

land, *Looking for America on the New Jersey Turnpike* (New Brunswick, N.J.: Rutgers Univ. Press, 1989); Steinbeck, *Travels with Charley,* pp. 25, 34; Salisbury, *Travels around America,* p. 2; Kuralt, *On the Road,* p. 53.

8. Quoted in Phil Patton, *Open Road: A Celebration of the American Highway* (New York: Simon and Schuster, 1986), pp. 235–36.

9. Pyle, *Home Country,* p. 93; Steinbeck, *Travels with Charley,* p. 234.

10. Steinbeck, *Travels with Charley,* p. 141; Kuralt, *On the Road,* p. 51; Moyers, *Listening to America,* p. 93; Salisbury, *Travels around America,* p. 3.

11. Kuralt, *On the Road,* p. 51.

12. Quoted in Peter Conrad, *Imagining America* (New York: Oxford Univ. Press, 1980), p. 4.

13. Patton, *Open Road;* Warren J. Belasco, *Americans on the Road: From Autocamp to Motel, 1910–1945* (Cambridge: MIT Press, 1979); Drake Hokanson, *The Lincoln Highway: Main Street across America* (Iowa City: Univ. of Iowa Press, 1988); Quinta Scott and Susan Croce Kelly, *Route 66: The Highway and Its People* (Norman: Univ. of Oklahoma Press, 1988); Gillespie and Rockland, *Looking for America on the New Jersey Turnpike;* David Brodsly, *L.A. Freeway: An Appreciative Essay* (Berkeley: Univ. of California Press, 1981); George R. Stewart, *U.S. 40: Cross Section of the United States of America* (Boston: Houghton Mifflin Co., 1953); Thomas R. Vale and Geraldine R. Vale, *U.S. 40 Today: Thirty Years of Landscape Change in America* (Madison: Univ. of Wisconsin Press, 1983); Thomas J. Schlereth, *U.S. 40: A Roadscape of the American Experience* (Indianapolis: Indiana Historical Society, 1985). In the state guides published by the Federal Writers' Project during the 1930s, special attention is placed on highway tours. See Federal Writers' Project, *A South Dakota Guide* (Pierre, S.Dak.: State Publishing Co., 1938). One of the books that emerged out of the project was *U.S. One: Maine to Florida* (New York: Modern Age Books, 1938). A recent book by an author who used the WPA guides as a jumping off point for journeys around the country is O'Gara, *A Long Road Home.* A good general introduction to interpreting local historical materials is David E. Kyvig and Myron A. Marty, *Nearby History: Exploring the Past around You* (Nashville: American Association for State and Local History, 1982).

14. John Brinckerhoff Jackson, *Discovering the Vernacular Landscape* (New Haven: Yale Univ. Press, 1984), p. xii; D.W. Meinig, ed., *The Interpretation of Ordinary Landscapes: Geographical Essays* (New York: Oxford Univ. Press, 1979), p. 6. See also John Fraser Hart, *The Look of the Land* (Englewood Cliffs, N.J.: Prentice-Hall, 1975); John A. Jakle, *The Visual Elements of Landscape* (Amherst: Univ. of Massachusetts Press, 1987); John A. Jakle, *The American Small Town: Twentieth-Century Place Images* (Hamden, Conn.: Archon Books, 1982); Robert F. Sayre, ed., *Take This Exit: Rediscovering the Iowa Landscape* (Ames: Iowa State Univ. Press, 1989); Wilbur Zelinsky, "The Pennsylvania Town: An Overdue Geographical Account," *Geographical Review* 67 (April 1977): 127–47; John C. Hudson, *Plains Country Towns* (Minneapolis: Univ. of Minnesota Press, 1985). There are also many useful handbooks available for travelers and people interested in landscapes and history, such as Rex C. Buchanan and James R. McCauley, *Roadside Kansas: A Traveler's Guide to Its Geology and Landmarks* (Lawrence: Univ. Press of Kansas, 1987); Ruth Kirk and Carmela Alexander, *Exploring Washington's Past: A Road Guide to History* (Seattle: Univ. of Washington Press, 1989); Carroll Van West, *A Traveler's Companion to Montana History* (Helena: Montana Historical Society Press, 1986).

15. Kuralt, *Dateline America,* p. 7.

16. Steinbeck, *Travels with Charley,* p. 69.

17. Jonathan Culler, "The Semiotics of Tourism," in *Framing the Sign: Criti-*

cism and Its Institutions (Norman: Univ. of Oklahoma Press, 1988), p. 160.

18. Gillespie and Rockland, *Looking for America on the New Jersey Turnpike.*

19. The search for meaning in cultural experience has been advanced especially by the work of Clifford Geertz. See his *The Interpretation of Cultures* (New York: Basic Books, 1973) and *Local Knowledge: Further Essays in Interpretive Anthropology* (New York: Basic Books, 1983).

20. On material culture, see Thomas J. Schlereth, ed., *Material Culture: A Research Guide* (Lawrence: Univ. Press of Kansas, 1985); Thomas J. Schlereth, ed., *Material Culture Studies in America* (Nashville: American Association for State and Local History, 1982); James Deetz, *In Small Things Forgotten: The Archaeology of Early American Life* (Garden City, N.Y.: Anchor Books, 1977); Ian M. G. Quimby, ed., *Material Culture and the Study of American Life* (New York: W. W. Norton, 1978); Dell Upton and John Michael Vlach, eds., *Common Places: Readings in American Vernacular Architecture* (Athens: Univ. of Georgia Press, 1986).

21. On uses of photographic and visual evidence, see William Stott, *Documentary Expression and Thirties America* (New York: Oxford Univ. Press, 1973); F. Jack Hurley, *Portrait of a Decade: Roy Stryker and the Development of Documentary Photography in the Thirties* (Baton Rouge: Louisiana State Univ. Press, 1972); James Curtis, *Mind's Eye, Mind's Truth: FSA Photography Reconsidered* (Philadelphia: Temple Univ. Press, 1989); Bill Ganzel, *Dust Bowl Descent* (Lincoln: Univ. of Nebraska Press, 1984); Alan Trachtenberg, *Reading American Photographs: Images as History, Mathew Brady to Walker Evans* (New York: Hill and Wang, 1989).

ELKTON

1. "Exploring the Real West," *Time* 134 (Aug. 7, 1989): 64–65; Pierre, S.Dak., *Capital Journal,* May 1, 4, 1989; Huron, S.Dak., *Plainsman,* May 11, 1989.

2. In 1986, eight years after Congress moved observances to the fourth Monday in May, South Dakota voters changed state law to conform with federal law. Pierre *Capital Journal,* May 23, 1989; "Memorial Day Observance," program, Elkton, S.Dak., May 29, 1989; Elkton, S.Dak., *Record,* May 25, 1989.

3. For descriptions of typical Memorial Day programs in towns on Highway 14, see Harrold, S.Dak., *Pioneer,* May 27, 1909; De Smet, S.Dak., *News,* June 3, 1910; Brookings, S.Dak., *Register,* May 14, 1914; Miller, S.Dak., *Press,* June 5, 1924.

4. Declining interest in commemorating Memorial Day and the transformation of the Fourth of July from a day of patriotic celebration to one of games and entertainment were increasingly evident by the 1920s. John E. Miller, "The Old-fashioned Fourth of July: A Photographic Essay on Small-town Celebrations prior to 1930," *South Dakota History* 17 (Summer 1987): 137. The editor of the Brookings *Register* noted on May 12, 1921, "It is uncomfortable to think that the actual patriotic observance of Memorial Day in past years has not been what it should. The sentiment of the people we know is full of patriotism but when the time comes for an expression or demonstration of it to honor the memory of fallen heroes, they feel a remoteness from it all and leave it up to the patriotic orders and societies to see that due honor is given to the nation's dead." The following year the De Smet *News,* June 2, 1922, reported growing criticism of ball games on Memorial Day and an increasing disregard for the spirit of the day.

5. James J. Flink, *The Car Culture* (Cambridge: MIT Press, 1975), p. 140; James J. Flink, *America Adopts the Automobile, 1895–1910* (Cambridge: MIT Press, 1970), pp. 109–12; Michael L. Berger, *The Devil Wagon in God's Country: The Automobile and Social Change in Rural America, 1893–1929* (Hamden, Conn.: Archon Books, 1979); Thomas J. Morain, *Prairie Grass Roots: An Iowa Small Town in the Early Twentieth Century* (Ames: Iowa State Univ. Press, 1988), pp. 109–32.

6. Anna Haper, who is ninety-one years old, agreed with Dick and Mary Seivert that Joe Noeth was the first person in the Elkton area to own a car. Anna Haper, interview with author, Elkton, S.Dak., Nov. 3, 1989. Dick Seivert told me that later he offered $5 for the old automobile, but the owner was asking $10 and finally sold it for that to a junk dealer. Dick and Mary Seivert, interview with author, Elkton, S.Dak., Nov. 3, 1989.

7. On the impact of the grid survey system, see Phil Patton, *Open Road: A Celebration of the American Highway* (New York: Simon and Schuster, 1986), pp. 32–34; Hildegarde Binder Johnson, *Order upon the Land: The U.S. Rectangular Land Survey and the Upper Mississippi Country* (New York: Oxford Univ. Press, 1976).

8. Patton, *Open Road,* pp. 44–47; Drake Hokanson, *The Lincoln Highway: Main Street across America* (Iowa City: Univ. of Iowa Press, 1988), pp. 5–21; Quinta Scott and Susan Croce Kelly, *Route 66: The Highway and Its People* (Norman: Univ. of Oklahoma Press, 1988), pp. 6–7; Stephen W. Sears, *The American Heritage History of the Automobile in America* (New York: American Heritage Publishing Co., 1977); Flink, *America Adopts the Automobile,* pp. 203–13.

9. Brookings County History Book Committee, *Brookings County History Book* (Freeman, S.Dak.: Pine Hill Press, 1989), p. 34; Donald Dean Parker, *Pioneering in the Upper Big Sioux Valley: Medary, Sioux Falls, Dell Rapids, Flandreau, Brookings, Watertown* (privately published, 1967), pp. 45–47, 51, 82, 172–73, 186; "Trails and Expeditions," *The Wi-Iyohi: Monthly Bulletin of the South Dakota Historical Society* 3 (June 1, 1949): 1–2; "Highways," *The Wi-Iyohi: Monthly Bulletin of the South Dakota Historical Society* 8 (Feb. 1, 1955): 1–7.

10. Donald Dean Parker, "Wagon Trails to the Pacific," Arlington, S.Dak., *Sun,* June 25, 1980; "The Nobles Trail," *South Dakota Historical Collections* 6 (1912): 183–201. On the early development of trails and roads in Dakota, see in Doane Robinson, "Highways," *Encyclopedia of South Dakota* (Pierre: privately published, 1925), pp. 347–52.

11. Gilbert C. Fite, *Peter Norbeck: Prairie Statesman* (Columbia: University of Missouri, 1948), p. 25.

12. Hokanson, *The Lincoln Highway,* pp. 5–21; Patton, *Open Road,* pp. 39–47.

13. There are a few materials and letters relating to the Yellowstone Trail Association and Parmley's activities in it located in SC10, folder 5, at the South Dakota State Archives in Pierre. Brief biographies of Parmley appear in L. M. Simons and James W. Cone, comp., *South Dakota Legislative Manual* (Pierre: State Publishing Co., 1907), p. 474; Lawrence K. Fox, ed., *Who's Who among South Dakotans: A Biographical Directory,* vol. 2 (Pierre, S.Dak.: Fox and Kindley, Publishers, 1928), p. 178. See also James Cracco, "History of the South Dakota Highway Department, 1919–1941" (Master's thesis, Univ. of South Dakota, 1970), pp. 16–19; Art Buntin, "20th Century Pioneering: The Road and Auto Frontier in Northern South Dakota," *18th Dakota History Conference Papers* (Madison: Dakota State College, 1987), pp. 134–49.

14. De Smet *News,* Aug. 15, 22, 1913; Brookings *Register,* Apr. 10, 1913.

15. Cracco, "History of the South Dakota Highway Department," pp. 22–29.

16. Minutes of the annual meeting of the Chicago, Black Hills and Yellowstone Park Highway Association, June 29–30, 1920, H75.343, folder 10, South Dakota State Archives, Pierre; Brookings *Register,* Aug. 26, 1920.

17. *Straight Away* 1, no. 1 (March 10, 1923), H75.343, folder 9, South Dakota State Archives, Pierre. Folders 9–11 contain a small number of brochures, records, and miscellaneous materials on the Black and Yellow Trail Association. Kyes also enlisted his children, Clifford as a drummer and Bernal as the pianist, in a six-piece orchestra that went to various towns to boost the trail. H. L. Kyes himself played the trombone. Pictures of the group are in *Straight Away* 1, no. 3 (1923).

18. *Straight Away* 1, no. 1 (March 10, 1923); Brookings *Register,* May 3, July 5, Sept. 20, 1923; Huron, S.Dak., *Evening Huronite,* Jan. 23, 1924.

19. Miller *Press,* Apr. 15, 1926; De Smet *News,* July 16, 1926.

20. Sioux Falls, S.Dak., *Argus Leader,* July 25, Sept. 14, 1934; Brookings *Register,* July 25, 1935; Volga, S.Dak., *Tribune,* Aug. 6, 1936.

21. Brookings *Register,* Oct. 24, Nov. 14, 1935; Cracco, "History of the South Dakota Highway Department," pp. 89–97. Besides Elkton and Aurora, two other towns were bypassed by the highway when it was resurfaced and rerouted during the 1930s—Hetland and Ree Heights.

22. Brookings *Register,* May 30, 1935.

23. Berger, *The Devil Wagon in God's Country,* pp. 31–52; John B. Rae, *The American Automobile: A Brief History* (Chicago: Univ. of Chicago Press, 1965), pp. 92–95; Reynold M. Wik, *Henry Ford and Grass-Roots America* (Ann Arbor: Univ. of Michigan Press, 1972), pp. 14–33.

24. Brookings *Register,* Feb. 26, 1920; U.S. Department of Commerce, *Statistical Abstract of the United States* (Washington, D.C.: U.S. Government Printing Office, 1929), p. 387.

25. Berger, *The Devil Wagon in God's Country,* pp. 59–60, 69–71, 95, 99; David B. Danbom, *The Resisted Revolution: Urban America and the Industrialization of Agriculture, 1900–1930* (Ames: Iowa State Univ. Press, 1979), pp. 126–28.

BROOKINGS

1. Gustav O. Sandro, "History of Brookings County" (Master's thesis, Univ. of South Dakota, 1936).

2. Several towns, including Brookings, Aurora, White, Bruce, and Sinai, did publish individual town histories. Ruth Alexander et al., *Brookings' Centennial Commemorative Book, 1879–1979* (Brookings, S.Dak.: Brookings Centennial Book Committee, 1979); *Aurora, South Dakota: Its First 100 Years, 1879–1979* (Aurora: Aurora Centennial History Committee, 1979); *Bruce, South Dakota, 1883–1983* (Bruce: Centennial Committee, 1983); *History of the Sinai Community: Sinai, South Dakota* (Sinai: Sinai Historical Committee, 1979); Charles Woodard and Linda Carlson, eds., *White, S.D., 1884–1984* (White: White History Book Committee, 1984).

3. Donald Dean Parker, *Writing Local History: How to Gather It, Write It, and Publish It* (New York: Social Science Research Council, 1944).

4. Manuscript, Donald Dean Parker Papers, box 2, Center for Western Studies, Augustana College, Sioux Falls, S.Dak.

5. John Beatty compiled several dozen of these articles in *Sharing Sharings: A Compilation of Stories about Early Settlers of South Dakota and Six Other Midwestern States* (Brookings, S.Dak.: Harold's Printing Co., 1989).

6. George and Evelyn Norby, interview with author, Brookings, S.Dak., Apr. 17, 1990.

7. "Brookings Historical Moments—1989" (calendar, Brookings Centennial Committee, S.Dak., 1988).

8. Carl L. Becker, "What Are Historical Facts?" reprinted in *The Philosophy of History in Our Time,* ed. Hans Meyerhoff (Garden City, N.Y.: Doubleday Anchor Books, 1959), p. 135.

9. For treatments of people's concepts of time, see G. J. Whitrow, *Time in History: The Evolution of Our Awareness of Time and Temporal Perspective* (New York: Oxford Univ. Press, 1988); Stephen Kern, *The Culture of Time and Space, 1880–1918* (Cambridge: Harvard Univ. Press, 1983), esp. chap. 1; Stephen Toulmin and June Goodfield, *The Discovery of Time* (New York: Harper and Row, 1965); Wyndham Lewis, *Time and Western Man* (Boston: Beacon Press, 1957).

10. The repetitive nature of town planning is discussed in Carole Rifkind, *Main Street: The Face of Urban America* (New York: Harper and Row, 1977); John W. Reps, *Cities of the American West: A History of Frontier Urban Planning* (Princeton: Princeton Univ. Press, 1979), pp. 543–47; David P. Handlin, *The American Home: Architecture and Society, 1815–1915* (Boston: Little, Brown, 1979), pp. 97–99.

11. For discussions of the influence of space and physical environment upon culture, see John Brinckerhoff Jackson, *Discovering the Vernacular Landscape* (New Haven: Yale Univ. Press, 1984); Michael Reed, ed., *Discovering Past Landscapes* (London: Croom Helm, 1984); D. W. Meinig, ed., *The Interpretation of Ordinary Landscapes: Geographical Essays* (New York: Oxford Univ. Press, 1979); Yi-Fu Tuan, *Topophilia: A Study of Environmental Perception, Attitudes, and Values* (Englewood Cliffs, N.J.: Prentice-Hall, 1974); David Lowenthal, "The American Scene," *Geographical Review* 58 (Jan. 1968): 61–88; Amos Rapoport, *The Meaning of the Built Environment: A Nonverbal Communications Approach* (Beverly Hills: Sage Publications, 1982).

12. Discussions of community gathering places are found in Lewis Atherton, *Main Street on the Middle Border* (Bloomington: Indiana Univ. Press, 1954), chap. 2; Everett Dick, *The Sod-House Frontier, 1854–1890* (New York: D. Appleton-Century Co., 1937), chap. 28.

13. For information on bird's-eye views of towns, see Seymour I. Schwartz and Ralph E. Ehrenberg, *The Mapping of America* (New York: Harry N. Abrams, 1980), pp. 298–99; Walter W. Ristow, *American Maps and Mapmakers: Commercial Cartography in the Nineteenth Century* (Detroit: Wayne State Univ. Press, 1985), pp. 261–63. For examples of bird's-eye views of South Dakota towns, see "Artists Draw South Dakota: Panoramic Views of Pioneer Towns," *South Dakota History* 8 (Summer 1978), pp. 221–49.

14. Brookings County, S.Dak., *Press,* Jan. 25, 1883, Dec. 15, 1887.

15. The Brookings County, S.Dak., *Press* ran a fourteen-part series by Robert F. Kerr on the early history of Brookings County between Oct. 14, 1897, and Mar. 10, 1898. See also the Brookings, S.Dak., *Register,* Sept. 7, 1899, Apr. 23, 1914.

16. Brookings *Register,* Aug. 9, 1923, June 12, 26, 1924, Sept. 17, 1925, Aug. 26, 1926. R. H. Williams, the first merchant to open a store on the Brookings town site, died in Santa Ana, California, in Dec. 1924. George West, another early pioneer in the county, died in Rhinebeck, New York, a few weeks later. W. H.

Roddle, who moved from Medary to Brookings in 1879, died in Sequim, Washington, in 1929. The following year, pioneer druggist J. T. Tidball died in Santa Ana, and early-day businessman George Rude died in Brookings. Brookings *Register,* Dec. 11, 1924, Jan. 15, 1925, Jan. 24, 1929, May 22, Sept. 11, 1930.

17. Ibid., July 2, 1925, Mar. 4, 15, June 3, July 1, 1926, Aug. 11, 1927.

18. Ibid., Feb. 28, Nov. 14, 1929.

19. Ibid., July 18, 1929.

20. Ibid., Sept. 7, 1899.

21. Ibid., Aug. 15, 1954, June 29, 1979; Alexander et al., *Brookings' Centennial Commemorative Book.*

22. Sandro, "History of Brookings County," is devoted almost entirely to the period before 1900. A series of newspaper interviews done by Arthur S. Mitchell, Jr., in 1939 and 1940 and later collected in *Pioneer Life: Dakota Territory, 1861–1889* (privately published) also emphasizes the early pioneer days. It is worth noting that pioneer history is almost entirely male-oriented. Stories about the early settlement period in Brookings focus almost exclusively on men's roles.

23. On small town boosterism, see Daniel J. Boorstin, *The Americans: The National Experience* (New York: Random House, 1965), pt. 3; Atherton, *Main Street on the Middle Border,* pp. 3–13, 330–32; Dick, *The Sod-House Frontier,* pp. 417–19; Sally Foreman Griffith, *Home Town News: William Allen White and the "Emporia Gazette"* (New York: Oxford Univ. Press, 1989), pp. 6–7, 139–58. Brookings, it should be noted, had plenty to boast about. See, for example, "Nine Happy Places," *Esquire* 74 (Dec. 1970): 146–53, which features Brookings as one of the best places to live in the United States.

24. Brookings League of Women Voters, *This Is Your Town* (1956), p. 5, Brookings Public Library vertical file, S.Dak.

25. Brookings's experience when he visited the town named after him to give a political speech must have reminded him of the biblical prophet who was not honored in his own country. He was called "an old sore-head" and criticized for being egotistical and bombastic and for "tooting his own horn." Brookings County *Press,* Oct. 26, 1882. On Brookings, see Donald Dean Parker, "Wilmot W. Brookings: Pioneer Promoter" (privately published pamphlet).

26. Brookings Area Chamber of Commerce, *Brookings, South Dakota: Someplace Special* (n.d.), p. 3, Brookings Public Library vertical file.

27. A three-page detailed synopsis of the 1954 production, *Harvest of the Years,* is included in *75th Anniversary Souvenir Program,* Aug. 15–19, 1954, Brookings Public Library vertical file, S.Dak.

28. Brookings Area Centennial Celebration Committee, *Brookings 100 Revue* (typescript), July 1979, Brookings Public Library vertical file, S.Dak.

29. David Lowenthal, "The Timeless Past: Some Anglo-American Historical Preconceptions," *Journal of American History* 75 (March 1989): 1279. See this whole special issue of the journal on the subject of memory and American history. On the use of historical pageants during the Progressive Era to define collective historical consciousness, see David Glassberg, "History and the Public: Legacies of the Progressive Era," *Journal of American History* 73 (March 1987): 957–80.

30. Brookings County History Book Committee, *Brookings County History Book* (Freeman, S.Dak: Pine Hill Press, 1989).

31. Elizabeth Fox-Genovese, "Literary Criticism and the Politics of the New Historicism," in *The New Historicism,* ed. H. Aram Veeser (New York: Routledge, 1989), pp. 217–18.

32. Brookings County History Book Committee, *Brookings County History Book,* p. 102.

ARLINGTON

1. On the history of Arlington see the special centennial edition of the Arlington, S.Dak., *Sun,* June 25, 1980.

2. South Dakota Newspaper Association, *1989 South Dakota Newspaper Directory* (Brookings: South Dakota Newspaper Services, Inc., 1989), p. 9; Watertown, S.Dak., *Public Opinion,* July 15, 1985; Sioux Falls, S.Dak., *Argus Leader,* July 27, Nov. 17, 1985.

3. In 1989 the governor's nephew, Larry Kneip, established a small museum honoring him in Arlington. "Arlington Exhibit to Chronicle Life of Late Gov. Richard Kneip," Huron, S.Dak., *Plainsman,* June 20, 1989.

4. After his father died, Schultz's mother moved to Arlington and spent her remaining years there.

5. The 1920 populations of these towns: Hetland, 248; Badger, 162; Lake Norden, 408; Erwin, 257. Arlington's was 1,011 and Lake Preston's was 1,008.

6. Most of the information about Schultz and his family comes from the author's interview with him in Chicago on Jan. 3, 1989. Additional information was obtained in interviews with his three living brothers—Leo ("Sparky"), Badger, Dec. 30, 1988, Aug. 15, 1989; Arthur ("Skinny"), Badger, Dec. 30, 1988; and Henry, Lake Norden, Dec. 30, 1988.

7. South Dakota State College, *Jackrabbit,* 1928, p. 61; on Hetland's history, see *Hetland: "My Home Town" Centennial Book, 1888–1988* (1988).

8. Badger history is recorded in *Backtracking to Badger, 1907–1982* (Badger: S.Dak.: Badger Diamond Jubilee Committee, 1982).

9. For biographical information on Schultz see D. Gale Johnson, "Theodore W. Schultz," in *International Encyclopedia of the Social Sciences: Biographical Supplement,* vol. 18, ed. David L. Sills (New York: Free Press, 1979), pp. 707–9; Tyler Wasson, ed., "Theodore Schultz," *Nobel Prize Winners* (New York: H. W. Wilson, 1987), pp. 938–40; Gustav Ranis, "The 1979 Nobel Prize in Economics," *Science* 206 (Dec. 21, 1979): 1389–91; Nick Eberstadt, "The Legacy of Theodore Schultz," *RF Illustrated,* Oct. 1980, pp. 8–9; "Selected Presentations from a Symposium with Theodore W. Schultz . . . September 21–22, 1981" (Brookings: South Dakota State University, 1981), mimeo.

10. Theodore W. Schultz, interview; South Dakota State College, *Jackrabbit,* 1927, pp. 93, 154–55, 157, 187, 204, 208; South Dakota State College, *Jackrabbit,* 1928, pp. 61, 196–97, 213–14.

11. Theodore W. Schultz interview.

12. Theodore W. Schultz, *Agriculture in an Unstable Economy* (New York: McGraw-Hill Book Co., 1945), pp. 30–32.

13. Ibid., pp. 32–33, 77, 88 (italics in the original).

14. Ibid., p. 247.

15. Theodore W. Schultz, *The Economic Organization of Agriculture* (New York: McGraw-Hill Book Co., 1953), pp. 285–95.

16. That some forms of community have declined or even disappeared is undeniable. Yet it is important to note that community continues to exist, even if in altered forms. Its geographical boundaries now are generally larger than they used to be. The historian Thomas Bender made a strong case for the persistence of community in twentieth-century America in *Community and Social Change in America* (Baltimore: Johns Hopkins Univ. Press, 1978), chap. 2.

17. "Alphabetical List of Members of the South Dakota Legislature Since Statehood," *South Dakota Historical Collections* 25 (1950): 421; Crothers was a local historian, too. See P. R. Crothers, "History of Badger Township," *South*

Dakota Historical Collections 13 (1926): pp. 158–80.

18. Sparky and Mary Ann Schultz's other son, Allan, farmed for seventeen years before high interest rates and declining prices forced him out of agriculture during the late 1970s. He now works at a college in Joplin, Missouri.

19. South Dakota Agricultural Statistics Service, *South Dakota Agriculture, 1988–89* (Pierre: South Dakota Department of Agriculture, 1989), p. 5; Sioux Fall *Argus Leader,* Apr. 21, 1985.

DE SMET

1. Laura Ingalls Wilder's five books set in and around De Smet, all published in New York by Harper and Row, are *By the Shores of Silver Lake* (1939), *The Long Winter* (1940), *Little Town on the Prairie* (1941), *These Happy Golden Years* (1943), and *The First Four Years* (1971).

2. Sinclair Lewis, *Main Street* (New York: Harcourt, Brace, 1920); Thornton Wilder, *Our Town: A Play in Three Acts* (New York: Coward McCann, 1938); Robert S. Lynd and Helen Merrell Lynd, *Middletown: A Study in American Culture* (New York: Harcourt, Brace, 1929).

3. Donald Zochert, *Laura: The Life of Laura Ingalls Wilder* (New York: Avon Books, 1976), pp. 71–73.

4. In the final television program, entitled "The Last Farewell," the entire set was blown up, ending the series with a bang and simultaneously clearing the location for a new series. "I think it makes for a good strong pioneer ending," Michael Landon, who portrayed Charles Ingalls in the series, was quoted as saying. "It was also a nice catharsis for the cast and crew." Stephen Farber, " TV's 'Little House' Set Is Dynamited for Finale," *New York Times,* Feb. 6, 1984, Arts and Entertainment section. For one viewer, who lived eleven miles from De Smet, this was the last straw. Several newspapers, including the Watertown, S.Dak., *Public Opinion* and the Sioux Falls, S.Dak., *Argus Leader,* printed the letter she wrote to the editor, which was also reprinted in *Laura Ingalls Wilder Lore* 10 (Spring–Summer 1984): 2. After recounting some of the facts about Laura Ingalls Wilder, the letter writer noted, "Many of the stories on television do not follow the books. Ma and Pa never adopted any children, neither did Laura and Almanzo. Mary, the blind sister, never married or had a child, nor taught school. Many of the television programs, I am sorry to say, did not follow the original Laura Ingalls Wilder stories."

5. Huron, S.Dak., *Daily Plainsman,* June 24, 1984; Vivian Glover, director, Laura Ingalls Wilder Memorial Society, interview with author, De Smet, S.Dak., Aug. 15, 1989. Laura Ingalls Wilder never wrote about the Third Street house, since she and Almanzo had married and moved to a homestead north of town in 1885, two years before Charles Ingalls started building it.

6. *Christian Science Monitor,* June 23, 1981; De Smet, S.Dak., *News,* May 18, 1988.

7. "Golden Years News," June 24–July 9, 1989 (pageant brochure).

8. During the 1989 pageant season, the De Smet Farm Mutual Insurance Company ran a survey of each car entering the pageant parking lot, inquiring what town, state, and country the people were from and publishing the results in the newspaper. On Sunday, July 2, there were 757 from South Dakota, 442 from other states, and 6 from foreign countries (2 from Sweden and 1 each from Japan, Germany, Denmark, and Costa Rica) for a total of 1,205. Ranking behind South Dakota were Minnesota (188), Missouri (23), California (21), Iowa (18), Washing-

ton (18), Illinois (17), Virginia (16), and Wisconsin (16). A grand total of 7,225 spectators attended the six performances in June and July. De Smet *News,* July 5, 19, 1989.

9. Janet Spaeth, *Laura Ingalls Wilder* (Boston: Twayne, 1987). See also Mary J. Mooney-Getoff, *Laura Ingalls Wilder: A Bibliography* (Southold, N.Y.: Wise Owl Press, 1981).

10. David Lowenthal, *The Past Is a Foreign Country* (Cambridge: Cambridge University Press, 1985), p. 218.

11. Laura Ingalls Wilder and Rose Wilder Lane, *Little House Sampler,* ed. William T. Anderson (Lincoln: Univ. of Nebraska Press, 1988), pp. 220–22.

12. Wilder, *The Long Winter,* pp. 298–307; De Smet *News,* Oct. 26, 1900, March 8, 1907, Oct. 14, 1921.

13. Wilder, *The Long Winter,* p. 67; De Smet *News,* Jan. 11, Dec. 20, 1907, Apr. 2, 1909, Apr. 21, 1911, Feb. 14, 1913; *South Dakota Legislative Manual,* 1903, pp. 235–36; *South Dakota Legislative Manual,* 1907, pp. 457–58.

14. Wilder, *Little Town on the Prairie,* pp. 243–51; De Smet *News,* May 30, 1919.

15. Wilder, *Little Town on the Prairie,* p. 71; Rapid City, S.Dak., *Daily Journal,* Mar. 17, 1889; Huron, S.Dak., *Daily Huronite,* Mar. 14, Aug. 28, 1889; George W. Kingsbury, *History of Dakota Territory,* vol. 2 (Chicago: S. J. Clarke Publishing Co., 1915), p. 1578, 1839, 1903.

16. The De Smet, S.Dak., *Leader* noted the arrival of the bird's-eye artist in its May 5, 1883 issue. A schematic map of residences and businesses in De Smet was printed in the *Leader,* Sept. 22, 1883. For bird's-eye drawings of other South Dakota towns, including Brookings, Huron, and Pierre, see "Artists Draw South Dakota: Panoramic Views of Pioneer Towns," *South Dakota History* 8 (Summer 1978): 221–49.

17. Rosa Ann Moore documented the close collaboration that existed between Laura Ingalls Wilder and her daughter Rose Wilder Lane and the way in which artistic considerations led Wilder to retell the stories she remembered from her childhood. See "Laura Ingalls Wilder's Orange Notebooks and the Art of the Little House Books," *Children's Literature* 4 (1975): 105–19; "The Little House Books: Rose-Colored Classics," *Children's Literature* 7 (1978): 7–16; "Laura Ingalls Wilder and Rose Wilder Lane: The Chemistry of Collaboration," *Children's Literature in Education* 11 (Autumn 1980): 101–9. William T. Anderson likewise noted the important contribution of Lane, especially to the early books, but he also emphasized the books' rootedness in historical experience. See "The Literary Apprenticeship of Laura Ingalls Wilder," *South Dakota History* 13 (Winter 1983): pp. 285–331; "Laura Ingalls Wilder and Rose Wilder Lane: The Continuing Collaboration," *South Dakota History* 16 (Summer 1986): 89–143. Ralph R. Dykstra called the books set in and around De Smet an "accurate autobiographical account." "The Autobiographical Aspects of Laura Ingalls Wilder's 'Little House' Books" (Ed.D. diss., State Univ. of New York at Buffalo, 1980), pp. 28, 258. Parallels between the books and contemporary newspaper accounts were noted by John E. Miller in "Place and Community in the 'Little Town on the Prairie': De Smet in 1883," *South Dakota History* 16 (Winter 1986): 351–72.

18. Diary entry, June 6, 1931, Rose Wilder Lane Diary, 1931–1935, Box 22, Item 37; and Laura Ingalls Wilder to Rose Wilder Lane, June 3, 1939, Box 13, Rose Wilder Lane Papers, Herbert Hoover Presidential Library, West Branch, Iowa.

19. Wilder and Lane, *Little House Sampler,* p. 217

20. For approximately a dozen other entries in the contest, see the file folder on the Pioneer Days contest, sponsored by the Huron *Daily Plainsman,* in the

Dakotaland Museum vertical file, state fairgrounds, Huron, S.Dak.

21. John E. Miller, "Freedom and Control in Laura Ingalls Wilder's De Smet," *Great Plains Quarterly* 9 (Winter 1989): 33.

22. In 1937, just as she was beginning the books set around De Smet, Laura Ingalls Wilder indicated that she would write about her experiences there "in the remaining volumes of my children's novel which ends happily (as all good novels should) when Laura of the *Little Houses* and Almanzo of *Farmer Boy* are married." Wilder and Lane, *Little House Sampler,* p. 220.

23. Wilder, *The Long Winter,* p. 65; and *These Happy Golden Years,* p. 153.

24. Wilder, *These Happy Golden Years,* p. 207.

25. Herbert S. Schell, *History of South Dakota,* 3d ed. (Lincoln: Univ. of Nebraska Press, 1975), pp. 223–24.

26. Wilder, *By the Shores of Silver Lake,* p. 254, *The Long Winter,* pp. 16, 68; *Little Town on the Prairie,* pp. 2, 49, 89, 97; and *The First Four Years,* pp. 4–5, 92, 119.

27. Wilder, *The First Four Years,* p. 119.

28. Wilder, *These Happy Golden Years,* p. 289; and *The First Four Years,* p. 22.

29. Zochert, *Laura,* pp. 193–95; For Wilder's account of the journey, see Laura Ingalls Wilder, *On the Way Home* (New York: Harper and Row, 1962).

30. Wilder, *By the Shores of Silver Lake,* p. 237; and *These Happy Golden Years,* p. 119.

31. Wilder, *The First Four Years,* pp. 133–34.

32. Ibid., p. 134.

33. Kenneth E. Hendrickson, Jr., "Some Political Aspects of the Populist Movement in South Dakota," *North Dakota History* 34 (Winter 1967): 77–92.

34. Whatever the nature of Laura and Almanzo Wilder's political views, their daughter Rose Wilder Lane turned into an avid ultraconservative, who detested not only big government but government intervention of almost any kind. Later in life, Rose informally adopted Roger MacBride, who ran as the presidential candidate of the Libertarian party in 1976. On Rose, see William T. Anderson, *Laura's Rose: The Story of Rose Wilder Lane* (De Smet: Laura Ingalls Wilder Memorial Society, 1976); Wilder and Lane, *Little House Sampler,* pp. 240–43; special issue on Rose in *Laura Ingalls Wilder Lore* 12 (Dec. 5, 1986).

MANCHESTER

1. Harvey Dunn has yet to receive the kind of critical and scholarly attention that has been devoted to contemporaries such as Grant Wood, John Steuart Curry, and Thomas Hart Benton. Robert F. Karolevitz, *Where Your Heart Is: The Story of Harvey Dunn, Artist* (Aberdeen, S.Dak: North Plains Press, 1970) is a solid biographical account containing many illustrations, including most of Dunn's prairie paintings. William Henry Holaday III, "Harvey Dunn: Pioneer Painter of the Middle Border" (Ph.D. diss., Ohio State Univ., 1970) catalogs every known Dunn painting and many of the drawings and reproduces the little book of notes taken from Dunn's lectures, *An Evening in the Classroom* (Tenafly, N.J.: Mario Cooper, 1934), and several other useful documents. Articles providing useful insights into Dunn's biography and paintings include Ernest W. Watson, "Harvey Dunn: Milestone in the Tradition of American Illustration," *American Artist* 6 (June 1942): 16–20, 31; Mari Sandoz, "Dakota Country," *American Heritage* 12 (June 1961): 42–53; Edgar M. Howell, "Harvey Dunn: The Searching Artist Who Came Home to His First Horizon," *Montana: The Magazine of Western History*

16 (Winter 1966), pp. 41–56. Aubrey Sherwood, the longtime editor of the De Smet, S.Dak., *News* who was instrumental in getting Dunn to donate his prairie paintings to South Dakota, wrote "Harvey Dunn: Master Mason" (n.p.: South Dakota Lodge of Masonic Research, 1964), pp. 51–64, and "I Remember Harvey Dunn" (privately published, 1984).

2. On the history of Manchester, see Janis G. H. Bowes, ed., *Manchester, S.D., History Book* (Huron, S.Dak.: Print Shop, 1989). Muriel Wallum also has a scrapbook filled with clippings and newspaper stories about the early history of Manchester. Information for this chapter was obtained primarily from interviews on May 24 and June 3 and 7, 1988, with Alferd and Muriel Wallum, who lived and worked and farmed for many years in the area; Joy "Smokey" Wallum, Alferd's brother and postmaster at Iroquois; Eldon Whites, a farmer near Iroquois; Noel "Toby" Toberman, who has lived all his life in town and runs a cattle operation right outside of town; John "Whitey" Woodall, who moved from Manchester at the age of eighteen in 1934; Harvey and Lucille Marx, who ran cafes and a grocery store in town after 1933; Eunice Moore, who has lived in the area all her life; and Bill Vincent, a De Smet High School student whose parents run Wallum's Corner.

3. Harvey Dunn, letter to H. Dean Stallings, Aug. 29, 1941, reprinted in Holaday, "Harvey Dunn," p. 288.

4. Ibid., p. 289.

5. De Smet *News,* June 6, 1930.

6. Quoted in Sherwood, "I Remember Harvey Dunn," p. 7.

7. Dunn, *An Evening in the Classroom,* p. 11.

8. C. J. Andres, "Notes on a Lecture of Harvey Dunn," in Holaday, "Harvey Dunn," pp. 229, 231, 234.

9. Quoted in Howell, "Harvey Dunn," p. 46.

10. Andres, "Notes on a Lecture," p. 224.

11. Ibid., p. 221.

12. Ibid., p. 233.

13. Watson, "Harvey Dunn," p. 18.

14. Dunn, *An Evening in the Classroom,* p. 11.

15. Some local people believe that it is Manchester that is depicted in the background of Harvey Dunn's painting for the cover of *American Legion Monthly,* in January 1934, but the image is so indistinct that it could have been almost any town.

16. Harvey Dunn, letter to H. Dean Stallings, Aug. 29, 1941, reprinted in Holaday, "Harvey Dunn," p. 290.

IROQUOIS

1. "Forget the Newspaper and TV—Local Cafe Is Where the News Is," *Wall Street Journal* June 7, 1985, p. 1. See also Ray Oldenburg, *The Great Good Place: Cafes, Coffee Shops, Community Centers, Beauty Parlors, General Stores, Bars, Hangouts and How They Get You through the Day* (New York: Paragon House, 1989).

2. Most of the information for this chapter was obtained from interviews on May 23–24, 1988, with Velma Leichtenberg; Josephine Stroub, a postal worker for thirty-four years; John "Whitey" Woodall, who ran a produce business; Wes Rounds, retired rural mail carrier; Joy "Smokey" Wallum, current Iroquois postmaster; B. C. Aughenbaugh, who continues to farm southeast of Iroquois; Maynard Sweet, teacher, sheep and cattle farmer, silo salesman, and real estate broker; and Nila Ondricek, a Huron resident who runs an antiques store in Iroquois.

3. "When Saturday Night Was the Best Night of the Week," *Dakota Farmer* 88 (May 4, 1968): 36. The relevance of Saturday night in more current contexts is treated in Susan Orlean, *Saturday Night* (New York: Knopf, 1990).

4. The story of the bell in the Catholic church is recounted in a pamphlet compiled by Josephine Stroub, "St. Paul's Catholic Church, Iroquois, South Dakota, 1885–1986, 101st Anniversary."

5. The Mark Brown quotation on the Congregational bell is from the De Smet, S.Dak., *Leader,* Dec. 29, 1883.

HURON

1. Kenneth Hammer, "Dakota Railroads" (Ph.D. diss., South Dakota State Univ., 1966), pp. 183–84; *Dakota Huronite,* May 18, 1936; Doane Robinson, *South Dakota: Sui Generis,* 3 vols. (Chicago: American Historical Society, 1930), p. 384.

2. Five of South Dakota's important towns (and four of the state's eight largest towns in the 1980 census) were located at or near points where railroads intersected with the James River. From north to south they were Aberdeen (third)–25,956, Redfield–3,027, Huron (seventh)–13,000, Mitchell (sixth)–13,916, and Yankton (eighth)–12,011.

3. On Huron's history see Dorothy Huss et al., *Huron Revisited* (Huron, S.Dak.: East Eagle Co., 1988); Stephen B. Plummer, "Huron, South Dakota, 1880–1900: Economic and Political Determinants" (Master's thesis, Univ. of South Dakota, 1969).

4. Brookings, S.Dak., *Register,* Sept. 5, 1986. The Dakota, Minnesota and Eastern headquarters are in Brookings, and its line runs from Winona, Minnesota, to Rapid City, South Dakota, with links to Mason City, Iowa, Watertown, South Dakota, and Oakes, North Dakota.

5. Huss et al., *Huron Revisited,* pp. 23, 87–88.

6. *Dakota Huronite,* Apr. 5, 1883.

7. Herbert S. Schell, *History of South Dakota,* 3d ed. (Lincoln: Univ. of Nebraska Press, 1975), p. 159.

8. Huss et al., *Huron Revisited,* pp. 16, 19.

9. John Elmer Dalton, *A History of the Location of the State Capital in South Dakota,* report no. 14 (Vermillion: Univ. of South Dakota, Government Research Bureau, Jan. 1945), p. 7. The desire to provide a larger area than was contained in the four square blocks downtown was probably behind the decision to offer land on the west edge of town for the location.

10. *Dakota Huronite,* May 10, 1883; Plummer, "Huron, South Dakota, 1880–1900," p. 73.

11. Ralph W. Wheelock, "The Tour of the Capitol Commission," *South Dakota Historical Collections* 5 (1910): 149.

12. On the origins of the statehood movement, see Howard R. Lamar, *Dakota Territory, 1861–1889: A Study of Frontier Politics* (New Haven: Yale Univ. Press, 1956), chap. 6; Schell, *History of South Dakota,* chap. 15; Carol G. Green, "The Struggle of South Dakota to Become a State," *South Dakota Historical Collections* 12 (1924): 503–40.

13. Sioux Falls ran a distant third in the balloting with 3,338 votes. Dalton, *A History of the Location of the State Capital,* p. 16

14. Plummer, "Huron, South Dakota, 1880–1900," chap. 2.

15. Ibid., pp. 34–36; Doane Robinson, *Encyclopedia of South Dakota* (Pierre, S.Dak.: privately published, 1925), p. 604.

16. Lynwood E. Oyos, "Gilbert A. Pierce," in *Over a Century of Leadership: South Dakota Territorial and State Governors* (Sioux Falls, S.Dak.: Center for Western Studies, 1987), p. 44; Pierre *Free Press,* Mar. 9, 12, 19, 1885.

17. Dalton, *A History of the Location of the State Capital,* pp. 17–20.

18. "Capital and Capitol History of South Dakota," *South Dakota Historical Collections* 5 (1910): 177.

19. Pierre *Free Press,* July 4, 1889.

20. John D. Unruh, "The Struggle for Statehood," *South Dakota Historical Collections* 35 (1970): 92.

21. Herbert T. Hoover, "The Sioux Agreement of 1889 and Its Aftermath," *South Dakota History* 19 (Spring 1989): 56–94; *Dakota Huronite,* quoted in Pierre *Free Press,* Oct. 2, 1890.

22. Plummer, "Huron, South Dakota, 1880–1900," pp. 82–84; Dalton, "A History of the Location of the State Capital, pp. 19–20.

23. Dalton, *A History of the Location of the State Capital,* p. 20.

24. Plummer, "Huron, South Dakota, 1880–1900," pp. 87–89.

25. Ibid., pp. 90–92. Pierre probably outspent Huron. John Elmer Dalton estimated that the temporary capital spent $1 million in its effort to hold onto its position. Dalton, *A History of the Location of the State Capital,* pp. 24, 28.

26. Plummer, "Huron, South Dakota, 1880–1900," pp. 94–95, 116–17; Dalton, *A History of the Location of the State Capital,* p. 33; Walter H. Hubbard, "John L. Pyle," *South Dakota Historical Collections* 3 (1906): 62.

27. Huss et al., *Huron Revisited,* chap. 3.

28. *Dakota Huronite,* Jan. 3, 1884.

29. Brochure put out by the Huron Chamber of Commerce Publicity Division, "Huron: The Market of Central South Dakota" (1930), Huron Public Library files, S.Dak.

30. Charles N. Campbell, comp., *Huron City Directory* (Huron, S.Dak.: Huronite Auxiliary Publishing House, 1883), p. 6

31. *Huron City Directory* (1905–6), pp. 17–95. The state census of 1905 showed Huron's population to be 3,783 at that time.

32. H. Roger Grant, ed., *We Got There on the Train: Railroads in the Lives of the American People* (Washington, D.C.: National Council on the Aging, 1989).

33. Lorna McMillan, *The Kent House Depot Hotel* (privately published, 1980), Huron Public Library, S.Dak.

34. Huss et al., *Huron Revisited,* pp. 84–86.

MILLER

1. The early history of Miller has been told in Scott Heidepriem, *Bring on the Pioneers: History of Hand County* (Pierre, S.Dak.: State Publishing Co., 1978); Louise Carroll Wade, "Small-town Survival on the Great Plains: Miller, Dakota Territory, in the 1880's," *South Dakota History* 16 (Winter 1986):317–50; Donald Dean Parker, *History of Our County and State: Hand County* (Brookings: South Dakota State College, n.d.); Myrna Cotton, *They Pioneered for Us* (Huron, S.Dak.: Huron Reminder Printing, 1956); Anna Mary Van Brunt Sessions, *Early History of Hand County, South Dakota* (privately published, n.d.).

2. Surveys of the right-of-way and siding locations had to be approved by the secretary of the interior. Many of these surveys and maps are available in collections of the National Archives Maps Division at Alexandria, Virginia.

3. Cotton, *They Pioneered for Us,* pp. 1–2; Heidepriem, *Bring on the Pioneers,* 447–49; Wade, "Small-town Survival," pp. 323–24.

4. Heidepriem, *Bring on the Pioneers,* 27–35; Wade, "Small-town Survival," pp. 334–36; Parker, *History of Our County and State: Hand County,* pp. 48–50.

5. Wade, "Small-town Survival," pp. 337–48.

6. Miller, S.Dak., *Press,* Dec. 14, 1939.

7. A full collection of South Dakota fire insurance maps is held by the South Dakota State Historical Society at Pierre. The Sanborn Company did maps of Miller in 1904, 1909, 1925, and 1934.

HIGHMORE

1. On F. C. W. Kuehn, the best-known local architect working in the towns on Highway 14, see Jeannette Kinyon, *Prairie Architect: F. C. W. Kuehn, His Life and Work* (Sioux Falls, S.Dak.: Center for Western Studies, 1984).

2. Midwestern small towns are especially useful in illuminating the meaning of the built environment. "Perhaps the clearest examples of objects that represent the intersection of community personality and physical substance, at least in the form of durable images in the popular and scholarly minds, are the New England village and Middle Western small town," noted Wilbur Zelinsky in "The Pennsylvania Town: An Overdue Geographical Account," *Geographical Review* 67 (Apr., 1977): 128 n. 6.

3. Edward T. Price, "The Central Courthouse Square in the American County Seat," *Geographical Review* 58 (Jan. 1968): 29–60. For studies of the roles of two other kinds of buildings, see Robert C. Ostergren, "The Immigrant Church as a Symbol of Community and Place in the Upper Midwest," *Great Plains Quarterly* 1 (Fall 1981): 225–38; Clark C. Spence, "The Livery Stable in the American West," *Montana: The Magazine of Western History* 36 (Spring 1986): 36–49.

4. Don Mason, "Hyde County Courthouse," in *Hyde Heritage* (Highmore, S.Dak.: Hyde County Historical and Genealogical Society, 1977), pp. 569–71.

5. Brookings County History Book Committee, *Brookings County History Book* (Freeman, S.Dak.: Pine Hill Press, 1989), pp. 77–78; Caryl L. M. Poppen, ed., *De Smet: Yesterday and Today* (De Smet, S.Dak.: De Smet Bicentennial Committee, 1976), pp. 128–29; Scott Heidepriem, *Bring on the Pioneers: History of Hand County* (Pierre, S.Dak.: State Publishing Co., 1978), pp. 35–37; Dorothy Huss et al., *Huron Revisited* (Huron, S.Dak.: East Eagle Co., 1988), pp. 17–18; Harold H. Schuler, *A Bridge Apart: History of Early Pierre and Fort Pierre* (Pierre, S.Dak.: State Publishing Co., 1987), pp. 66–67, 107–8.

6. John B. Perkins, *History of Hyde County, South Dakota: From Its Organization to the Present Time* (privately published, 1908), pp. 71–75.

7. James A. Schellenberg, *Conflict between Communities: American County Seat Wars* (New York: Paragon House, 1987), p. 40. See also Daniel J. Boorstin, *The Americans: The National Experience* (New York: Random House, 1965), pp. 164–67; Everett Dick, *The Sod-House Frontier, 1854–1890* (New York: D. Appleton-Century Co., 1937), chap. 32.

8. Schellenberg's *Conflict between Communities* focuses on the Midwest in the 1870s and 1880s, when most of the bitterest county seat battles erupted. In Schellenberg's count, South Dakota (the counties that later became part of it) ranked highest in violent conflicts, with twelve between 1881 and 1904, ten of them during the 1880s. Hyde County's confrontation was not violent enough to

rank among the forty-nine episodes he devotes major attention to nor did any other county on Highway 14 rank in that category. But Hyde County's contest was conspicuous enough to be given a paragraph (p. 68). (Kansas ranked second behind South Dakota with eleven violent episodes, Minnesota had eight, Nebraska had five, North Dakota had four, and other states had three or fewer [pp. 28–31]).

9. Herbert S. Schell, *History of South Dakota,* 3d ed. (Lincoln: Univ. of Nebraska Press, 1975), p. 204; Brookings County History Book Committee, *Brookings County History Book,* p. 49; Poppen, *De Smet: Yesterday and Today,* p. 9; Stephen B. Plummer, "Huron, South Dakota, 1880–1900: Economic and Political Determinants" (Master's Thesis, Univ. of South Dakota, 1969), p. 47; Heidepriem, *Bring on the Pioneers,* pp. 29–35; Anna Mary Van Brunt Sessions, *Early History of Hand County, South Dakota* (privately published, n.d.), pp. 19–22.

10. Perkins, *History of Hyde County,* p. 8

11. Ordway, in fact, was later indicted by a grand jury for alleged irregularities in the process of organizing Hyde and Faulk counties. Howard R. Lamar, *Dakota Territory, 1861–1889: A Study of Frontier Politics* (New Haven: Yale Univ. Press, 1956), pp. 202–4, 236–40. See also Lynwood E. Oyos, "Nehemiah G. Ordway," in *Over a Century of Leadership: South Dakota Territorial and State Governors* (Sioux Falls, S.Dak.: Center for Western Studies, 1987), pp. 35–40.

12. Perkins, *History of Hyde County,* pp. 8–9. On Ordway's machinations generally, see Schellenberg, *Conflict between Communities,* pp. 64–68; J. Leonard Jennewein and Jane Boorman, eds., *Dakota Panorama* (Sioux Falls, S.Dak.: Midwest Beach, 1961), pp. 192–93; Dick, *The Sod-House Frontier,* pp. 478–79.

13. Perkins, *History of Hyde County,* pp. 10–15.

14. Ibid., p. 18.

15. Schell, *History of South Dakota,* p. 214; Mason, *Hyde Heritage,* pp. 4, 36–38.

16. Ree Heights, located between Highmore and Miller, also had two rival groups contesting for dominance, but the competition there was much less intense than it was at Highmore. Heidepriem, *Bring on the Pioneers,* pp. 16–17.

17. The maps showing these sidings are located in the National Archives Maps Division in Alexandria, Virginia.

18. George W. Kingsbury, "Abram E. Van Camp" and "Andrew Nelson Van Camp," in *History of Dakota Territory,* vol. 4 (Chicago: S. J. Clarke Publishing Co., 1915) pp. 1229–30, 1240–41.

19. Perkins, *History of Hyde County,* pp. 81, 95, 101, 165–66.

20. Plats for each town are contained in the town lot record books in the county courthouses. On the layouts of plains towns, see John C. Hudson, *Plains Country Towns* (Minneapolis: Univ. of Minnesota Press, 1985), pp. 87–90; John E. Miller, "Place and Community in the 'Little Town on the Prairie': De Smet in 1883," *South Dakota History* 16 (Winter 1986): 351–72.

21. Town layouts on the Chicago and North Western lacked the cookie-cutter sameness that characterized towns laid out earlier on the Illinois Central Railroad. John Brinckerhoff Jackson, *American Space: The Centennial Years, 1865–1876* (New York: W. W. Norton, 1972), pp. 67–68.

22. Main Street is "uniquely American, a powerful symbol of shared experiences, of common memory, of the challenge and struggle of building a civilization," wrote Carole Rifkind in *Main Street: The Face of Urban America* (New York: Harper and Row, 1977), p. xi. On small town morphology and the appearance of Main Streets, see also Lewis Atherton, *Main Street on the Middle Border* (Bloomington: Indiana Univ. Press, 1954), pp. 43–49; John A. Jakle, *The Ameri-*

can Small Town: Twentieth-Century Place Images (Hamden, Conn.: Archon Books, 1982), pp. 18–22; Christopher Tunnard and Henry Hope Reed, *American Skyline: The Growth and Form of Our Cities and Towns* (Boston: Houghton Mifflin, 1953); John Fraser Hart, *The Look of the Land* (Englewood Cliffs, N.J.: Prentice-Hall, 1975), pp. 158–60.

23. Plat of Highmore, by Thomas F. Nichol, recorded July 3, 1882, *Hyde County Town Lot Platbook,* book 1, pp. 5–6; see also Hyde County Centennial Committee, *Staying Power* (Pierre, S.Dak.: State Publishing Co., 1989), pp. 79–81.

24. *Hyde County Town Lot Platbook,* book 1, pp. 7–10, 15–16, 19–20.

HARROLD

1. Hugh Sidey notes the importance of cafes as community centers in "Chewing the Fat in Iowa," *Time* 123 (Feb. 27, 1984), p. 24.

2. Highmore, S.Dak., *Herald,* May 22, 1986; Pierre, S.Dak., *Capital Journal,* Jan. 17, 1986.

3. The story of the Bohning store derives primarily from an interview with Claude ("Jack") Bohning in Harrold on November 6, 1985. Also see the family history that he wrote for the Harrold Centennial Committee in *Siding No. 6: The History of Harrold, 1886–1986* (Harrold, S.Dak.: Harrold Centennial Committee, 1986), pp. 118–21.

4. Harrold Centennial Committee, *Siding No. 6,* p. 119.

5. My characterization of small town Saturday nights is derived from dozens of interviews with South Dakotans over the years. See also Ellen Rebecca Fenn, "When Saturday Night Was the Best Night of the Week," *Dakota Farmer* 88 (May 4, 1968): 36.

6. Groton, S.Dak., *Independent,* reprinted in Webster, S.Dak., *Reporter and Farmer,* Nov. 11, 1936.

PIERRE

1. "St. Charles Hotel Gets New Lease on Life," Huron, S.Dak., *Plainsman,* Sept. 15, 1985; "St. Charles' Opening Was 1911's Most Pleasant Social Event," Pierre, S.Dak., *Capital Journal,* May 28, 1985.

2. Pierre *Capital Journal,* Nov. 2, 1906, June 26, 1987; Pierre, S.Dak., *Rustler,* Nov. 1906.

3. Pierre *Capital Journal,* Mar. 15, July 28, 1906.

4. Ibid., Apr. 19, 1906.

5. Ibid., Mar. 7, 9, 1914.

6. Ibid., Jan. 4, 1907.

7. Ibid., Mar. 23, 1907, Jan. 18, Feb. 18, July 7, 1910, Nov. 22, 1911.

8. Ibid., June 25, 1909.

9. A story on big fortunes in South Dakota reprinted in the Pierre *Rustler,* June 1903, and in the Pierre *Capital Journal,* June 15, 1903, profiled Hyde along with four other men who were considered to be among the wealthiest men in the state. For biographical information on Hyde see "Charles Leavitt Hyde," in *National Cyclopedia of American Biography,* vol. 34, (New York: James T. White and Co., 1948), pp. 27–28; Lawrence K. Fox, ed., "Charles Leavitt Hyde," in *Who's Who among South Dakotans: A Biographical Directory,* vol. 2 (Pierre, S.Dak.: Fox and Kindley, Publishers, 1928), pp. 115–16; George W. Kingsbury,

"Charles Leavitt Hyde," in *History of Dakota Territory,* vol. 5 (Chicago: S. J. Clarke Publishing Co., 1915), pp. 443–45; Doane Robinson, "Charles L. Hyde," in *History of South Dakota,* vol. 1 (Logansport, Ind.: B. F. Bowen and Co., Publishers, 1904), pp. 829–30.

10. Charles Leavitt Hyde, *Pioneer Days: The Story of an Adventurous Life* (New York: G. P. Putnam's Sons, 1939); on the self-made man in America, see Irvin G. Wyllie, *The Self-Made Man in America: The Myth of Rags to Riches* (New York: Free Press, 1966); John G. Cawelti, *Apostles of the Self-Made Man* (Chicago: Univ. of Chicago Press, 1965); Richard M. Huber, *The American Idea of Success* (New York: McGraw-Hill Book Co., 1971).

11. He moved to Pierre to be near his son and died there several months later. Pierre *Capital Journal,* Aug. 4, 1911; Pierre *Rustler,* Sept. 1911.

12. Hyde, *Pioneer Days,* pp. 20–21.

13. Ibid., pp. 19–20, 79–83.

14. Ibid., pp. 94, 98–99.

15. Ibid., pp. 21–22.

16. Ibid., pp. 56–58.

17. Ibid., pp. 60–61.

18. Ibid., pp. 84–85.

19. Pierre *Rustler,* Jan. 1892.

20. Ibid., Feb. 1901, Mar. 1902.

21. Pierre *Capital Journal,* Feb. 16, 18, 1905; John Elmer Dalton, *A History of the Location of the State Capital in South Dakota,* report no. 14 (Vermillion: Univ. of South Dakota, Government Research Bureau, Jan. 1945), p. 42.

22. Pierre *Capital Journal,* Apr. 24, May 8, 13, Nov. 7, 1903; Pierre *Rustler,* Apr., Oct. 1902.

23. Pierre *Capital Journal,* Sept. 14, 15, Dec. 7, 9, 1905, Nov. 5, 24, 1906, Feb. 19, Mar. 19, Oct. 14, 1907.

24. Ibid., Mar. 20, Apr. 15, May 18, July 26, 1907, Feb. 24, 1908.

25. Pierre *Rustler,* May, Dec. 1902, May 1903; Pierre *Capital Journal,* June 10, Aug. 15, 1903, May 21, 1904, May 11, 1905, Oct. 9, 1906.

26. Pierre *Capital Journal,* Sept. 13, 1905.

27. See photograph of Capitol Avenue facing p. 90 in Hyde, *Pioneer Days.*

28. Paula M. Nelson, *After the West Was Won: Homesteaders and Town-Builders in Western South Dakota, 1900–1917* (Iowa City: Univ. of Iowa Press, 1986), chap. 8.

29. Pierre *Capital Journal,* Oct. 29, 1910.

30. Ibid., Nov. 23, 1912.

31. "Report of Attorney General George W. Wickersham to President Taft on the Hyde Case," reprinted in Sioux City, Iowa, *Journal,* Apr. 4, 1913.

32. "Reply of Chas. L. Hyde, Pierre, S.D., to Charges of Violating Sections 3929 and 4041 of the Revised Statutes," to the postmaster general of the United States, typescript, n.d., Hyde Papers, South Dakota State Archives, Pierre.

33. Pierre, S.Dak., *Weekly Free Press,* Nov. 17, 1910; "Statement of Chas. L. Hyde," n.d., Hyde Papers.

34. Information on the case is summarized in Wickersham's report listed in n. 31; See also Hyde's "Reply" and "Statement" cited in nn. 32 and 33.

35. Ibid.

36. J. E. Mallery to whom it may concern, Nov. 17, 1910, and S. W. Clark to whom it may concern, Nov. 18, 1910, Hyde Papers.

37. P. F. McClure to whom it may concern, Nov. 22, 1910, and Coe I. Crawford statement, Nov. 23, 1910, Hyde Papers.

38. Pierre *Capital Journal,* Dec. 20, 22, 1911; Doane Robinson to the attorney general, Jan. 20, 1913, Hyde Papers.

39. Pierre *Capital Journal,* Dec. 20, 1911.

40. Ibid., Nov. 23, 1912, Jan. 27, Mar. 4, 1913; *New York Times,* Jan. 3, 1913, p. 18.

41. Pierre *Capital Journal,* Oct. 23, 1911.

42. The prison sentence was commuted, but Hyde agreed to pay the fine and court costs. Ibid., Mar. 4, 13, 1913.

43. Pierre *Rustler,* Mar. 1913.

44. Hyde, *Pioneer Days,* pp. 84–85.

45. Pierre *Capital Journal,* Sept. 12–13, 1938; Sioux Falls, S.Dak., *Argus Leader,* Sept. 11, 1938. Pierre's population in 1940 was 4,322.

FORT PIERRE

1. Harold Schuler, *A Bridge Apart: History of Early Pierre and Fort Pierre* (Pierre, S.Dak.: State Publishing Co., 1987), p. 5; Harold Schuler, *Fort Pierre Chouteau* (Vermillion, S.Dak.: Univ. of South Dakota Press, 1990), pp. 17–27; Doane Robinson, *A History of South Dakota from Earliest Times* (Mitchell, S.Dak.: Educator School Supply Co., 1907), pp. 10–11; Robinson, *Encyclopedia of South Dakota* (Sioux Falls, S.Dak., 1925), pp. 37, 587.

2. Charles E. DeLand, "Editorial Notes on Old Fort Pierre and Its Neighbors," *South Dakota Historical Collections* 1 (1902): 344; "The Most Historic Spot," Pierre, S. Dak., *Capital Journal* (editorial), June 17, 1987.

3. Larry Zimmerman, *Peoples of Prehistoric South Dakota* (Lincoln: Univ. of Nebraska Press, 1985), p. 103; Robinson, *A History of South Dakota from Earliest Times,* p. 8.

4. DeLand, "Editorial Notes on Old Fort Pierre," p. 344.

5. On Father De Smet, see John Upton Terrell, *Black Robe: The Life of Pierre-Jean De Smet, Missionary, Explorer and Pioneer* (Garden City, N.Y.: Doubleday and Co., 1964); Louis Pfaller, *Father De Smet in Dakota* (Richardton, N.Dak.: Assumption Abbey Press, 1962).

6. Stephen Return Riggs, "Journal of a Tour from Lac-Qui-Parle to the Missouri River," *South Dakota Historical Collections* 13 (1926): 341–43.

7. Jesse P. Williamson, "Stephen Return Riggs," *South Dakota Historical Collections* 13 (1926): 324.

8. On the Verendryes, see Martin Kavanagh, *La Verendrye: His Life and Times* (Brandon, Manitoba: privately published, 1967); Charles E. DeLand, "The Verendrye Explorations and Discoveries," *South Dakota Historical Collections* 7 (1914): 99–322; Doane Robinson, "The Verendrye Plate," *Proceedings of the Mississippi Valley Historical Association for the Year 1913–1914,* vol. 7 (Cedar Rapids, Iowa: Torch Press, 1914), pp. 244–53.

9. "The Chevalier Verendrye's Journal, 1742–3," *South Dakota Historical Collections* 7 (1914), pp. 356–57.

10. Ibid.

11. Sioux Falls, S.Dak., *Argus Leader,* Feb. 19, 1913; "Verendrye Plate," *Bulletin of South Dakota State Historical Society* (July 1955), p. 2; Robinson, "The Verendrye Plate."

12. Robinson, *A History of South Dakota from Earliest Times,* p. 13.

13. DeLand, "The Verendrye Explorations and Discoveries," p. 250.

14. "Talk by George Philip at Dedication of Verendrye Monument," type-

script, Sept. 1, 1933, in "Verendrye Monument," South Dakota State Archives vertical file, Pierre.

15. Fort Pierre, S.Dak., *Times,* Sept. 7, 1933.

16. Letter, Will G. Robinson to mayor of Fort Pierre, Apr. 25, 1951, in "Verendrye Monument," South Dakota State Archives vertical file, Pierre.

17. Fort Pierre *Times,* Oct. 7, 1954.

18. Pierre, S.Dak., *Capital Journal,* Aug. 31, 1989.

19. Ibid., Aug. 28, 1989.

20. Herbert T. Hoover, "The Sioux Agreement of 1889 and Its Aftermath," *South Dakota History* 19 (Spring 1989): 56–94.

21. Pierre, S.Dak., *Free Press,* July 9, 1889.

22. In his classic interpretation of the plains region, Walter Prescott Webb stressed the importance of the ninety-eighth meridian as a dividing point. *The Great Plains* (Boston: Ginn and Co., 1931), chap. 2. The East River–West River division has occasioned continual speculation over what it is that divides the two areas. See, for example, John Milton, *South Dakota: A Bicentennial History* (New York: W. W. Norton, 1977, chap. 7; James D. McLaird, "From Bib Overalls to Cowboy Boots: East River/West River Differences in South Dakota," *South Dakota History* 19 (Winter 1989): 454–91.

23. On the Missouri River, see Stanley Vestal, *The Missouri* (Lincoln: Univ. of Nebraska Press, 1964).

24. Hyman Palais, "A Study of the Trails to the Black Hills Gold Fields," *South Dakota Historical Collections* 25 (1950): 221–26.

25. Donald Dean Parker, "Early Explorations and Fur Trading in South Dakota," *South Dakota Historical Collections* 25 (1950): 60.

26. On Manuel Lisa, see Richard Edward Oglesby, *Manuel Lisa and the Opening of the Missouri Fur Trade* (Norman: Univ. of Oklahoma Press, 1963).

27. Doane Robinson, "Lewis and Clark in South Dakota," *South Dakota Historical Collections* 9 (1918): 561–71; Gary E. Moulton, ed., *The Journals of the Lewis and Clark Expedition,* vol. 3 (Lincoln: Univ. of Nebraska Press, 1987), pp. 113–14; James P. Ronda, *Lewis and Clark among the Indians* (Lincoln: Univ. of Nebraska Press, 1984), pp. 27–41.

28. DeLand, "Editorial Notes on Old Fort Pierre," pp. 373–74.

29. Ibid., p. 337; Doane Robinson, *History of South Dakota,* vol. 1 (Logansport, Ind: B. F. Bowen and Co., Publishers, 1904), pp. 829–30.

30. William H. Truettner, *The Natural Man Observed: A Study of Catlin's Indian Gallery* (Washington, D.C.: Smithsonian Institution Press, 1979), p. 12.

31. Quoted in Doane Robinson, *South Dakota: Sui Generis,* 3 vols. (Chicago: American Historical Society, 1930), p. 200.

32. Ibid., pp. 200–201; Harold McCracken, *George Catlin and the Old Frontier* (New York: Dial Press, 1959), pp. 47–63.

33. Davis Thomas and Karin Ronnefeldt, eds., *People of the First Man: Life among the Plains Indians in Their Final Days of Glory* (New York: E. P. Dutton and Co., 1976), pp. 28–32; David C. Hunt and Marsha V. Gallagher, *Karl Bodmer's America* (Lincoln: Joslyn Art Museum and Univ. of Nebraska Press, 1984), pp. 182–90; John Chancellor, *Audubon* (New York: Viking Press, 1978), pp. 215–16; Mary Durant and Michael Harwood, *On the Road with John James Audubon* (New York: Dodd, Mead and Co., 1980), pp. 561–65; Ferol Egan, *Fremont: Explorer for a Restless Nation* (Garden City, N.Y.: Doubleday and Co., 1977), pp. 27–33; Allan Nevins, *Fremont: Pathfinder of the West* (New York: D. Appleton-Century Co., 1939), pp. 37–44.

34. Herbert S. Schell, *History of South Dakota,* 3d ed. (Lincoln: Univ. of Nebraska Press, 1975), pp. 66–68.

35. On Scotty Philip see James M. Robinson, *West from Fort Pierre: The Wild World of James (Scotty) Philip* (Los Angeles: Westernlore Press, 1974); Wayne C. Lee, *Scotty Philip: The Man Who Saved the Buffalo* (Caldwell, Idaho: Caxton Printers, 1975).

MIDLAND

1. Midland Pioneer Museum, *Historic Midland, 1890–1986* (Pierre, S.Dak.: State Publishing Co., 1986), pp. 131–34; historical scrapbook located in the Midland Pioneer Museum.

2. On the places where activity concentrated in small towns, see Lewis Atherton, *Main Street on the Middle Border* (Bloomington: Indiana Univ. Press, 1954), pp. 33–64; John A. Jakle, *The American Small Town: Twentieth-Century Place Images* (Hamden, Conn.: Archon Books, 1982), pp. 18–35.

3. Charles W. Bohi and H. Roger Grant, "Country Railroad Stations of the Milwaukee Road and the Chicago and North Western in South Dakota," *South Dakota History* 9 (Winter 1978): 3–4, 12.

4. Kingsbury County, S.Dak., *Independent,* Apr. 28, 1905.

5. H. A. Stimson, *Depot Days* (Boynton Beach, Fla.: Star Publishing Co., 1972), p. 1.

6. Nat Stimson interview with author, De Smet, S.Dak., Jan. 8, 1987.

7. H. Roger Grant and Charles W. Bohi, *The Country Railroad Station in America,* rev. ed. (Sioux Falls, S.Dak.: Center for Western Studies, 1988), p. 3. See also Jakle, *The American Small Town,* pp. 16–18. The studies done on American depots tend to concentrate on the larger and more monumental depots. See, for example, Carroll L. V. Meeks, *The Railroad Station: An Architectural History* (New Haven: Yale Univ. Press, 1956); Edwin P. Alexander, *Down at the Depot: American Railroad Stations from 1831 to 1920* (New York: Clarkson N. Potter, 1970); Jeffrey Richards and John M. MacKenzie, *The Railway Station: A Social History* (New York: Oxford Univ. Press, 1986).

8. Brookings County, S.Dak., *Press,* Apr. 29, May 20, 1880; Laura Ingalls Wilder remembered playing games with other children at Ben Woodworth's birthday party in the De Smet depot. *Little Town on the Prairie* (New York: Harper and Row, 1941), pp. 243–51.

9. Lorna McMillan, *The Kent House Depot Hotel* (privately published, 1980), Huron Public Library, S.Dak.; Brookings, S.Dak., *Register,* Feb. 20, 1913.

10. Flora Ziemann, interview with author, Fort Pierre, S.Dak., Fall 1985.

11. De Smet, S.Dak., *News,* May 23, 1919; Brookings *Register,* Apr. 22, 1920.

12. Harold Fritzl, interview with author, De Smet, S.Dak., Fall 1985; De Smet *News,* July 29, 1917.

13. Highmore, S.Dak., *Herald,* Nov. 13, 1919.

14. The story of the shooting is related in an exhibit at the Midland Pioneer Museum.

15. Annual death rates among U.S. railroad employees during the early 1900s generally ranged between 2,500 and 3,700. *Historical Statistics of the United States: Colonial Times to 1970* (Washington, D.C.: U.S. Bureau of the Census, 1975), part 2, p. 740.

16. De Smet *News,* July 29, 1904.

17. Brookings County *Press,* Dec. 1, 1887.

18. Ibid., Mar. 17, 1904.

19. Yi-Fu Tuan, *Place: An Experiential Perspective* (Minneapolis: Univ. of Minnesota Press, 1975), p. 152.

20. Elsie Hey Baye, comp., *Haakon Horizons* (Pierre, S.Dak.: State Publishing Co., 1982), p. 159.

21. Miller, S.Dak., *Press,* Dec. 12, 1988, June 19, 1989; Huron, S.Dak., *Plainsman,* June 25, 1989; "Promoting with Paint: Signs of the Times," *Centennial Sentinel* 2 (Oct./Nov. 1988): 5.

22. *Siding No. 6: The History of Harrold, 1886–1986* (Pierre, S.Dak.: State Publishing Co., 1986); *Aurora, South Dakota: Its First One Hundred Years* (Aurora: Aurora Centennial History Commitee, 1979); Midland Pioneer Museum, *Historic Midland, 1890–1986.*

23. Daniel J. Boorstin, *Hidden History* (New York: Harper and Row, 1987), pp. 150–52.

PHILIP

1. Information on Gustav Johnson came primarily from an interview on July 26, 1988, with Evelyn Johnson Haberly, his eldest daughter and the only person still living in Philip who was there when the town originated. Reproductions of Gustav Johnson's photographs can be found in *A Pictorial History of the Philip Area: Featuring the Photographic Art of Gustav Johnson* (Dallas: Taylor Publishing Co., 1988); Elsie Hey Baye, comp., *Haakon Horizons* (Pierre, S.Dak.: State Publishing Co., 1982), pp. 296–321. Some of his pictures were also used to illustrate the fiftieth anniversary history of the town, Curt Satzinger, ed., *Philip, South Dakota: First Half Century, 1907–1957* (Philip: Pioneer Publishing House, 1957).

2. On the settlement of the West River region during the early 1900s, see Paula M. Nelson, *After the West Was Won: Homesteaders and Town-Builders in Western South Dakota, 1900–1917* (Iowa City: Univ. of Iowa Press, 1986).

3. History of the town of Philip is recorded in Baye, *Haakon Horizons,* pp. 280–92; Satzinger, *Philip, South Dakota;* Clara Roseth, ed., *Prairie Progress in West Central South Dakota* (Sioux Falls, S.Dak.: Midwest Beach, 1968).

4. Utilizing photographs for historical interpretation is discussed in Susan Sontag, *On Photography* (New York: Dell Publishing Co., 1978); Alan Trachtenberg, "Introduction: Photographs as Symbolic History," in *The American Image: Photographs from the National Archives, 1860–1960* (New York: Pantheon Books, 1979). See also Walter Rundell, Jr., "Photographs as Historical Evidence: Early Texas Oil," *The American Archivist* 41 (October 1978): 373–98; Marsha Peters and Bernard Mergen, "Doing the Rest: The Uses of Photographs in American Studies," *American Quarterly* 29 (1977): 280–303; Andreas Feininger, *Photographic Seeing* (Englewood Cliffs, N.J.: Prentice-Hall, 1973); John Collier, Jr., and Malcolm Collier, *Visual Anthropology: Photography as a Research Method* (Albuquerque: Univ. of New Mexico Press, 1986).

5. Sontag, *On Photography,* p. 23.

6. Ibid., pp. 108–9.

7. Trachtenberg, "Introduction: Photographs as Symbolic History," p. xxviii.

8. Satzinger, *Philip, South Dakota,* pp. 6, 96.

9. Ibid., p. 30.

10. Details about the building of the Philip Auditorium are taken from Kevin Kuchenbecker, "Philip Auditorium: A Stop and Go Project" (history paper, South Dakota State University, Spring 1988).

11. Information about ball games and other activities in the Philip Auditorium came largely from interviews on July 26–27, 1988, with Jim Ingram, who bought the building and remodeled it for use as a hardware store; Ray Baker, who was mayor when the city sold the old auditorium; Luverne Larson and Bernard O'Connell, longtime residents who recall activities in the auditorium; Duane McWilliams, one of the workers on the remodeling project; and Howard Phillips, who coached the Philip High School basketball team during the 1944–46 seasons.

WALL

1. *Eastern Pennington County Memories* (Wall, S.Dak.: American Legion Auxiliary, Carroll McDonald Unit, 1965), pp. 9–12.

2. Ted Hustead, interviews with author, Wall, S.Dak., Oct. 22, 1985, July 27, 1988.

3. See John E. Miller, "Two Visions of the Great Plains: 'The Plow That Broke the Plains' and South Dakotans' Reactions to It," *Upper Midwest History* 2 (1982): 1–12.

4. Quoted in "Welcome to Wall Drug and the Badlands!" (brochure distributed at Wall Drug).

5. Dana Close Jennings, *Free Ice Water: The Story of Ted and Bill Hustead's Wall Drug* (Aberdeen, S.Dak: North Plains Press, 1987), chaps. 5, 6.

6. Richard D. James, "Wall, S.D., Has Population of Only 800, but Its Drug Store Draws 10,000 a Day," *Wall Street Journal,* Sept. 5, 1973, p. 12; see also Constance Mitchell, "Some Stores Branch out by Staying Put," *USA Today,* Feb. 26, 1985, pp. 1–2B; *Eastern Pennington County Memories,* pp. 75–76.

7. Todd Murphy, "Wall Drug: Free Water Hole Has Plenty to Sell," Sioux Falls, S.Dak., *Argus Leader,* Sept. 11, 1986, p. 9A.

8. Hustead interview, July 27, 1988.

9. "The Western Art at Wall Drug" (booklet sold at Wall Drug).

10. Dean S. Nauman, ed., *The Vanishing Trails Expedition: 16 Years* (Wall, S.Dak.: The Vanishing Trails Committee, 1976).

11. Al Strandell, interviews with author, Wall, S.Dak., Oct. 22, 1985, July 26, 1988; Pennington County, S.Dak., *Courant,* Dec. 10, 1981, May 15, 1986; Rapid City, S.Dak., *Daily Journal,* Sept. 13, 1983; *Eastern Pennington County Memories,* p. 50.

12. On the impact of the drought in West River South Dakota, see Paula M. Nelson, *After the West Was Won: Homesteaders and Town-Builders in Western South Dakota, 1900–1917* (Iowa City: Univ. of Iowa Press, 1986), pp. 120–41.

13. Donald Worster observed that the optimism that helped see plains people through such disasters, while heroic and useful in many ways, was also often naive and counterproductive when it blinded them to the need for changing to better agricultural practices. *Dust Bowl: The Southern Plains in the 1930s* (New York: Oxford Univ. Press, 1979), pp. 26–28, 42–43.

MOUNT RUSHMORE

1. Robert Hipple, interview with author, Pierre, S.Dak., Aug. 22, 1989; Harold Schuler, interview with author, Pierre, S. Dak., Aug. 22, 1989.

2. Gilbert C. Fite, *Mount Rushmore* (Norman: Univ. of Oklahoma Press, 1952), pp. 131, 162, 210.

3. Ibid., p. 52.

4. The total cost came to $989,992.32. Congress appropriated $836,000.00 of this sum. The Mount Harney Memorial Association solicited $54,670.56 from various businesses and individuals. People in Rapid City contributed $13,896.36, and citizens of Lead added $7,000.00. Hot Springs and Belle Fourche each gave over $1,000.00. Ibid., pp. 210, 224.

5. Ibid., p. 232.

6. Ibid., p. 6.

7. Ibid., pp. 6–9.

8. Huron, S.Dak., *Huronite,* Jan. 22–23, 1924; Minutes of South Dakota state meeting of Black and Yellow Trail Association, Huron, Jan. 22, 1924, H75.343, folder 9, South Dakota State Archives, Pierre.

9. Rapid City, S.Dak., *Daily Journal,* Feb. 1, 1924. Fite, *Mount Rushmore,* pp. 9–10.

10. Fite, *Mount Rushmore,* pp. 10, 54–55; Rex Alan Smith, *The Carving of Mount Rushmore* (New York: Abbeville Press, 1985), p. 26; *Queen City Mail,* quoted in Rapid City *Daily Journal,* Feb. 8, 1924; Yankton, S.Dak., *Press and Dakotan,* Jan. 31, 1924.

11. Fite, *Mount Rushmore,* pp. 16–17.

12. Ibid., p. 22; Smith, *The Carving of Mount Rushmore,* pp. 32–33; In a signed statement released to the press, Borglum made clear his position that the mountain should memorialize not just state or regional history but national history: "The characters chosen should preferably be national in the largest sense. One group, alone, of this character would signal out your great national park and give it a place entirely its own. It would relate itself at once with our national impulse which is greater than state development." Rapid City *Daily Journal,* Sept. 26, 1924.

13. Fite, *Mount Rushmore,* p. 50.

14. "Mount Rushmore" was officially recognized by the United States Board of Geographic Names in June 1930. Ibid., pp. 52–53.

15. Ibid., p. 46.

16. Quoted in Robert J. Dean, *Living Granite: The Story of Borglum and the Mount Rushmore Memorial* (New York: Viking Press, 1949), pp. 17–18.

17. Ibid., pp. 87–88.

18. Fite, *Mount Rushmore,* p. 200.

19. Ibid., p. 99.

20. Ibid., pp. 75, 88, 100–106.

21. Ibid., p. 101.

22. Ibid., pp. 205–6.

23. Ibid., p. 206

24. Ibid., pp. 209–10.

25. Ibid., pp. 45, 85, 230.

26. Sioux Falls, S.Dak., *Argus Leader,* May 19, July 5, 1989; Huron, S.Dak., *Daily Plainsman,* May 18, 31, 1989.

27. Fite, *Mount Rushmore,* p. 45.

28. Note, for instance, Bernard Bailyn in his 1981 presidential address to the American Historical Association: "Modern historiography in general seems to be in a stage of enormous elaboration. Historical inquiries are ramifying in a hundred directions at once, and there is no coordination among them." "The Challenge of Modern Historiography," *American Historical Review* 87 (Feb. 1982): 2; See also John Higham, *History: The Development of Historical Studies in the United States* (Englewood Cliffs, N.J.: Prentice-Hall, 1965); Peter Novick, *That*

Noble Dream: The 'Objectivity Question' and the American Historical Profession (Cambridge: Cambridge Univ. Press, 1988).

29. Fite, *Mount Rushmore,* p. 80.

30. Ibid., pp. 128–29, 210.

INDEX

All of the cities and towns are in South Dakota, unless otherwise noted.